BRIDGING SONIC BORDERS

BRIDGING SONIC BORDERS

Popular Music in Contemporary Dominican/
Dominicanyork Literature

SHARINA MAÍLLO-POZO

UNIVERSITY OF TEXAS PRESS
Austin

Requests for permission to reproduce material from this work should
be sent to permissions@utpress.utexas.edu.

♾ The paper used in this book meets the minimum requirements of
ANSI/NISO Z39.48–1992 (R1997) (Permanence of Paper).

Library of Congress Cataloging-in-Publication Data

Names: Maíllo-Pozo, Sharina, author.
Title: Bridging sonic borders : popular music in contemporary
Dominican/Dominicanyork literature / Sharina Maíllo-Pozo.
Description: First edition. | Austin : University of Texas Press, 2025. |
Series: Latinx: the future is now | Includes bibliographical
references and index.
Identifiers: LCCN 2024034039 (print) LCCN 2024034040 (ebook)
ISBN 978-1-4773-3154-5 (hardcover)
ISBN 978-1-4773-3155-2 (paperback)
ISBN 978-1-4773-3156-9 (pdf)
ISBN 978-1-4773-3157-6 (epub)
Subjects: LCSH: Popular music in literature. | Dominican literature—
20th century—History and criticism. | Dominican literature—
21st century—History and criticism. | American literature—Caribbean
American authors—History and criticism. | LCGFT: Literary criticism.
Classification: LCC PQ7400 .M35 2025 (print) | LCC PQ7400 (ebook) |
DDC 860.9/3578—dc23/eng/20250117
LC record available at https://lccn.loc.gov/2024034039
LC ebook record available at https://lccn.loc.gov/2024034040

doi:10.7560/331545

TO MY DEAR PRIMO JOSHUA, THE COOLEST DOMINICANYORK
WHO LEFT US WAY TOO SOON.

TO ALL THE WOMEN WHO CAME BEFORE ME AND THE
FANTASTIC WOMEN WHO LIFT ME UP DAILY.

TO LEONEL, FOR BEING AN EXEMPLARY DAD TO MY DEAR
FRIEND ILEANA.

CONTENTS

BRIDGING SONIC BORDERS

Bridging Sonic Literary Borders between the Dominican Republic and New York City

In the 1996 article "Dominican Writers at the Crossroads: Reflections of a Conversation in Progress," Daisy Cocco De Filippis ruminates about the direction of Dominican literature in the twenty-first century and whether diasporic writers would have a lasting impact on the transformation of Dominican identity.[1] Almost three decades later, the answer to this question is affirmative: the literature produced by Dominicans on the island and in the diaspora has had a noticeable effect on not only Dominican but also Latinx, US American, Caribbean, and Latin American identities. Dominican Latinx writers such as Julia Álvarez, Loida Maritza Pérez, Rhina Espaillat, Junot Díaz, Josefina Báez, Angie Cruz, Nelly Rosario, Elizabeth Acevedo, Raquel Cepeda, Chiqui Vicioso, Marianela Medrano, Ana-Maurine Lara, Naima Coster, and Lorraine Ávila have been seminal in the reframing of gender, sexuality, racial, ethnic, linguistic, and cultural discourses on dominicanidad and latinidad.[2] The emergence and prominence of transnational Dominican writers such as Francis Mateo, Aurora Arias, Emmanuel Andújar, Rita Indiana, Frank Báez, and Juan Dicent illustrate what Fernanda Bustamante Escalona describes as an "all inclusive: todos y todas incluidos, y todo permitido." Their works counternarrate official discourses of dominicanidad, recognizing and visibilizing cultural heterogeneity and a "dominicanidad 'otra,' 'anónima,' de 'abajo'"[3] ("other" Dominicanness, "anonymous," "from below").

In the epilogue of *The Cambridge History of Latina/o Literature* (2018), María Josefina Saldaña-Portillo explains that within the last few decades, Latinx literature has come to include traditions beyond Chicanx and Puerto Rican works.

> The category of Latina/o literature and its criticism is no longer bound by the colonialist geography of the United States, which originally included the Mexican-American Southwest and Puerto

Rican, but also the immigrant literatures of the Hispanic Caribbean. It is not simply that Latina/o authors in the United States now come from a wide array of Latin American countries. It is also that heuristic practices now exceed the nationalist borders of the U.S. and of American literary studies, as critics place Latina/o literature in its proper hemispheric context for interpretation.[4]

Bridging Sonic Borders: Popular Music in Contemporary Dominican/ Dominicanyork Literature responds to this shift, attesting to the need to address and include the literature produced by Dominicans in the Latinx literary canon. In this sense, this book recovers and visibilizes Dominican/dominicanyork writings. It foregrounds how the literary production of the last three decades relates to Dominicans' migratory movements to the United States and considers the impact that translocation and access to US American popular culture and new technologies have had in the rewriting of literary history in Dominican and US Latinx literary traditions.

Works written in the Dominican Republic and the Dominican diaspora in New York are brought together in this book; sound and words coalesce to make subjects and experiences that have been sidelined in official discourses of Dominican and Latinx identities audible and visible. The works analyzed are anchored in the particularities of Dominican transnational and diasporic life. They offer a space and place to conceptualize and assess the deployment of sound (popular music, noise, and silence) in Dominican/dominicanyork literature. The book examines the interconnections between popular music and literature produced by Dominican/ dominicanyork writers and brings to the forefront a collective transnational cultural history that has remained marginalized in dominant discourses on Dominican and Latinx identities on the island nation and in the United States. Through an interdisciplinary analysis of Dominican, Caribbean, and Afro-diasporic popular music and Dominican/dominicanyork literature produced between 1990 and 2020, the book emphasizes the ways in which transnational interchanges are central to creating an archive that challenges fundamentalist and reductionist constructions of Dominican identity.

By foregrounding the understudied intersections between popular music and literature by canonical and noncanonical authors who write from different geographic locations and different generations, and whose works are written in Spanish, English, and Dominicanish, this book prompts further thinking about the effects of cultural interactions between the Dominican Republic and New York City in the consolidation of an alternative cultural archive that extends its geographic borders to account for island and diasporic Dominicans' understanding of gender, race, ethnicity, class, and other intersections of identity. Thus the book centers overlooked aspects of dominicanidad through narratives that have been excluded and silenced in Dominican and US cultural histories.

This is not an exhaustive study of transnational and Latinx Dominican literature. Rather, through a comparative approach, the book highlights key connections between the literary corpuses from both spaces that use popular music to articulate alternative scripts of dominicanidad. This study demonstrates that the link between popular music and literature in Dominican/dominicanyork literary production plays a major role in epistemological shifts in contemporary Dominican literature: new aesthetics and *nuevos saberes* (new ways of knowing). The literary production I examine diverts from the ways literature has, as Lorgia García-Peña writes, "produced violence and exclusion of actual human beings throughout the history of the nation."[5] In this sense, the deployment of popular music in what I call "sonic literary texts" becomes vital to questioning the role of literature, in the words of Frances Aparicio, "as a new reality that can substitute for and transcend the social spaces of the masses."[6] Latinx studies scholar Juan Flores describes Puerto Rican music as "the vernacular expression of people and communities seeking, and finding, their own voice and rhythm."[7] With the integration of popular music, Dominican/dominicanyork literature aligns with Flores's reflections.

In the Spanish-speaking Caribbean, Luis Rafael Sánchez's *La guaracha del Macho Camacho* (1976) ushered in the postmodern tradition to incorporate popular music in literature as a tool to critique and reframe national identity. The novel marks the course of a literary subgenre in the Caribbean region that I dub sonic literary texts. According to Lorraine Ben-Ur, with *La guaracha del Macho Camacho*, "asistimos actualmente a la edad de la nueva novela del Caribe, la que ha de cifrar, a través de una visión personal, las esencias de la cultura antillana: su lenguaje, su ritmo y su modo de reaccionar ante las formas foráneas"[8] (we are currently witnessing the age of the new Caribbean novel, which must encrypt, through a personal vision, the essences of Antillean culture: its language, its rhythm and their way of reacting to foreign forms). Similarly, Héctor López points out that in the late 1960s and 1970s, writers from the Spanish-speaking Caribbean found new alternatives to examine and re-create national imaginaries though the integration of sonic cultures in their writings. This synergy is necessary to understand how music, which López denominates "submundo de la sentimentalidad del Caribe"[9] (underworld of Caribbean sentimentality), is a useful resource to challenge cultural and disciplinary purism in contemporary Caribbean literature.

In the Dominican Republic, this postmodern integration of popular music in literature occurred about a decade later, a delayed effect caused by the sociopolitical junctures that restricted Dominican literary production during the *Trujillato* and *Balaguerato*. Shifting away from a literary tradition that sustained the nation-building pillars of Hispanophilia, heteronormativity, and geographic delimitations of Dominicanidad to the nation-state, which prevailed during the Trujillato and to a similar extent during *los doce años* de Balaguer (1966–1978), post-1970s Dominican literature—more precisely, the corpus that emerged after the 1980s—explores the continuities and discontinuities of hegemonic discourses of transnational Dominicanidad by Latinx Dominican writers and Dominican writers who write from the island nation. It is during this decade that a collection of sonic literary texts began to consolidate, especially in the context of mass migration to the US.

Although created from different geographic spaces, the writings of Dominican Latinx and transnational authors from the late 1980s to today have been influenced by the traumatic political turbulence that shaped Dominican history in the twentieth century (two US occupations, thirty-one years under the dictatorship of Rafael Leonidas Trujillo, and the twelve years of terror of Joaquín Balaguer), as well as the migration of Dominicans post-1965 and the influx of technological innovations, global connectivity, and US American popular culture.[10] The post-1980s literary corpus imagines the Dominican nation beyond its geographic and metaphorical borders; it is a gateway to consider how new social and cultural conditions offer a unique opportunity to conceptualize transnational dominicanidad. To this effect, the book looks at the interstitial cultural spaces creating multiple forms of knowledge and possibilities for human agency.[11] I draw from the vast body of critical works that highlight the circulation of cultural expression, fluid notions of identity formation, solidarity networks, and, considering that Dominicans are the largest diasporic/Latinx immigrant group in New York City, the constant economic, political, and cultural exchanges between the islands of Manhattan and Hispaniola to assess the role of sonic literary texts in these transborder dynamics.[12]

Since my analyses consider how transnational dynamics have shaped the cultural production of Dominicans *aquí y allá* (here and there), Juan Flores's approach to Caribbean music as one form of "cultural remittance" in constant flux between the homeland and hostlands is fruitful for extending my study beyond the borders of the Dominican Republic. I look at sonic literary texts as examples of "negotiation across the 'insular-diasporic barrier,'" cultural expressions that "cannot be understood today in isolation from the diasporic pole of their translocal realities, nor of course strictly from the vantage point of the diaspora alone."[13] As one such example, the connections that Yolanda Martínez-San Miguel establishes in *Caribe Two Ways: Cultura de la migración en el Caribe insular hispánico* among popular music, visual arts, and literature produced by migrants from the Spanish-speaking Caribbean have benefited my work. In particular, her readings of local and official representations of homeland and receiving communities has been useful in addressing the Caribbean migrant culture that results from the cultural interactions of homeland and diasporic communities.[14] Similarly, Lorena Alvarado's methodology in "Listening to Literature: Popular Music, Voice, and Dance in Latina/o Literary Imagination, 1980–2010" has been important for me to situate this book within a burgeoning field of research within Latinx studies.[15] Finally, and more specific to the Dominican literary tradition, *El sonido de la música en la narrativa dominicana: Ensayos sobre identidad, nación y performance*, edited by Médar Serrata, has been a constant reference for understanding the historical intersections between popular music, literature, and performance from the Dominican Republic and its diaspora in the United States.[16] The comprehensive analysis of a diverse body of works by scholars of transnational Dominican cultural and literary studies in this anthology reflects the growing interest in the intersections between literature and popular music as a necessity for a new generation of writers and intellectuals to challenge homogeneous and exclusionary discourses of Dominican cultural and national identities. The insertion of popular music and local and global music icons in literature creates a space of coexistence between these two fields. Therefore, sonic literary texts act as conciliatory platforms in which different cultural registers converge and collude to build heterogeneous discourses of identity.

While these seminal works have paved the way for the theoretical foundations I develop, this is the first book-length study dedicated solely to transnational literature by Dominican authors on the island and in the diaspora through the foregrounding of the fusion between literary texts and popular music. Although it was conceived in a different format and from a different critical perspective, the edited volume by Médar Serrata is an analogue to this book; however, my book examines island and diaspora literary production not as separate but rather as complementary and in light of each other. Moreover, my study extends and departs from previous critical works by centering the epistemological shifts in the conceptualization of dominicanidad as represented in the transnational literature produced over the last three decades. Further, it highlights the works of Dominican/dominicanyork women to whom popular music is central to define their individual and collective identities as Afro-Latinxs, Dominicans, and dominicanyorks. My foregrounding of women's experiences in the book attest to what Silvio Torres-Saillant describes as "the gender-inflected texture of Dominican-American literature," or the unprecedented growth of dominicanas writing about experiences of Dominican Latinxs and subjects constantly moving between Manhattan and the Dominican Republic. In the words of Torres-Saillant, "The construction of Dominican cultural identity that has thus far gained currency in the literary imagination draws largely from the perspective, the location, the sensibility, and the historical experience of women."[17]

Since I take an interdisciplinary approach, Aparicio's reflections on the role of women as listeners of popular music and the function of this music in identity formation in *Listening to Salsa: Gender, Latin Popular Music, and Puerto Rican Culture* and George Lipsitz's theorizations on popular music as dialogical spaces in *Footsteps in the Dark: The Hidden Histories of Popular Music* have been central to the development of my argument throughout the book.[18] So has María Elena Cepeda's *Musical ImagiNation: U.S.-Colombian Identity and the Latin Music Boom*, which explores the vital role of popular music in the enactment and reimaginings of Colombian identity both in the homeland and in the United States.[19] I have also drawn valuable insights from Flores's understanding of Caribbean music as traveling rhythms that have accompanied the multidirectional mass migrations of Caribbean people and have given way to the opening of "new sites of creolization and transculturation, unimagined in earlier periods of cultural definition and self-definition, and catalyzing unimagined changes in both lands of origin and places of arrival and settlement."[20] His work is seminal to conceiving New York City as a new site of "creolization and transculturation" for Dominicans.[21]

For Dominican merengue, I have relied on three ethnomusicological classic studies on the genre: Paul Austerlitz's comprehensive history, *Merengue: Dominican Music and Dominican Identity*, and Sydney Hutchinson's "Merengue Típico in Santiago and New York: Transnational Regionalism in Neo-Traditional Dominican Music" and *Tigers of a Different Stripe: Performing Gender in Dominican Music*.[22] Hutchinson's transnational framing and understanding of merengue and Dominican popular music has been vital to my argument that the different processes I associate with bridging occur not only in literary texts but also in the history of Dominican musical genres. Similarly, Deborah Pacini Hernández's "*La lucha sonora*: Dominican Popular Music in the Post-Trujillo Era" helped me understand the system of Dominican popular music as a battleground of genres and styles, tightly linked to socioeconomic and political conjunctures.[23]

Although my book does not engage in the methodology of sound studies, my work is indebted to the field. Sound studies scholars and their publications have honed my sensibility to listen to sound beyond strictly musical objects. Jonathan Sterne's *The Audible Past: Cultural Origins of Sound Reproduction* and *The Sound Studies Reader* provided concepts such as sonic textures, modes of listening, and acoustic architectures that have been useful for helping me understand the historicity of sonic worlds by underscoring the roles of technology, urban growth, and other aspects of modernity.[24] Some topics of my study are more closely related to Leonardo Cardoso's *Sound-Politics in São Paulo*, from which I borrow notions of urban soundscapes in my readings of Santo Domingo's sonic culture in the 1980s and 1990s.[25]

When considering the current shifts in narratives of dominicanidad, my book dialogues with the vast work of Silvio Torres-Saillant on the cultural production of the Dominican diaspora. Lorgia García-Peña's notion of contra*dictions* and her approach to El Nié as a theoretical site have been vital in my conceptualizations of dominicanidad from the margins. Following both scholars, rather than look at the diaspora as the sole space where narratives of contradictions emerge, I turn to the island and its literary production to bridge two literary corpuses that contradict, challenge, negotiate, and open the possibility for alternative discourses to show that the works I analyze impinge on the most traditional definitions of dominicanidad.

Throughout my study, I use two interconnected concepts that require clarification. *Sonic literary texts* refers to forms of verbal creativity (short stories, novels, poems, and performances) in which sound is central. When using this term, I also refer to texts that appeal to and interpellate the sonic memories of readers and audiences. *Sonic archives* describes a sort of collective memory, a variety of sources and forms in which sound appears in the texts, an open field of experimentation and dissent, and archival work. I do not call it a music archive, as that would not reflect the variety of forms I analyze throughout the book, including multiple music genres, lyrics, the cultural impact of popular music icons, concerts, oral history, and album covers, as well as a consideration of noise, silence, and sound that is not defined strictly in musicological terms.

The archive becomes a dynamic repertoire when it is used and embodied in particular works. It is an open field of exploration in which the specific choices of each artist make polemical interventions. Two outstanding examples of this are the shifting perceptions of merengue and the impact of African American and Afro-diasporic musical expressions on the whole sonic archive of Dominican/dominicanyork literary production. My use of the term *archive* also relates to the archival research I have done to write this book. I have conducted research at the Dominican Studies Institute and Columbia University in New York, the Biblioteca Nacional de España in Madrid, and the Archivo General de la Nación in Santo Domingo. In addition, the oral histories I have been able to gather from interviews with some of the writers I study in this book have given me an entry into very specific histories and registers of spoken dominicanidad.

Another concept that recurs throughout this book is *bridging*, which conjures having multiple interconnections, but not without conflict. It stands for processes that both unite and link but also produce dissonances. There is a historicity of bridging that responds to different stages of migration and the experience of first-generation immigrants versus first-generation US-born Dominicans. My conceptualization of bridging considers particularly the idea of specific forms of popular music and technologies (for example, Madonna, US Black jazz musicians, and Johnny Pacheco in Josefina Báez's *Dominicanish*[26]). I bridge the literary production of the island and New York City, and I also deal with bridging between different genres of popular music that affect identities, subjectivities, and understandings of nation.

The concept of bridging is partially informed by Gloria Anzaldúa's understanding of borderlands and the history this concept has had in diasporic and Latinx studies. Beyond the specificity of the physical border between Mexico and the United States, Anzaldúa's revision of a nonbinary understanding of phenomena, which she sometimes refers as "queering," is akin to my conceptualization of how bridging blurs cultural borders. Bridging as a process is also equivalent to a triangulation in which a third element either destabilizes binaries or emerges from the unsettling of binaries (as in the notion of El Nié [neither here nor there], the interruptions of hip-hop culture in relation to Dominican Latinx, and the multifold critical approaches to merengue). This bridging happens in what Anzaldúa terms "rajadura," which she defines as "a third point of view, a perspective from the cracks and a way to reconfigure ourselves as subjects outside binary oppositions, outside existing dominant relations."[27] El Nié is also an in-between, ambiguous, uncomfortable, painful, liberatory, and communal third space that "forge[s] a hybrid consciousness that transcends the 'us' versus 'them' mentality and will carry us into nos/otras position bridging the extremes of our cultural realities."[28]

Finally, the sonic literary texts I analyze bridge generations and experiences of islanders and Dominicans in New York, as well as multiple genres of popular music from different periods and geographies. In their engagement with popular music, the writers I consider do diverse kinds of bridging by seeking common ground and simultaneously contesting, subverting, and criticizing the continuities of conversative ideologies of gender, ethnicity, nationality, and language. Throughout this study, I do not use *Latinx* and *Latina/o* interchangeably but adopt the term each writer uses to refer to their identities and poetics. Similarly, my use of *Dominican American*, *dominicanyork*, and *dominiyorkian* follows and honors the ways the writers represent themselves.

CHAPTER DESCRIPTIONS

Paul Austerlitz notes that merengue has been deemed the quintessential cultural symbol of Dominican national identity since its beginnings, when it emerged during the battles for independence from Haiti in 1844.[29] In chapter 1, I analyze how various writers have revisited merengue to destabilize and decenter its historical links to univocal and uncritical discourses of dominicanidad. I examine Francis Mateo's "Cañemo Revival Blues" (2010), Rita Indiana's *Papi* (2011), and Rey Andújar's "Merengue" (2013). These three texts use merengue in radically different and distinct ways. Mateo draws on *merengue típico cibaeño* from the rural zone of Mao, Valverde, to reflect on masculinity and the feelings of nostalgia of male returnees from New York City to rural areas in the Dominican Republic.[30] In contrast, Indiana highlights and celebrates late 1970s and 1980s postdictatorial merengue that emerged from the vibrant interchanges between Dominicans on the island and the diaspora. In Indiana's novel *Papi*, merengue appears in reference to iconic figures of what I call *merengue de ruptura* (a version of the music genre transformed in the aftermath of the dictatorship and during Balaguer's authoritarian regime) and a visual culture that highlights the dominicanyork aesthetics. I contend that Indiana values this type of merengue as a countercultural tradition of resistance (in *Papi*, merengue is associated with shared and cherished moments with the young protagonist's father), but at the same time, the merengue tradition needs to be overcome as it replicates gender ideologies Indiana criticizes. Andújar makes a radical critique of merengue as it perpetuates male chauvinistic and heteronormative gender ideologies. The title of his story, "Merengue," is itself a provocation—the antagonist to the protagonist, "la loca," a queer person who, borrowing from Carlos Decena, goes from being a "tacit subject" to assuming a nonheteronormative sexuality,[31] destroying the cultural symbols that have excluded them and continue to do so.

In my analysis of these three texts, I show the continuities and discontinuities of merengue as the quintessential cultural and national symbol of dominicanidad. These authors negotiate and resist hegemonic notions where working-class, Afro-Dominican, rural, migrant, and queer people tend to be excluded, silenced, and buried. I underscore how none of the forms of continuity or rupture with merengue are "pure"; they all experiment in different ways with fusions or hybridity.

Over the last three decades, a significant number of texts have moved away from merengue and instead attempted to reconfigure the cultural landscape of dominicanidad by delving into rock, pop, and modern folk music and their iconic artists. Thus a new alternative sonic archive for protest and resistance has appeared. In chapter 2, I first discuss narratives from the late 1990s and the early 2000s that revolve around rock and folk musician Luis "Terror" Días, who became an iconic figure for countercultural Dominican movements in the 1970s and 1980s. In "Poco Loco" (2000) and "Invi's Paradise" (1998), Aurora Arias fictionalizes anecdotes of Días's concerts and vividly reconstructs the atmosphere of Santo Domingo in the 1980s. Her short stories confer a mythical dimension to Días and simultaneously narrate the emergence of a popular icon as a social and cultural phenomenon.

In two texts by Josefina Báez, the memory of Días goes beyond his iconicity and relates to a more complex set of affects including friendship, admiration, mourning, and a common experience of living in the margins and the in-betweenness of the Dominican Republic and New York. In the poem "Lista del Terror" (2009), Báez's multifaceted enumeration of Días's life and persona conveys a complex contradictory and endearing mosaic of how he lived and affected the lives of others. In a fragment of the text for performance *Levente no. Yolayorkdominicanyork* (2011), Báez describes how a Dominican girl in New York, fascinated by the aura of the icon, discovers the human and intimate dimensions of a man. Although Báez's accounts of Días are marked by mourning, absence, and loss, there is a general tone of warmth, tenderness, and solidarity between the two artists. In contrast to Báez, Andújar's account of Días is notably more spectral. In his short story "Terror" (2013), Andújar depicts the almost ghostly existence of the music icon during his time in New York and the subjectivity of disillusionment of Dominicans living in the diaspora in the 1990s. As with Báez's account, the memory of "Terror" in Andújar's story is determined by the dissonances, fragmentation, and dislocations of diasporic life.

While Arias, Báez, and Andújar center on Días to foreground alternative scripts of dominicanidad at home, abroad, and between urban Santo Domingo and New York City, in the last text I analyze in this chapter, Rita Indiana shifts her attention to the Dominican urban youth of the 1990s.

Although there are no direct references to Días in *La estrategia de Chochueca* (2003), the phantomlike existence of the young characters who populate the novella shows a continuity in the attempts to amplify new voices and sounds to the Dominican imaginary in post-1980s literature. Further, Indiana revisits an emblematic transnational music concert of *canción protesta* that took place in Santo Domingo under the repressive government of Balaguer in 1974. Her writing about the concert is of particular significance to the reframing of national narratives by establishing links with protest songs of Latin America and leftist political ideologies. In sum, *La estrategia de Chochueca* and the other works examined in this chapter present more expansive and inclusive sounds of dominicanidad that bridge the experiences between Dominicans on the island and the diaspora in New York City.

The third and fourth chapters focus on the literary production of three Afro-dominicanyork Latina women who write from New York City. Their creative processes and works privilege their experiences as 1.5 generation (migrants who arrived in the United States as children or teenagers) and first US-born generation dominicanas in New York. For these groups, the cultural effervescence of the city, US popular culture, and the social transformations that had an impact on Latinx identity formations play a vital role in how their identities are reconfigured and reimagined. The incipient years of hip-hop culture in New York City were crucial for reflecting on Black and Brown struggles in the city and became one of Afro-diasporic and US Black American urban youth's most influential cultural expressions. I understand the shift to hip-hop as a sign of changes in the identitarian formations that mark when sons and daughters of Dominicans born or raised in the United States began to search for forms to express their conflicts and desires, as well as their complex feelings of community belonging and exclusion.

In chapter 3, I analyze Raquel Cepeda's memoir, *Bird of Paradise: How I Became Latina* (2013), and Elizabeth Acevedo's novel in verse, *The Poet X* (2018). Both writers establish connections between "atypical" sonic archives, poetry, and memoir in the articulation of Dominican and Latinx cultural identities. Cepeda's memoir is a site of dissension and contestation, demonstrated in part by the prominent role of hip-hop in her text and its portrayal as an empowering tool that bridges and connects urban youth of her generation across the US. Hip-hop is also crucial to the ethnoracial affiliation of Cepeda as an Afro-diasporic subject vis-à-vis her father's Hispanophilia and desire to be regarded as white. Although they were written in different eras and belong to different literary genres, both *The Poet X* and *Bird of Paradise* amplify the voices of Black and Brown urban disenfranchised youth, particularly Afro-Latina girls and women. Throughout *The Poet X*, rap and some of the iconic figures of today's hip-hop culture coalesce and empower the protagonist, Xiomara, to confront cultural, religious, familial, and social expectations as she finds her own voice as a Black Latina girl entering womanhood in a world in which Black women are constantly fighting for self-representation. Both texts analyzed in this chapter highlight the oft-ignored role of girls and women as producers and carriers of Afro-diasporic and US American cultures. Borrowing from Omaris Zamora's reflections on Afro-Latinas as knowledge creators, this chapter evinces how Cepeda and Acevedo "possess multiple understandings of blackness (i.e., Caribbean, transnational, diasporic), womanhood, and feminist epistemologies," which disrupt essentialist and hegemonic notions of Blackness, Latinidad, and Americanness in both the United States and the Dominican Republic.[32]

In chapter 4, I continue analyzing texts produced in New York. However, I take a different direction in my methodology, dedicating this chapter to a single writer, Josefina Báez. After more than ten years of archival research on the life and legacy of Báez in the Dominican Studies Institute, Columbia University's recent acquisition of the Josefina Báez Papers, and a series of interviews from 2016 to 2023, I decided that having a final chapter solely dedicated to Báez and her prolific trajectory not only made sense but was also the most logical way to connect the threads that make up the fabric of this book. Báez's works bridge sound (or the complete absence of it), literature, and popular culture. They move us closer to alternative forms of knowledge that challenge essentialist definitions of Dominicanidad, Latinidad, and US Americanness by tapping into a hybrid and heterogeneous sonic archive that includes blues, jazz, opera, US American pop, bolero, merengue, bachata, hip-hop, reggaetón, and dembow.

Báez's texts also display her extensive knowledge of popular culture, keen social awareness, and hyperconsciousness of her surroundings. Her historical savviness and insights are essential tools for her characters, readers, and audiences to navigate the intricacies of immigration vis-à-vis present and past events that have affected the lives of Dominicans and Latinxs in their homelands and in the diaspora in the United States. In *Dominicanish* (2000), a young protagonist and narrator speaks of her processes of translocation, adaptation, and immersion into new cultural systems. The stories narrated are intertwined with Black and Latinx sonic archives, as well as key political events and social transformations that influenced Báez's cultural, linguistic, racial, and social consciousness while straddling life in the borderlands between La Romana and New York.

In the second text I analyze, *Levente no. Yolayorkdominicanyork,* dominicanidad is conceptualized as an ongoing project embodied and enunciated by everyday women who inhabit El Nié. Here I follow García-Peña's theorizations of El Nié as a place of discomfort from where Dominican subjects—mostly women—interject US and Dominican histories, emerging as agents of their own histories and identities while also finding hope and even bliss in discomfort.[33] Thus in my discussion of the text, I highlight how the shift in social, gender, and racial dynamics that result from migratory movements to the United States enables the characters of *Levente no. Yolayorkdominicanyork* to reframe the embodied experiences of multiple generations of women and decenter hegemonic and patriarchal narratives of Dominican and US identities that deem the voices of working-class diasporic women invisible.

In the final section of this chapter, I turn to silence, love, and community as the main axis of the third text I examine, *Comrade, Bliss Ain't Playing* (2009). Grounded in Black feminist scholarship, my analysis of this last text demonstrates that the revolutionary and transformative power of silence is a necessity for the poetic voice to create steady and strong bridges with her surrounding communities.

On October 5, 2023, I was part of a panel of five women scholars who spoke about the relevance of Báez's life and work during the public celebration of the acquisition of the Josefina Báez Papers at Columbia University. The room was filled with the sounds of over one hundred people who gathered to celebrate Báez. I was the last of the panelists to speak, and coincidentally, my remarks were about silence in the midst of noise: silence as yet another way to honor her; silence as the ultimate tool to look inward and bring joy outward. Immediately after I spoke, there was beautiful noise from the audience, standing ovations for Báez, and music in the background as she read her poetry. The last verses she read were from *Comrade, Bliss Ain't Playing*, and at that moment, her voice, the cadence of the verses, and the music in the background all became one. Love emanated, and La Maison Française was filled with hugs, tears, laughs, and a sense of community and communion that can only be explained with silence, as words can't encapsulate the magic of that moment.

In *Bridging Sonic Borders*, I seek to create literary bridges between sonic literary texts produced on the island and the Dominican diaspora in New York City by establishing a dialogue between Dominican transnational and US Latinx writings. Rather than filling a void, this book is a viaduct connecting *dos orillas*. It creates a space, as Esther Hernández-Medina cogently notes, "entre espacios que habitan las personas o comunidades que no 'encajan' por ser migrantes o por ser 'diferentes' por la razón que sea"[34] (between two spaces inhabited by the people and communities that "do not fit" for being migrants or for being "different" for whatever reason). My hope is that the sonic literary texts I analyze throughout the chapter open new paths to approach the study of the intersections between popular music and Dominican/dominicanyork literature. The book creates a sort of Nié, where two cultural expressions give birth to a third space.

CHAPTER 1

Merengue Makes It to *los Países*—with a Twist

The first time I heard the word *dominicanyork* was in 1986, when I was six years old. I remember it vividly because it was used to refer to my soon-to-be uncle, *tío* Pache, a *barbú* with curly hair, a swagger, and a New York Dominican accent who stole my aunt's heart—and ultimately "stole" my aunt from me. The infamous family story of how I ran away from the church where they were getting married while holding the tail of her white dress still haunts me at every family gathering. The reasons for my tantrum are still debated, but now, in my forties, I realize that instead of saying the dreaded "I oppose this union," six-year-old me simply decided to run away from the marriage that would mark the fragmentation of the only side of my family that was somehow still together. Shortly after the big celebration, my *tía* took a direct flight to New York City via Pan Am— *el dominicanyol se la llevó.* Three years later, my *tía* brought my *abuela* to los países,[1] and in 1989, at age nine, my circular migration cycle began.

Some Christmases and summers, I would listen to Fernandito, Bonny Cepeda, Los Kenton, Johnny Ventura, Milly, Jocelyn y Los Vecinos, Los Hermanos Rosario, La New York Band, and other merengue bands in my grandmother's living room in her one-bedroom apartment in the Bronx or watch them on *El Show del Mediodía* in my mother's house in Santo Domingo. Reflecting on my constant *vaivenes* between the borderlands of New York and Santo Domingo, and as a self-identified dominican-york currently living in the US South, I am still trying to understand my crossing, inhabiting, and bridging of the borderlands between the US and the DR not as fragmentation or loss, but as a redemptory and unifying condition. Relying on individual and collective sonic memories has been vital to conceptualizing my transnational and borderless embodiment of dominicanidad. In this light, reading the texts of the three authors I analyze in this chapter has been a conscious act: piecing together and recovering parts of my individual and collective identities that were lost in the rush of packing and unpacking with every return and departure. It is also a way to dialogue with others, like Francis Mateo, who speak of the transnational connections between the rural Dominican Republic and urban New York. Finally, this chapter is a space of reckoning and acknowledging *las heridas abiertas* (the open wounds) that remain on the bodies of Dominican migrants.

In *The Diaspora Strikes Back*, Juan Flores writes, "The history of Puerto Rican migration, community formation, and returning home provides an especially rich field for studying modern-day processes of transnational identity formation, trans-locality, circular migration, and diasporic communities."[2] The same could easily be said of Dominicans. Yet, while much has been said about transnational Dominican identity, circular migration remains understudied. In the field of cultural studies, with the exceptions of Yolanda Martínez-San Miguel, Silvio Torres-Saillant, Angelina Tallaj, Lorna Torrado, and Sydney Hutchinson, little attention has been paid to the impact of remigrants on the cultural landscape of the homeland.[3] In this regard, my intervention with Mateo's "Cañemo Revival Blues," Rita Indiana's *Papi*, and—to a lesser extent—Andújar's "Merengue" centers the experiences of circular migrants. While I focus on broad cultural dynamics in the homeland and hostlands, my reading of these texts considers other layers of transnational dynamics by showing the impact of return on the culture of the homeland, especially as it relates to music and dominant scripts of Dominican identity.

"Cañemo Revival Blues" (2010) and *Papi* (2011) center merengue típico cibaeño and what I call merengue de ruptura, respectively: a variation of the genre that emerged in the postdictatorial Dominican Republic and gained momentum with the nation's sociopolitical and economic reconfiguration, as well as with the massive migration of Dominicans to the United States. Mateo's and Indiana's texts conceptualize dominicanidad as fluid and borderless. They present a less common narrative: the "ongoing remittance of cultural values and practices" from the diaspora to the island, where ideas, values, and expressive forms have been "introduced into societies of origin by remigrants and their families as they return 'home,' sometimes for the first time, for temporary visits or permanent re-settlement, and as transmitted through the increasingly pervasive means of telecommunications."[4] Similarly, and even more literally, Andújar's short story "Merengue" produces a narrative in which symbolic ties connecting the Dominican migratory subject to merengue are questioned, challenged, and ultimately severed. Andújar delegitimizes merengue as *the* cultural marker of Dominican identity, which I read as a social critique of the heteronormative character embodied in merengue, rather than a direct attack on the genre. All these texts demonstrate how the merengue continuum not only "'returns' to those ancestral origins and has a dynamic relation with musical and broader cultural life in the home-lands,"[5] but also reconfigures the way we understand the "broader cultural life" and values in the homeland and hostlands.

The sonic literary texts I examine here use merengue to propose new approximations of a more encompassing and inclusive conceptualization of dominicanidad. They record the changes to merengue as it moves trans-nationally and can be construed as attempts to disrupt dominant scripts of Dominican identity. They also bridge literary efforts on the island and in the Dominican diaspora, inscribing alternative narratives that challenge the Hispanocentric foundations and pervasive homogeneity still preva-lent in the dominant understanding of dominicanidad. Thus the presence of merengue in these fictional narratives purposely shifts away from the reification of merengue as the symbol of cultural cohesion and presents it as a site of alternative knowledge production.

These sonic literary texts also extend the authors' readerships through different means of distribution. The integration of familiar, and in some cases popular and recognizable, sonic archives lures readers that might not otherwise read these texts. Mateo, for instance, integrates meren-gue típico cibaeño and rap, which may appeal to multiple generations of readers both on and off the island. Further, "Cañemo Revival Blues" was originally published digitally on the Cielo Naranja website and distributed through Facebook posts. The digital accessibility both on a site often vis-ited by Dominican studies scholars and on Mateo's Facebook page entices readership among academic spheres globally, as well as Facebook follow-ers who, like Mateo, have ties to La Línea, a rural borderland between Haiti and the Dominican Republic where the story takes place.[6] In gen-eral, Mateo's texts record the cultural transformations of Dominicans in the borderlands between New York and the Dominican Republic, or what he refers to as *la media isla*. He taps into an unofficial archive that blurs the borders between urban and rural spaces, merengue típico cibaeño and rap, and digital and print culture.

Similarly, Rita Indiana's *Papi* has garnered attention from critics and readers across generations and around the world, in great part because of her multimedia work, pastiche approach to art creation, online presence, and transgressive engagement with sonic archives in narrative fictions. In *Papi*, she makes sonic and visual archives of merengue from the seven-ties and eighties—the golden age of postdictatorial merengue and its con-tinuation throughout and after the period of los doce años—audible and legible. In doing so, she appeals to the collective memory of multiple generations of Dominicans in New York, which may extend the readership of the novel in the diaspora. Rita Indiana's participation in music festivals and literary events in New York City has also contributed to the phenomenon of music fans turned readers and vice versa. One such case is music journalist and host of the radio show *Beat Latino*, Catalina Marie Johnson, who interviewed Rita Indiana during the Latin Alternative Music Conference in New York City in 2011. In the introduction of their conversation, Johnson disclosed that she had been a fan of Rita Indiana's music for a while and that it was through this interest that she discovered Rita Indiana was a writer too and was introduced to her literary production "Desde hace mucho tiempo soy fan, Rita, de tu música, pero al investigar más, me enteré, pues, que has escrito, eres autora . . ."[7]

Finally, Andújar's "Merengue" is part of the collection *Saturnario*, which was reedited and reprinted with translations in English in 2013 as the product of a collaborative crowd-source effort under the title *Saturnalia / Saturnario*. I see this communal approach to reassembling the text, as well as the translation to English, as a crucial step toward reintroducing a raw and less romanticized version of merengue, particularly in the story "Merengue," to English-speaking audiences in the US. Andújar is also the author of a weekly cultural column in the digital version of the widely read Dominican newspaper *Acento*, which has disseminated his diasporic musings across the Dominican Republic.[8]

My analyses of "Cañemo Revival Blues," *Papi*, and "Merengue" in this chapter evince how the synergy between music and literature tell a borderless, transnational story in which "border-crossing by marginal 'others'" can be construed as "efforts by ordinary people to escape control and domination 'from above' by capital and the state."[9] The stories of the "marginal 'others'" centered in these texts are intertwined with merengue típico cibaeño and postdictatorial merengue in an effort to contest and legitimize alternative narratives of dominicanidad in the transnational consciousness. Or, as Flores puts it, these narratives are "converting New York *merengue* from what has been a 'transplant' into a 'transnational circuit.'"[10] I read these texts by Francis Mateo, Rita Indiana, and Rey Andújar as "transnational texts from below," emphasizing the ways these authors "ponen de manifiesto los núcleos de un ser, sus angustias, sus sueños y sus máscaras"[11] (reveal the nucleus of their being, their anguish, their dreams, and their masks). I highlight how the relationship between popular music and literature articulates alternatives to dominant identity discourses regarding dominicanidad in the Dominican Republic and the United States.

Dominican actor and writer Francis Mateo was born in 1977 in Santiago de los Caballeros, Dominican Republic. He grew up in Mao, Valverde, the same area where part of his short story "Cañemo Revival Blues" takes place. He arrived in the United States in 1994 and has since lived in New York City. In addition to writing, Mateo has worked as an actor with a wide array of theater companies, including the Public Theater, Repertorio Español, Puerto Rican Traveling Theater, Hudson Shakespeare Company, Urban Stages, Harlem Classical Theatre in New York, and Folger Theatre in Washington, DC.

Mateo's forays into theater preceded and often coincide with his writing. Since the publication of "Cañemo Revival Blues" in 2010, Mateo has cemented himself as a chronicler of everyday life and cultural dynamics of the Dominican community in Washington Heights, which used to be the Dominican enclave par excellence and "remains the symbolic heart of the city's Dominican community."[12] He has dabbled in poetry, storytelling, and multimedia projects. His first book, a collection of poems titled *Ubre Urbe* (2013), and his collection of vignettes, *El Alto* (2019), have circulated successfully within the Dominican community in Washington Heights and the cultural scene of Santo Domingo's Zona Colonial.

Ubre Urbe draws attention to realities that are rarely explored in transnational Dominican literature: the poverty, loneliness, corruption, and disenchantment that pervade the Dominican community of Washington Heights. In this sense, Mateo follows the tradition of poets such as Miguel Piñero, whose works demarcate a hostile and unkind Latino cartography of the city that has become his home.[13] Yet Mateo is not detaching himself from the DR to declare a New York Latinx identity that shuns the homeland, as Piñero did in his works. Rather, his dominicanyork, Latinx experience is heavily influenced by his memories of and contact with the island and its cultural dynamics. Mateo's works can be read through Lorgia García-Peña's theorizations of El Nié as an "uncomfortable place that hurts and makes the subject bleed, creating an open wound of historical rejection: 'una herida abierta.' Yet this discomfort also offers the possibility of finding a poetics of dominicanidad ausente, from which to interject both US and Dominican histories."[14] In this light, Mateo's literary interventions become a sort of Nié: a redemptory and empowering space where Dominicans from the diaspora legitimize their experiences vis-à-vis dominant identity discourses from the nation-state and the US.

With an inquisitive tone, the poems in *Ubre Urbe* confront us with uncomfortable truths that reflect on the quotidian struggles of Dominicans as borderland subjects who oscillate between *el aquí y el allá*. Mateo becomes a sort of flaneur, "a figure of the modern artist-poet, a figure keenly aware of the bustle of modern life, an amateur detective and investigator of the city, but also a sign of the alienation of the city and of capitalism."[15] This modern artist-poet and his narrators stroll along the northern tip of Manhattan, otherwise known as El Alto or Washington Heights, investigating parts of the city that remain invisible to map new cartographies of dominicanidad in the transnational circuit between New York and the Dominican Republic.

Throughout the collection, the poetic voice wanders through the shadows of the night, through the streets of Washington Heights and the northern tip of Manhattan. This wandering uncovers an after-hours New York filled with the broken dreams of young prostitutes, drugs, and a cacophonic concert of ghostly voices. The book's opening marks the trajectory of a nomadic and solitary body who loses himself in the daily gloom, constantly battered by the brutality of a merciless city: "I slip through the wide gutters / of the first world / while needles fall from the sky / and no-one feels my wound."[16] The author consistently puts a conscious emphasis on the many heridas abiertas that accompany migration and find a way to penetrate the Dominican community of Washington Heights. In this sense, the act of walking creates, to expand on José David Saldívar's notion, a "*Transfrontera* contact zone" that blurs the geopolitical separations between people in both the Dominican Republic and New York, invoking "the heterotopic forms of everyday life whose trajectories cross over and interact."[17]

Mateo's writing blurs the borderlines between el aquí y el allá, creating new bridges that connect the Dominican diasporic community in New York City with the homeland. These connections become fundamental to accessing cultural, political, and historical archives and approaching them from a critical stance. The sequential poems "Opus 2" through "Opus 9" close *Ubre Urbe* with a critical and scathing tone. In them, the poetic voice wavers between the streets of Washington Heights and those of la media isla to denounce the transnational structures that have rendered him, a dominicanyork, invisible in both spaces. Mateo rummages through the borderlands to glue together the pieces of dominicanyorks—"I'm broke. It's so hard, so hard, real hard"—to find, perhaps, "a sign": "something that keeps the vital fire from being extinguished."[18] Here a transnational Dominican subjectivity emerges that is no longer anchored in nostalgia for the homeland and vilification of the hostland. Rather, Mateo's sharp and penetrating voice delves into the wound of transnational dominicanidad, and though he celebrates its hybrid nature, he also dismantles the idealized image of the two geographic and metaphorical spaces that are consubstantial to individual and collective Dominican identity formation in the borderlands between la media isla and New York City.

In "Cañemo Revival Blues," Mateo also foregrounds the dynamics between Dominican rurality and US urbanity, speaking from the intersection of New York and the rural Dominican—from the intersection of rap and merengue típico cibaeño to counteract invisibility and carve new spaces from which to understand and enunciate dominicanidad from the borderlands.[19] This story, as its title suggests, is a return to a specific place in the homeland, a modern-day journey heavily mediated by social media platforms. It focuses on La Línea Noroeste, commonly referred to as La Línea, a region of the Dominican Republic that traverses the northern areas of the island. Its narrator is a young Dominican migrant, native to this region, who accesses the everyday life and culture of his hometown, Mao, Valverde, through a social media page on which news from La Línea and the diasporic community in New York converge—a virtual transnational circuit between the homeland and hostlands.

"Cañemo Revival Blues" originates from a real-life Facebook post wherein the wife of a man named Cañemo warns him that if he continues to cheat, drink, and lead a life of debauchery and excess, he'll end up dead. In Mateo's fictionalized extension of this post, the narrator opens the story by asserting, "He's dead, / or so I've heard."[20] Seeking proof of the alleged death, the narrator takes to social media, finding the news of Cañemo's passing is trending. As the story progresses, it refers to the various ways the news was conveyed through Twitter and Facebook:

La noticia se regó en una hemorragia virtual, Twitter silbaba tantas letras que se había perdido el cómo y el cuándo de su muerte. En el Facebook se tejían telarañas en los posteos que llevaban su nombre, llamadas, e-mails. "No jodas" "¿Quién? ¿El Cañemo?" Expresiones como estas eran palpables en cada rincón donde fue conocido. De repente los medios tecnológicos-sociales se hicieron eco de una carta que flotaba en el ciberespacio huérfano y con letras que más que un poema, parecían lágrimas de alambique.[21]

(The news broke in a virtual hemorrhage; Twitter whistled so many letters that it lost the how and when of his death. On Facebook, cobwebs were woven in posts that bore his name, calls, emails. "Stop messing around" "Who? El Cañemo?" Expressions such as these popped up in every corner where he was known. Suddenly, social media echoed with a letter that floated in the orphan cyberspace and with lyrics that, more than a poem, resembled alembic tears.)

These forms of news propagation, what Mirca Madianou and Daniel Miller dub "polymedia," open new avenues to understanding how the convergence between transnationalism and new virtual communicative outlets is an essential bridge connecting migrants with their homelands.[22] Thus "Cañemo Revival Blues" demonstrates how technology connects diasporic subjects with their countries of origin in the age of new media.[23] It also shows the details that get lost in the tangled net of posting and reposting.

The narrator takes it upon himself to recount every detail related to Cañemo's death. Further, his commentary during the procession in Cañemo's honor illustrates the material limitations of rural access to technology. In doing so, the fictional narration of events makes visible the marginalization of rural subjects in modern-day communication both within their local communities and between homeland and hostlands. In the words of the narrator, "Muchas de las personas que no se habían enterado por falta de acceso al internet, vagancia u otra razón lógica y prudente, salían ahora de sus casas, algunos a medio vestir o que recién despertaban de sus siestas debido a la conmoción armada en la calle."[24] (Many of the people who had not heard the news because of a lack of access to the internet, vagrancy, or other logical and prudent reason were now leaving their homes, some of whom were half dressed or had just woken up from their naps due to the armed commotion in the street.) While the story acknowledges the usefulness of technology in connecting migrants with their homelands, it also considers the shortcomings of technology in rural areas, which put residents at a disadvantage in their engagement with local, transnational, and global dynamics. The story is a reminder that narratives about migration and cultural transformation are not exclusive to urban spaces and that the impact of transnational dynamics extends to rural life and culture.

In "Merengue Típico in Santiago and New York: Transnational Regionalism in a Neo-Traditional Dominican Music," ethnomusicologist Sydney Hutchinson highlights the role of merengue típico cibaeño in the transnational cultural exchange between specific rural zones of the Dominican Republic and New York City. Hutchinson writes, "The constant reference of typical merengues to local places reinforces listeners' ties to their regional and local origins, creating a Dominican space in New York even while emphasizing the fact that roots have not been planted in the city, but remain in the soil of Santo Domingo."[25] Merengue típico cibaeño is an essential cultural tool that connects the transnational subject not with the whole island, but with a fraction of it.

In "Cañemo Revival Blues," the genre is the central subtext of the story—it infiltrates the story from beginning to end. It plays in the background of Cañemo's funeral procession, a sort of invitation to the neighbors to partake in the ceremony. The role of merengue típico cibaeño in the story could be construed as serving a historical purpose that has been tied to the genre: amplifying news of public events to gather masses and proselytize, though in this case, the news is not related—at least in an evident way—to political endeavors. Instead, this version of the musical genre is the personal story of a local neighbor told through the lyrics: "Se murió El Cañemo / por allá por Dajabón. / Quién lo diría? sí, señor / con una Morena y un trago 'e ron / el Cañemo se murió.[26] (El Cañemo died / Over there by Dajabón. / Who would say it? Yes, sir / With a *morena* and a drink o' rum / el Cañemo died.) This use of merengue típico cibaeño inserts a personal narrative into the public eye to ventilate the hedonistic and hypermasculine tendencies that permeate Dominican rurality and are all too familiar to a narrator who may be speaking from the diaspora.

In an interview, I asked Mateo about this characterization of Cañemo as a hypermasculine prototype consumed by rum, women, and partying. He replied, "This is super normal. *Eso somos nosotros*. It is what I saw when I traveled to Mao, Valverde. It's what I hear from stories my abuela tells me. *Romo* [rum] is in our cultural consciousness; it's men's way of withstanding the constant infringement of our rights; our constant emasculation. And women and partying become part of *esa manera de soportar* [the way to survive it]."[27] Dominican men have been historically anesthetized and silenced with rum, women, and popular music. Understanding the characterization of Cañemo as part of this genealogy is key to seeing and understanding how the complexity of the present in Mateo's short story is somehow linked to, as Michel Foucault puts it, "the errors, the false appraisals, and the faulty calculations that gave birth to those things that continue to exist."[28] "Cañemo Revival Blues" conflates the past and present, evincing some of the historical repetitions that have delineated *lo que somos* (what we are). It is not a story of nostalgia, but one that looks back at the rural homeland, showing how behaviors learned, witnessed, and experienced in these remote rural spaces also find their way into transnational flows between New York and the DR.

The story also brings attention to the impact of migration in the cultural transformations of La Línea, where merengue típico cibaeño and rap coalesce. The integration of two musical genres in the same short story tells a narrative of cultural hybridization that results from transnational flows between urban New York and the rural Dominican Republic. This is illustrated in the narrator's description of La K, a famous local rapper who embodies the urban music aesthetic imported from hip-hop culture during Cañemo's burial, where he is sporting "una gorra de medio lado de los Yankees de Nueva York"[29] (a sideways New York Yankees baseball cap).

By integrating merengue típico cibaeño and rap into the text, the story itself becomes a representation of a musical style that boomed within the Dominican community in New York City in the 1990s: *merenhouse/merenrap*.[30] Although the short story does not include a direct example of this style, by integrating merengue and rap—two key components of merenhouse/merenrap—"Cañemo Revival Blues" ultimately speaks to the hybridized cultural trends that resulted from Dominican migration to the United States. New generations of Dominican and dominicanyork writers are interrupting and reframing national narratives that have ousted marginalized subjects, cultural expressions, and spaces from official dominicanidad.

In Mateo's case, this is accomplished in part through the foregrounding of Dominican rurality and regional musical tradition—merengue típico cibaeño—which was eclipsed by the more urban and "modern" *merengue de orquesta* pushed by Trujillo. Rossy Díaz notes that the circulation of merengue in the twenty-first century "has been largely viable because of new musical styles, largely mediated by urban youth cultures and transnational dominicanidad, as well as by musical and communicational technology and hip-hop culture."[31] I would also argue that by centering merengue típico cibaeño, Mateo is moving away from the Eurocentrism embedded in merengue de orquesta during the Trujillo Era. As Hutchinson reminds us, "Although Trujillo's racism meant that the European aspects of merengue have long been overemphasized, merengue típico [cibaeño] still maintains many elements typical of African-derived musics, such as polyrhythmic complexity, call-and-response structure, a focus on improvisation, and communal participation."[32] "Cañemo Revival Blues" highlights interactions between the musical traditions of a specific rural zone of the homeland and new music styles—such as rap—encountered via migration, connecting urban and rural life across time and geographic locations and engaging with a renewed sense of racial consciousness that privileges Afro-derived and Afro-diasporic musical expressions.

In "Cañemo Revival Blues," rap becomes a part of the cultural identity of the Dominican (trans)nation. Its presence does not conflict with merengue típico cibaeño, nor does it attempt to dissolve it, but rather the two forms together amplify and mourn the death of Cañemo. In the song that Cañemo's friend, local rapper La K, improvises for the occasion, he expresses sadness for the loss of Cañemo: "Eto no e vaina de maquillaje y delienador / Eto e' pa' llorar y beber ron / Eto no e' vaina de Emo / Ete é el entierro del Cañemo."[33] (This not a makeup and eyeliner thing / This is to cry and drink rum / This is not an emo thing / This is Cañemo's burial.) The improvised rap unearths some of the wounds of Cañemo's ethos. It mourns a life consumed by an excess of leisure, women, and rum. Although the lyrics of the song still have some of the misogynistic and hypermasculine undertones that have been associated with post-1980s rap music, such as "mujere, ajutence lo' blumen"[34] (women, tighten up your panties), the song is an emotional outlet through which La K pours his sadness and elicits emotions from his predominantly male audience. Thus the presence of rap, an Afro-diasporic genre birthed in New York to ventilate the social struggles of marginalized communities, is "deterritorialized" and "reterritorialized" in a northern rural area of the DR.

Mateo's short story bridges various borderlands: homeland and hostland, physical and virtual spaces, urbanity and rurality, merengue típico cibaeño and rap. It also confronts the reader with the role of circular migration in the transformations of Dominican cultural identity in rural DR and the urban diasporic community in New York. In "Cañemo Revival Blues," merengue típico cibaeño and rap are key to (re)conceptualizing cultural flows in the borderlands between the Dominican Republic and New York, as well as to creating alternative narratives in which a local story told through social media and popular music bridges time and geographic borders. By traversing these spaces, Mateo integrates popular music to, as George Lipsitz puts it, "provide evidence about change over time in public life."[35] The sounds emanating from the text counter the absence of rural stories and their protagonists in the sociocultural and historical archives of the (trans)nation.

In 1998, Silvio Torres-Saillant and Ramona Hernández foresaw that "the trend of the Dominicans of the next generation will probably not continue to be that of replicating the established forms from the home country. Rather, it will be the creation of alternative forms, combining the rhythms of the native land with those of the host country."[36] This prediction materializes in Mateo's "Cañemo Revival Blues," with the author's creation of an "alternative form" that encompasses the local rhythms of Mao, Valverde, and New York. This story, like the novel *Papi*, which I turn to next, foregrounds transnational and global readings of dominicanidad that consider spaces, narratives, and subjectivities that remain unseen and unaccounted for in current imaginations of Dominican identity.

Dominican writer, performer, and bandleader Rita Indiana is no stranger to life in the borderlands, as she has been in constant migration to and from the Dominican Republic, New York, and Puerto Rico. Although Puerto Rico and, most recently, New York have become her permanent residences for the last two decades, her work—musical and literary—is very much informed by Dominican local politics and culture, as well as by her circular migratory movements. Over the last decade, Rita Indiana has become a trans-Caribbean and transnational cultural icon, contesting, blurring, disrupting, and transforming the notion of dominicanidad. With her prose and music, she creates alternative cultural archives in which working-class émigrés, queer and Afro-Dominican subjects, and their syncretic traditions are no longer ausentes in the conceptualization of Dominican identity. In this section, I consider how Rita Indiana's vaivenes between genres and geographic spaces are central to her (re)articulation of dominicanidad. While her bridging and blurring of borders between and within music and literature may be read as "ignor[ing] divisions between artistic disciplines,"[37] as Hutchinson suggests, this also allows her to provide a more accurate depiction of the ways we have ignored the in-between spaces that make up the multitextured and diverse fabric of Dominican identity.

Rita Indiana's literary career began in the mid-1990s with the publication of her poems "El legado," "La caída," and "La división" in the cultural magazine *Vetas*.[38] Her contribution to Dominican prose began with her short-story collections *Rumiantes* (1998) and *Ciencia succión* (2002). With the novella *La estrategia de Chochueca* (2003), she embarked on what she refers to as "la trilogía de las locas," which continued with *Papi* (2005; 2011) and concluded with *Nombres y animales* (2013). *La mucama de Omicunlé* (2015) was awarded the Grand Prize for Literature by the Caribbean Writers Association in 2017 and translated into English as *Tentacle* (2018) by Achy Obejas. Her most recent book is *Hecho en Saturno* (2018).

Rita Indiana's artistic reach and versatility are reflected in her diverse performance projects, video art, literature, and popular music. Along with literature, her contributions to Latin American, Caribbean, and Latinx music have gained her international renown.[39] After the viral success of her YouTube single "El blu del ping-pong" (2009)—in her words, "the song that started it all"—Rita Indiana y los Misterios' *El juidero* (2010) became an instant musical phenomenon.[40] The album, like her literary works, incorporates a wide array of genres, rhythms, and global and local references that define the heterogeneous nature of her artistic work.

Similar to *Papi* and *La estrategia de Chochueca*, in *El juidero*, Indiana, an innate storyteller, narrates the effects of migration, the ever-present specter of Trujillo and Balaguer, neoliberalism, and capitalism on the Dominican national, diasporic, racial, and gender and sexuality imaginaries. These constant themes, eclectic references to local and US pop culture, fusions of diverse musical and literary genres, and the masterful re-creation of the Dominican vernacular are some of the recognizable characteristics of Indiana's creative universe. When asked to place her work in a specific genre, she responded that in both music and literature, she aims to create her own category.[41] So Indiana's trademark is her conscious employment and integration of US and Caribbean sounds, movements, and language to put forward "a new and more politicized way of listening" that summons her readers and audiences "to confront other points of view, and, in particular, to reflect on their own feelings about marginalized groups, thus producing potential for change."[42]

Rita Indiana's prose pairs music and literature, a phenomenon that Fernando Valerio-Holguín refers to as a product of "la tradición *órfica del Caribe*" (the Orphic tradition of the Caribbean) or the tendency to integrate popular music into literature.[43] In fact, the organic interaction across genres is a constant in Rita Indiana's writing; the presence of music in the author's daily life has influenced her literary creative process to such an extent that it has become innate to her fiction. As the author asserted in her 2011 interview with Jasmine Garsd and Félix Contreras on NPR's Alt.Latino, "If you read my novels, there is a lot of music in there, not just reference to it but also in the shape of these works, in the form of these works, there is music in them."[44] She also states that literature has made an undeniable imprint on her music and refers to the influence of Lezama Lima present in her song "El juidero." For instance, before ping-pong became the center of her song "El blu del ping-pong," it was the focal point of her short story "Ping pong vals."[45]

The intersection between music and literature in Rita Indiana's work is not exclusive to her. Rather, it is a continuation of a literary tradition in Dominican/Dominican American letters that can be traced back to the late-nineteenth century.[46] In this sense, one could argue that Rita Indiana's sonic texts and musical compositions are a clear effort to revisit the past to open social wounds that have yet to heal. Her works reclaim forgotten, marginalized, and buried histories and subjects that have been made invisible in the ruins of decades of instability and political intransigence in the Dominican Republic, massive internal migration within and external immigration to the United States and Puerto Rico, and the social impacts of neoliberalism.

Discussing Rita Indiana's writing without considering the incidence of popular music in her works would not present an accurate depiction of her literary production. She has repeatedly stressed in interviews that the organic interaction and continuous dialogue between music and literature is a constant and insists the two nourish one another.[47] These influences, cross-pollinations, and permutations—the dialogue between her literary and music production and her recycling and borrowing of images—produce new narratives of dominicanidad through cultural syncretism and repetition.

Rita Indiana's multilayered cultural productions and the bridges she builds among them counter official narratives and afford visibility to peripheral, marginalized, and silenced subjectivities and experiences.[48] This is clearly illustrated in the novel *Papi*, in which Rita Indiana's universes collapse, tracing the effects and ideological burdens of political repression on Dominican migrant communities, the dynamics of circular migration, and cultural hybridization. The interaction between music and prose creates an archive in which "music draws and builds on her written work, often exploring similar themes, employing same metaphors, and even having similar sonic qualities," and vice versa.[49] In *Papi*, Rita Indiana builds an innovative and heterogeneous vision of Dominican national and cultural discourses that go beyond the confines of the island.

This inclination toward fusion, a characteristic of post-1980s Dominican literature, "evidencia un asedio frontal a los vestigios de ese saber uniformador"[50] (evinces a frontal siege on the vestiges of this standardized knowledge). In other words, the tendency to integrate popular music reformulates the homogeneous and Hispanophilic foundations that have served as the basis for conceptualizing and building Dominican cultural identity. This new approach to rethinking national narratives defies what cultural and literary critic Miguel D. Mena describes as "una visión fundamentalista de la dominicanidad. La misma nos reduce a una historia, una lengua, una cultura, que operan como una especie de traje de fuerza, dentro de un lenguaje apocalíptico de que, si te sales de ahí, te perderás"[51] (a fundamentalist vision of dominicanidad. The same reduces us to a story, a language, a culture, which operates as a type of power suit within an apocalyptic language that if you deviate from this vision, you will get lost). Thus Rita Indiana's *Papi* legitimizes narratives, subjectivities, and sonic archives that challenge outdated ideological foundations of dominicanidad. Through the re-creation of spaces infused with sonic memories and the centering of transborder subjects in constant movement, this text unearths subjectivities and cultural expressions in the transnational Dominican imaginary.

Since its publication in 2005, Rita Indiana's second novel, *Papi*, has become a transnational literary phenomenon. It has garnered the attention of literary critics, ethnomusicologists, and cultural studies scholars across Latin America, the Caribbean, Spain, and North America.[52] The novel conveys the fragmented and ever-evolving condition of dominicanidad; its transience and spatial mobility invite reflection on the diaspora's essential role in the historical and cultural evolution of the island. In *Papi*, the eight-year-old narrator anxiously awaits the return of her father, a Dominican living in New York. Using hyperbole, the young narrator describes the material excesses and *machista* behavior of her father with a certain degree of admiration that, to readers, verges on mockery.

Focusing on the characteristic organic exchange between music and literature in Rita Indiana's works, I read *Papi* as a sonic archive that registers the sociocultural transformations of Dominicans at the crossroads between the DR and New York. I look particularly at the chapters that illustrate the centrality of popular music in narratives of dominicanidad. The novel presents merengue from the seventies and eighties, and *merengueros* from both decades, as a valuable archive with which to reclaim marginalized subjectivities and silenced histories in official scripts of dominicanidad. The characters and merengueros embody some of the social values and aesthetics attributed to the dominicanyork, a subjectivity that is the product of Dominican immigration to New York. Throughout the novel, papi fits the profile of the stereotypical dominicanyork, a subjectivity that Angelina Tallaj describes as "working class and rural Dominican migrants who were returning from New York but had acquired the money to access American items of luxury."[53] The term can be applied to the totality of the group of dominicanos ausentes living in los países, but it is usually linked to the Dominican community in New York, which was, and is, the enclave par excellence of Dominicans in the US.

Papi records the linguistic transformations, cultural exchanges with the outside world, and diversification of transnational cultural codes that rule Rita Indiana's literary and sonic universe. The novel is also inserted into a context of technological advances and the irruption of US popular culture in the DR via telecable. Thus *Papi* destabilizes the univocal foundations of nationalist literature and "se inscribe en el discurso de apertura y movilidad textual"[54] (is inscribed in the discourse of openness and textual mobility) that challenges a homogeneous discourse of Dominican identity. With *Papi*, the author shows that the rigidity of spatial and cultural borders is a convention anchored in outdated ideologies that do not reflect the current reality of Dominican subjects. *Papi* thus revitalizes a fluidity of dominicanidad, a result of hybridization processes stemming from globalization and Dominican immigration to the United States. US American culture that filters in through music and television also contributes to the Dominican cultural transformation presented in *Papi*.[55] Rita Indiana deploys the transnational cultural dynamics of working-class immigrants and Afro-Dominican musical icons from the seventies, eighties, and to a lesser extent nineties as a tactical tool to show that although identities forged "from below" may not be naturally subversive or counterhegemonic, they differ from hegemonic identities, as "subaltern identity formations produce narratives of belonging, resistance, or escape."[56] *Papi* is a sonic literary text that foregrounds dominicanyork subjectivities and experiences, and in doing so, it transgresses and subverts scripts of the Dominican and US nations that deem this subaltern subjectivity invisible.

Papi's centering of dominicanyork culture as it relates to post-trujillian merengue—a transformative period for the genre—is not fortuitous, but rather a point from which merengue and its symbolic value in Dominican identity emerge from new sociohistorical and cultural junctures and subjectivities. Thus *Papi*'s fictional universe offers new paradigms and frameworks for thinking about dominicanidad through the aesthetics, subjects, and experiences in the book. It presents characters that are in constant movement between the Dominican Republic and the United States and the new social orders they encounter in this *vaivén* (coming and going). The novel proposes a fluid and postinsular conceptualization of Dominican identity in the process of disassociation from the dictatorial past.[57]

WHAT DOES *PAPI*'S SONIC ARCHIVE SAY ABOUT DOMINICANIDAD?

Toward the end of the sixties and throughout the seventies and eighties, merengue made its way onto the international music scene. This was a period of great sociocultural and political redefinition in the Dominican Republic and the United States.[58] In this context, merengue became a metaphor for change in both countries as their ties became more visible and material in the aftermath of the second intervention of the United States in the DR and the passage of the Immigration and Nationality Act of 1965 in the US.[59] As ethnomusicologist Peter Manuel notes, the late sixties brought "a spiffed up merengue, invigorated by the foreign influences that threatened it, [which] became a triumph not only in its homeland, but abroad as well."[60] *Papi* captures this triumph and also shows the influences that threatened postdictatorial merengue: competition from foreign music genres and the imposition of capitalism, which dictated an accelerated pace of production and promotion, as well as the constant movement of merengueros between the Dominican Republic and New York. Further, the novel confronts the reader with the effects of the economically and politically driven emigration of Dominicans that occurred during Joaquín Balaguer's doce años.[61]

Merengue, which runs through the subtext of *Papi*, represents a less commonly told story of the social and political events that culminated in the disruptive and revolutionary shifts in the genre within transnational circuits I discuss below. Thus the Dominican diasporic community, and the circular migrations of both a sonic archive and musical icons that center the immigrant experience in New York, contextualize transnational dominicanidad *desde esta orilla*. In other words, in *Papi*, the diaspora speaks and carves a space for subjects, narratives, and renewed perspectives in the transnational Dominican imaginary.

Juan Duchesne-Winter maintains that papi, the main character of the novel, is "un robot cuya única señal de vida es su capacidad de putrefacción continua y renovable"[62] (a robot whose only sign of life is his capacity for continuous and renewable putrefaction). I believe what papi represents is more complex than that; his association with dominicanyork culture and merengue de ruptura points to a gradual deviation from the way dominicanidad has been conceptualized, represented, and reproduced. While papi's "sign of life" may, indeed, reproduce putrefied and decayed structures, it also centers peripheral bodies, such as that of the dominicanyork and renewed sounds in new scripts of dominicanidad that capture, record, and reproduce the experiences of working-class, racialized Dominicans in the borderlands between New York City and the DR.

From the beginning, music accompanies papi. In the opening chapter, the narrator awaits her father's arrival from the United States and compares him to Jason Voorhees, an icon of US American horror films: "Papi es como Jason, el de *Viernes trece*. O como Freddy Krueger. Más como Jason que como Freddy Krueger. Cuando uno menos lo espera se aparece."[63] (Papi is like Jason, from *Friday the 13th*. Or like Freddy Krueger. More like Jason than Freddy Krueger. When you least expect it, he appears.) A background melody anticipates each appearance of her father and fuels the narrator's illusions: "Yo a veces hasta oigo la musiquita de terror y me pongo muy contenta porque sé que puede ser *él* que viene por ahí."[64] (I sometimes even hear scary music and it makes me so happy because I know that he's coming.) The music of *Friday the 13th* intertwines a well-known horror icon with the ever-present haunting of (neo)trujillian phantoms, such as Balaguer. Like Jason Voorhees—who always returns to torment his victims—Balaguer always returned to the Dominican political landscape, a truism immortalized in his 1986–1990 campaign slogan, "Vuelve y vuelve, Balaguer" (Comes back and comes back, Balaguer). Beginning the story this way highlights the repetition of multiple forms of violence that assaulted Dominicans on and off the island during and after the balaguerista regime of the doce años.

The novel traces papi's circular journey. He is a Dominican immigrant who sells cars in New York and whose repetitive homecomings and fragmented presence "deviene un conflicto irresuelto que debe ser constantemente retomado y procesado por la niña desde la espera, la promesa del retorno y la imposibilidad del regreso del padre con la que concluye la novela"[65] (become an unresolved conflict that must be revisited and processed constantly by the little girl, from her longing for her father, the promise of return, and the impossibility of going back with which the novel ends). This is evident early in the novel:

> Pero Jason sabe más que eso y se desaparece por meses y hasta años, hasta que a mí se me olvida que existe, entonces la musiquita de terror es el mismo papi dando bocinazos desde su carro y yo bajo los escalones de cuatro en cuatro para que él me vuelva carne molida lo más pronto posible.
>
> Pero en lo que más se parece papi a Jason no es que se aparece cuando una menos lo espera, sino es que vuelve siempre. Aunque lo maten.[66]

> (But Jason knows better than that and disappears for months and even years, until I forget that he exists, then the horror music is the very same papi honking from his car and I go down the stairs four at a time so that he will turn me into ground beef as soon as possible.
>
> But what most likens papi to Jason is not that he appears when you least expect him, but that he always comes back. Even if they kill him.)

The reappearances of papi—with his horror music accompaniment— perpetuate dominant forms of masculinity but are also sites of disruption. The almost caricaturized representation of papi confronts the reader with hegemonic notions entrenched in the transnational Dominican imaginary. In this case, though, the hypermasculine portrayal of a man in the Dominican diaspora, rather than a mere reproduction of hegemony, becomes useful to reflect on how the notion of masculinity among Dominicans is central to their legitimacy within and outside the nation-state.[67] Maja Horn's reading of *Papi* exhorts us to nuance Rita Indiana's approach to Dominican masculinity by considering that the novel renders "strange and even utterly absurd what often is thought of as common sense in the Dominican Republic" rather than approaching it as a mere replica and perpetuation of hegemonic and paternalist (neo)trujillian masculinity.[68] This becomes evident in the narrator's ironic tone and use of hyperbole to describe the pandemonium generated by the numerous women who besiege her and compete with her for her father's attention:

> Y cuando no son niñeras son las novias mismas. . . . Porque me han hecho esconderme adentro de sus pantihoses. Para que mami no me vea, para que las otras novias de papi no me vean. Se disfrazan de mujeres policía, de compañeras de la universidad de mami, de saloneras, de muchachitas que van al colmado con shores y bajimamas.[69]

> (And when it's not nannies it's the girlfriends themselves. . . . Because they've made me hide inside their pantyhose. So Mami would not see me, so that Papi's other girlfriends would not see me. They disguise themselves as policewomen, as classmates from Mami's college, as hairdressers, as young women who go to the grocery store wearing shorts and tube tops.)

Papi stands as an archetype of opulence and excess, whose "hyperbolic masculinity, material riches, and power go hand in hand, one appearing to reinforce the other, and him at the apex of the country's power structure."[70] At first glance, this rhetoric of abundance could place papi as an heir to the (neo)trujillian legacy. However, this performance of excess has more to do with his migratory movements as a working-class immigrant and the expectations of upward economic mobility: he returns to the DR from the US and thus must present the successes in los países as a kind of prodigal (capitalist) son. This presentation not only is about flaunting success but also is due to the socioeconomic demands placed on migrants by their families in the homeland. Thus papi facilitates the economic stability and procurement of material goods for his counterparts on the island: "Y se sueñan contigo llenando la maleta con regalos para ellos y se sueñan que tú solo trabajas para ellos, solo vives para ellos, sueñan que tú les debes todo en la vida, en sus sueños."[71] (And they dream of you filling your suitcase with gifts for them, and they dream that you only work for them, only live for them, they dream that you owe them everything in life, in their dreams.)

Before his departure to the United States, papi was a low-stratum sailor. After his move to New York, his economic situation changes, and he becomes the owner of several car dealerships. He returns to the island on numerous occasions to show off the material goods he has acquired, such as boats, pianos, and overcoats. Although this depiction is highly caricaturized, it is consistent with the stereotypical dominicanyork, boasting about prosperity acquired abroad. Gold chains, cars, and expensive clothing validate his new status and place him at the crest of the economic ladder in his country of origin: "Ya todo el mundo sabe que estás volviendo, que vas a regresar, que vuelves triunfante, con más cadenas de oro y más carros que el diablo. Ya todo el mundo lo sabe."[72] (Everyone knows that you are coming back, that you will return, that you will return triumphantly, with more gold chains and more cars than the devil.) This almost grotesque representation is consistent with the view Dominicans from the island had (and some still have) regarding Dominican emigrants who settled in the United States. For the people papi is returning to, his racialized immigrant body can be triumphant only if it fulfills the burden of the stereotype. This is evident in the way the narrator boasts on his behalf:

Mi papi tiene más carros que el diablo. Mi papi tiene tantos carros, tantos pianos, tantos botes, metralletas, botas, chaquetas, chamarras, helipuertos, mi papi tiene tantas botas, tiene más botas, mi papi tiene tantas novias, mi papi tiene tantas botas, de vaquero con águilas y serpientes dibujadas en la piel, botas de cuero, de hule, botas negras, marrones, rojas, blancas, color caramelo, color vino, verde olivo, azules como el azul de la bandera. Botas feas también. Botas para jugar polo y para cortar la grama. Botas de hacer motocross, mi papi tiene motores, motonetas, motores ninja, animales domésticos, four wheels y velocípedos. Papi tiene el pelo rizado, negro y rizado, porque cuando era marino y tenía uniformes, blancos, kakis, botas, una escopeta de palo, una escopeta de mentira para hacerse fotos, mi papi tenía el pelo muy corto, porque en la Marina de Guerra se lo cortaban a caco, con una navaja eléctrica que hacía zum zum y le quitó lo que le quedaba de rubio en la cabeza, porque es que papi cuando era niño era muy rubio, con el pelo casi blanco, casi albino, y muy lacio y muy largo.[73]

(My papi has more cars than the devil. My papi has so many cars, so many pianos, so many boats, machine guns, boots, jackets, overcoats, heliports, my papi has so many boots, he has more boots, my papi has so many girlfriends, my papi has so many boots, cowboy boots with eagles and snakes drawn on the leather, leather boots, rubber boots, black boots, boots that are brown, red, white, caramel-colored, wine-colored, olive-green, blue like the blue from the flag. Ugly boots too. Boots to play polo and to cut the grass. Motocross boots, my daddy has motorcycles, scooters, ninja motorcycles, pets, four-wheelers, and bicycles. Papi has curly hair, black and curly, because when he was a sailor and had white and khaki uniforms, boots, a wooden shotgun, a fake shotgun to pose in pictures, my papi had very short hair, because in the navy they would shave his head with an electric razor that went zum zum and it took away whatever blond was left on his head, because as a child, papi was very blond, with almost white hair, almost albino, and very straight and very long.)

The descriptions of papi are often negative and describe his pompous attire and tasteless appearance: "mi papi tiene tantas botas, de vaquero con águilas y serpientes dibujadas en la piel. . . . Botas feas también" (my papi has so many boots, cowboy boots with eagles and snakes drawn on the leather. . . . Ugly boots too). Rita Indiana distances papi from the *tíguere* aesthetics embodied by Trujillo, instead favoring a transnational tíguere aesthetic that centers the "underclass styles of masculinity embodied by Papi."[74] I read this and other descriptions as reflections of the tendency of islanders—especially upper-class Dominicans and the political elite—to stigmatize and chastise dominicanyorks.

The descriptions of papi's body can also be read as a rupture with the Hispanophilic foundations of dominicanidad, establishing a direct connection with more Afro-centric aspects of Dominican identity. Before he left the island, papi had straight blond hair, but following his arrival in the United States, his hair became "negro y tupido y corto, un mini afro"[75] (black, thick, and short, a mini afro).

Wendy Roth explains that immigration as a social process adds new racial schemas to immigrants, their host societies, and their home societies. She also argues that by interacting with others in host societies, migrants/immigrants learn new racial schemas predominating there.[76] In the case of *Papi*, the juxtaposition between racial schemas privileged on the island (a continuum schema) and the new ones prioritized in the novel (the binary US schema) expounds how Dominican immigration to the US affects the way race is performed to assimilate to the new context where migrants are in proximity to US Blacks or to situate themselves in the Black/white binary paradigm of the US. The textual example cited above demonstrates how physical features usually associated with whiteness (straight blond hair) and Blackness (black, thick, and short, a mini afro) situate papi within the binary US schema and evidence his assimilation to US Black aesthetics.

Papi presents a myriad of experiences and realities of marginal voices at the crossroads of migratory movements between the Dominican Republic and New York—*los que se quedan y los que se van* (those who stay and those who leave). By looking at los que se van (*y vuelven*), *Papi* presents the reader with non-white, working-class subjectivities that have not been acknowledged and represented in Dominican and US imaginaries. At first glance, the depiction of papi, a working-class dominicanyork who is immersed in a world of schemes and violence, may be considered problematic—another misrepresentation and marginalization—since the novel reproduces some of the stereotypes associated with this social group. However, as Torres-Saillant pointed out in a 1995 exchange with Patricia Pessar, dominicanyorks "are as ugly and as beautiful, as good, and as evil as everyone else."[77] In other words, *Papi* does not offer a glorified counter to the stereotypical dominicanyork; rather, it complicates papi's character, creating a humanized and comprehensive picture by also showing intimate moments with his daughter and providing his backstory. Further, read through the lens of García-Peña's conceptualization of "*El Nié*," the emphasis on papi's body, his belongings, and his many excesses speak to "the ways in which dictions are projected and performed on racialized bodies to sustain exclusionary borders of the nation." The repetition of the stereotype (the diction) is ultimately "contested, negotiated, and even redefined" in a fictional narrative (the contra*diction*) that centers the life, experiences, and inclinations of a dominicanyork.[78]

A DOMINICANYORK SONIC ARCHIVE

In "*La lucha sonora*: Dominican Popular Music in the Post-Trujillo Era," Deborah Pacini Hernández meditates on the role of popular music in reframing discourses of dominicanidad. She looks at the impact of public cultural dialogues in the post-Trujillo era on the reconstruction of discourses on Dominican identity and concludes that "these public discussions about traditional culture, race, national identity, and popular music—particularly in relation to merengue—were not fortuitous; they served as a convenient excuse for a necessary dialogue about issues of race, tradition, and national identity."[79]

Likewise, I see Rita Indiana as using merengue to nuance and reconfigure Dominican nationalism.[80] In *Papi*, she expands the parameters of *lo dominicano* by creating a cultural bridge between the Dominican Republic and its diasporic community in New York through merengue de ruptura, a version of the genre transformed in the aftermath of the dictatorship and during Balaguer's authoritarian regime. Her inclusion of merengueros such as Johnny Ventura, Cuco Valoy, Wilfrido Vargas, Los Kenton, Bonny Cepeda, and Fernando Villalona reinforces the symbolic divorce from the official homogeneous sound of an official sonic archive of the Trujillo regime. In addition to leaving their mark on the music industry and contributing to the dismantling of cultural homogeneity, these icons and their renewed sonic archive become key to restoring "popular music's ability to address a wide range of topics."[81] They address the social realities of a historical present that was no longer delimited to the island and—intentionally or not—reflect issues of race and racism. In this way, they replace "nationalism as a major concern in the process of definition [of dominicanidad]" with sonic narratives that redefine, as Yolanda Martínez-San Miguel reminds us, "unos vínculos comunitarios y familiares que rebasan los límites tradicionales de un lugar y modos de ser que significan la 'esencia' de lo nacional"[82] (community and family ties that go beyond the traditional limits of a place and ways of being that signify the "essence" of the national).

Further, the post–Civil War period, which also coincided with the beginning of Balaguer's doce años (1966–1978), was characterized by a ruthless, liberal, and evasive attitude in which entertainment was one of the most effective means for burying the memories of a political past marked by dictatorship, intransigence, and instability. These changes had a definite impact on the music industry and resulted in an explosion of merengue bands that deviated from the solemnity that characterized trujillian merengue. These new orquesta groups introduced dances and daring musical lyrics to entertain and evade reflection on past political events. They also contested the past and reflected on the immigrant experience of Dominicans, especially in New York. The merengueros who parade through the pages of *Papi* are framed within this context. Rita Indiana's choice of specific representative figures, far from fitting the evasive trend, are deployed in the novel to meditate on the impact of sociocultural transformations on the Dominican imaginary that result from Dominican migration to the United States.

The references to papi's musical predilections throughout the novel appeal "a una estética política de visibilización y el reconocimiento de lo ignorado, del margen"[83] (to a political aesthetic of visibility and the recognition of the ignored, from the margins). For example, during a visit to one of his houses, the narrator discovers papi's love of music, noticing the house is full of cassette players and turntables. She enters the rooms designated for the sole purpose of storing papi's record and cassette collection:

"Hay una habitación para los merengues, y los estantes llegan al techo. Hay otras habitaciones para la música americana y hay una habitación pequeñita para la música clásica o música de muertos, como dice papi, que realmente es el baño."[84] (There's a room for merengues, and the shelves go up to the ceiling. There are other rooms for American music and there's one tiny room for classical music, or as papi says, music of the dead, which is really the bathroom.) The eclecticism of papi's music collection articulates a poetics of dominicanidad that considers the triangulation of Dominican, US American, and European cultures through the appreciation of popular musical trends from these three spaces. Yet it is evident that merengue occupies a privileged place: in the room dedicated to the merengue collection, the shelves go up to the ceiling.

Lipsitz calls the blues a "social institution" that "played a crucial role in creating ways of knowing and ways of being vital to African Americans."[85] I believe a similar argument could be made for merengue in *Papi* and that it is possible that Rita Indiana's privileging of this genre may be a way to amplify the role of merengue de ruptura as a social institution that creates ways of being vital to Dominican people in the borderlands.

As the narrator explores papi's record collection, she mentions various records papi owns. Her perusal of the collection is primarily visual, noting the album art. In many cases, the images on the album covers correspond with her father's own physical description:

Pero más que los discos a mí lo que me gustan son las carátulas. Las fotos y los dibujos de los cantantes haciendo poses en trono de mimbre o sosteniendo un micrófono como un muslo de pollo. Fotos en blanco y negro para que una sepa quién canta y quién es que toca qué. Algunos traen hasta la letra de los merengues para los que no pueden aprendérsela de oído. Fernandito el Mayimbe sentado en una roca con un sombrero de vaquero, a Cuco Valoy un policía le cae a macanazos, a Fausto Rey un gatico le trepa por el hombro y los Vecinos tienen botines blancos y peinados que combinan. Los Kenton se están separando, culmina papi mientras mira una carátula en la que se unían a Bonny Cepeda para un concierto con trajes de karatecas y con afros que cada año van disminuyendo en tamaño.[86]

(But what I like more than the records are the album covers. The pictures and drawings of the singers striking poses in a wicker throne or holding the microphone like a drumstick. Photos in black and white so that one knows who sings and plays what.

Some even have the merengue lyrics for those who can't learn it by ear. Fernandito el Mayimbe sitting on a rock wearing a cowboy hat, Cuco Valoy clubbed down by a policeman. A cat climbs up Fausto Rey's shoulder, and Los Vecinos wear matching white boots and hairstyles. Los Kenton are breaking up, concludes papi while looking at a cover in which they joined Bonny Cepeda for a concert in karate uniforms and with Afros that get smaller every year.)

This accumulation of images allows the narrator to place her father in an explicit social group and appeals to readers who have a certain familiarity with a sonic archive that is embedded in the collective consciousness of generations of Dominicans in the cultural borderlands between the DR and the US to locate the character within a particular context. It also becomes a fertile opportunity to redefine what we understand as American culture, as it presents to readers aspects and experiences that are not commonly registered in the American consciousness.

The physical equivalences between papi and the merengue aesthetic of the seventies and eighties situate the visual alongside the sonic archive foregrounded in *Papi*. This cross-pollination is an example of how Rita Indiana conveys Dominican identity through a kind of collage. As Celiany Rivera-Velázquez explains, Rita Indiana creates "imágenes visuales de los pedazos a veces contradictorios, circulares o irracionales del Caribe que ella captura perfectamente en la página"[87] (visual images of the pieces— at times contradictory, circular, or irrational—of the Caribbean that she captures perfectly on the page). The visual aspects integrated in the novel reproduce the vulgar and bizarre tastes of the dominicanyork that prompt the repudiation of Dominican society. The extravagant images on the album covers coincide with some of the characteristics attributed to this subjectivity, confronting the reader with the aesthetics of an abject group in the Dominican imaginary. The details emphasized on Fernando Villalona's, Fausto Rey's, and Los Vecinos' album covers correspond with papi's bizarre taste. However, the album covers of Los Virtuosos (led by Cuco Valoy), Los Kenton, and Bonny Cepeda delve into the complexity of Dominican racial dynamics in a transnational context. In the case of Los Kenton and Cepeda, the narrator notes that their *pajones* (Afros) are less pronounced on some covers.[88] This observation implies that the physical acceptance of Blackness may be contingent on aesthetics imposed by the music industry that are more palatable to audiences. It could also be a product, as Rachel Quinn argues, of Rita Indiana's strategic deployment of Blackness "to produce a consumable Dominican cultural aesthetic."[89]

FIGURE 1.1. *Cover of Los Virtuosos album* ¡No me empuje! *(1975).*

Regardless, Rita Indiana's visual archive does not attempt to homogenize the Black experience of Dominicans in the transnational circuit. Rather, her approach exhorts the reader to consider how Dominican subjects at the crossroads between the Dominican Republic and New York negotiate Blackness. The inclusion of the 1975 Los Virtuosos album *¡No me empuje!*, for example, more overtly relates Blackness to social discrimination (see fig. 1.1). The album cover shows a Black man, Cuco Valoy, being battered by a light-skinned police officer while a group of mixed-race men witness the action as passive bystanders. Although we can clearly locate this action within the context of Balaguer's reign of terror, the violence inflicted on the Black body aligns Dominican anti-Blackness with the discrimination against Black people in the US. Valoy, like many other merengueros of his generation, was entangled in the webs of transnational racial discrimination, and his experiences outside the island awakened in him an understanding of his Black ethnoracial identity in a transnational and global context.[90] Looking at this cover from the United States, it is impossible not to establish connections with the historical violence enacted by US police officers that has resulted in the death of so many Black people. In drawing this parallel, I wish to amplify the global historical abuse of Black bodies. *Papi* captures a structural social reality that has haunted Black bodies globally since the advent of the colonial project. The incorporation of this visual element—these album covers—becomes a site from which to reflect on las heridas abiertas of anti-Blackness and violence in the very old and busy bridge between the Dominican Republic and the US.

The complementarity between the sonic and visual archives of the novel also amplifies the ways Johnny Ventura, Cuco Valoy, Wilfrido Vargas, Fernando Villalona, Los Kenton, Bonny Cepeda, and Los Vecinos contributed to the dismantling of cultural homogeneity through the aesthetic and thematic innovations they brought to merengue. Johnny Ventura was one of the pioneers in the creation and diffusion of fast-paced merengue with dance moves inspired by James Brown. By including Ventura in the novel, Rita Indiana highlights an aesthetic and musical link to "sonic blackness," which is extended through the inclusion of Wilfrido Vargas, who integrated freestyle rap into merengue.[91] This is instantiated in the way that *Papi*'s young narrator establishes an important contrast between the idols she prefers and her papi's preferences:

> A papi Cuco Valoy le gusta mucho, a mí no tanto, sobre todo cuando saca su campanita y dice: y ahora es que vamos a hacer brujería! A mí me gusta más Johnny Ventura y su Combo Show, todos con pantalones muy apretados, que según mi tía Leysi se meten en los pantaloncillos para que se les vea más grande y bailan al mismo tiempo, con camisas de color con los botones abiertos hasta el ombligo y los pelos y la cadena de oro afuera.[92]

> (Papi really likes Cuco Valoy, but me, not so much, especially when he takes out his little bell and says, "And now we're going to do some brujería!" I like Johnny Ventura y su Combo Show more, all with tight pants, and according to my aunt Leysi, they put socks in their pants so that they look bigger while they dance, with colored shirts unbuttoned to their navels and their hair and gold chains out.)

The narrator's preference for Johnny Ventura y su Combo Show emphasizes the men's aesthetics and dance moves as the main attraction. Although she does not explain why papi prefers Cuco Valoy, she asserts that she does not like Cuco Valoy so much because he mentions *brujería* (witchcraft). Considering that she is a young girl living on the island, we can attribute her attitude toward brujería to the stigmatization of Afro-Caribbean religious practices still prevalent in the Dominican imaginary. Rita Indiana's juxtaposition of the young girl's openness to an aesthetic that is directly related to African American funk and her simultaneous rejection of Afro-Dominican religious practices speaks to the complexities of racial identity in the Dominican Republic, where US Black American cultural practices are embraced while local ones are rejected, despite the racial implications of the former. This juxtaposition contributes to a more nuanced understanding of Dominican Blackness in which two attitudes about Afro-derived cultural expressions are at odds, yet it is clear there is a Black awareness resulting from the musical influences of US Black American funk, a genre tied to the Black liberation movement in the United States.

Further, the narrator's references to Wilfrido Vargas, a central figure in the transformation of merengue in the 1970s, also emphasize fractures in fundamentalist notions that reduce dominicanidad to one language.[93] Vargas is known for integrating English into his lyrics. Thus his presence in the novel can be read, in the words of Chicana feminist Gloria Anzaldúa, as "linguistic terrorism" in which the "illegitimacy" of the mixture between English and Spanish overcomes the silencing of diverse aspects that challenge the homogeneous dimensions of Dominican identity.[94] Additionally, Vargas's merengues were often fast-paced, and some included improvised phrasings reminiscent of freestyle rap. His presence might also be read as a metaphor for post-trujillian cultural transformation in a transnational context. With the hybrid, fluid, and less "pure" musical proposition of Vargas and the other merengueros cited in the novel, Rita Indiana creates new cognitive maps in which, one hopes, "the music that once emblematized the ideal of a unified and racially homogeneous nation-state now reveals the multiracial character of the country and registers the inexorable interconnectedness of contemporary culture and commerce in a transnational frame."[95] Ultimately, these have been relevant starting points from which to begin new discussions about Dominican identity.

Rita Indiana articulates Dominican identity as "una construcción 'en tránsito,' fluida y trasnacional"[96] (a construct "in transit," fluid and transnational). In addition to Ventura and Vargas, Fernando Villalona illustrates a dominicanidad that transcends geography. Villalona was in constant movement between the Dominican Republic and Manhattan—an iconic transnational merenguero. He transgressed rigid geographic and cultural boundaries of Dominican identity, and the scope of his music reflected the life and experiences of Dominicans on the island, as well as the immigrant community in the United States. The diasporic experience and the longing for *regreso* (return) that were themes in his music contributed to his popularity in New York. Songs like "Cuando pise tierra dominicana," "Dominicano soy," and "Quisqueya" are still inscribed into what García-Peña calls a "poetics of dominicanidad ausente," anchored in nostalgia.[97]

In *Papi*, Rita Indiana appeals to nostalgia by revisiting a sonic archive of the golden age of merengue, yet there is a shift in her deployment. The iconicity and affect elicited by Fernando Villalona and his oeuvre reflects the ambivalent value of border crossers like Villalona and papi. Although in the novel both are portrayed as desired, revered, and idolized, they are also depicted as criminalized subjects, a threat to Dominican mores and values. This is instantiated in the constant fluctuations between Villalona, who was imprisoned for alleged possession of marijuana, and the icon loved and cherished by an audience that demanded his release to see him perform.[98] In this sense, Villalona and papi interrupt and destabilize hegemonic notions of dominicanidad circumscribed by the geography of the island and the social stigmatization of border-crossing subjects. Thus by referring to Villalona's transgression, Rita Indiana reflects on the stigmas that border crossers carry when returning to the island and the ways they embrace new scripts of dominicanidad in which, as Anzaldúa proposes when referring to the "new mestiza consciousness," "nothing is thrust out, the good the bad and the ugly, nothing rejected, nothing abandoned."[99]

Some scholars have categorized *Papi* as a dictator novel.[100] For literary critic Rita De Maeseneer, *Papi* reflects two historical-political moments that still affect Dominican society: the Trujillato and the Balaguerato.[101] As Rita Indiana told De Maeseneer a year after the novel was published, "Ojalá que mis intenciones subversivas no sean en realidad una trampa que transparente mi legado literario dominicano, o sea, que la diarrea novelera trujillista no sea, a fin de cuentas, el motor que mueva a *Papi*."[102] (I hope that my subversive intentions are not really a trap that betrays my Dominican literary legacy, or rather, that the trujillista imaginative diarrhea is not, after all, the engine that moves *Papi*.) De Maeseneer's reading of the novel is a resourceful meditation on Rita Indiana's relationship to the Trujillato and its imprint on contemporary writers. However, her statement suggests that even if the novel is read from this perspective, the text is perhaps better suited to other interpretations; the reader is encouraged to examine unexplored coordinates of Dominican identity, though it is difficult to escape the specter of (neo)trujillian ideologies. I hope that my reading of the novel evinces the transformations that result from the hyperactive cultural flows between the Dominican Republic and the United States post-1965.

MERENGUE MAKES IT TO *LOS PAÍSES*

Suffice it to say that the end of the Trujillato started a period of change, rupture, and openness within the nation-state. Permanent contact with the outside world via the increased circulation of media, emigration, and the rapid development of the technological and telecommunications industries in the Dominican Republic also arrived in the mid to late 1960s, especially during and after the 1965 US military intervention in the Dominican Republic.[103] *Papi* reflects the sociocultural changes that resulted from the late twentieth-century political interconnections that predate mass migration from the Dominican Republic and the US. It presents cultural flows between la media isla and New York not as a phenomenon that resulted exclusively from mass immigration to the US, but as a product of the complex historical interconnections between the two nation-states. Thus *Papi* is a symbolic deconstruction of homogeneous, hegemonic, and simplistic narratives that have prevailed in Dominican cultural and literary production.

In *Papi*, the borders of Dominican and US American popular culture collide. We see the coexistence of *El Show del Mediodía*, *El Sabroshow*, and MTV and, through them, the collision between merengue and US American popular music. By including these platforms and genres in the novel, Rita Indiana puts forth a pluralistic model of dominicanidad. In the words of Néstor García Canclini, this shows that "en un mundo tan fluidamente interconectado, las sedimentaciones identitarias organizadas en conjuntos históricos más o menos estables (etnias, naciones, clases) se reestructuran en medio de conjuntos interétnicos, transclasistas y transnacionales"[104] (in a world so fluidly interconnected, identity sedimentations organized in more or less stable historical groups [ethnic groups, nations, classes] are restructured in the midst of interethnic, transclass, and transnational groups). In the case of *Papi*, popular music plays an important role in the articulation of a hybrid dominicanidad; the novel reinscribes and reformulates narratives of dominicanidad by centering sonic archives that are the result of the fluid interconnections between the DR and New York. In this fictional universe, merengue de ruptura—often associated with working-class Dominicans and the immigrant community in New York—and US American popular culture clash and coalesce, becoming Dominicans' symbolic salvation from the rigid state structures that have defined dominicanidad.

The incorporation of merengue in *Papi* lends itself to multiple interpretations. By revisiting and highlighting the sonic archive of the late 1970s and 1980s, Rita Indiana taps into the collective memory of generations of Dominicans on and off the island. She centers the experiences of diasporic Dominicans in New York, extending the Caribbean to the island of Manhattan, and from there "la diáspora tiene el potencial para ayudar a moderar los parámetros conceptuales vigentes en el discurso sobre la dominicanidad"[105] (the diaspora has the potential to help moderate the prevailing conceptual parameters in discourses of dominicanidad). Through the novel, the existence and experiences of dominicanyorks expand and complicate stagnant and exclusive paradigms of dominicanidad that have excluded working-class immigrants and their experiences. Borrowing from Torres-Saillant, *las yolas regresan* (the makeshift boats return) with a sonic archive that undergoes constant renovations and adaptations post-1965. Further, Rita Indiana's positioning of papi as a dominicanyork centers the experiences of underprivileged subjects at the crossroads of migratory flows between the Dominican Republic and New York. In doing so, she dismantles the conceptualization of dominicanidad "en función de una definición física de isla"[106] (based on a physical definition of an island). *Papi* conjures personal and collective memories in which merengue de ruptura was most certainly the soundtrack of our lives in the borderlands.

REY ANDÚJAR: QUEERING MERENGUE

Rey Andújar's short story "Merengue" offers a different approach to merengue. Although the genre is central to the story, its presence is a reminder of how New York is not an emancipatory space free from the Dominican nation-state's dominant ideologies of gender and sexuality. In Andújar's "Merengue," the rhythm remains a heterosexist domain in which queer bodies have no place on the dance floor.

While queerness has long been a taboo subject in Dominican literature, queer representation has been steadily increasing in Dominican and Dominican American literature. In the late 1990s and early 2000s, in particular, the queer body has been evoked in the construction of new Dominican identity discourses in literature.[107] This shift has resulted in the consolidation of a counternarrative in which the stories of abject and marginalized subjects highlight the exclusionary nature of hegemonic notions of dominicanidad, disarticulating the matrixes of an imaginary that isolates, represses, and renders invisible bodies that threaten the homogeneous and heterosexist foundations of Dominican identity.[108] Andújar's story uses the eponymous genre to meditate on and challenge hegemonic discourses that still prevail in the transnational Dominican imaginary. "Merengue" strikes back, revealing the impossibility of transcending the rigid confines of gender and sexuality established in the DR, even in the diaspora.

Andújar is considered one of the most refreshing and transgressive voices in contemporary Dominican and Caribbean literature. He has published several novels, including *El hombre triángulo* (2005) and *Candela* (2007), as well as short-story collections, among them *El factor carne* (2005), *Amoricidio* (2008), *Saturnario* (2011), *Saturnalia / Saturnario* (2013), and *UGDU y otros relatos* (2011). His work critiques and challenges hegemonic foundations of Dominican identity and suggests alternative scripts of dominicanidad that transcend the borders of patriarchy, heteronormativity, and geography. Some of his most recent work—like that of his peers Rita Indiana and Francis Mateo—focuses on the experiences of Dominican immigrants in the United States, especially in New York. In the collection *Saturnalia / Saturnario*, stories such as "Merengue" make legible queer and abject bodies that have been marginalized, violated, and silenced in the Dominican imaginary.

In "Queer Diasporas, Boricua Lives: A Meditation on Sexile," cultural studies critic Lawrence La Fountain-Stokes expands on Manolo Guzmán's definition of "sexile" and theorizes that the concept of "sexile," or sexual exile—exile driven by one's gender or sexuality—"can be the result of implicit family rejection that leads to personal anxiety and unhappiness, or individual and collective (family, church, government) aggressions that entail outright physical and emotional abuse, censorship, punishment, public harassment, job discrimination, and violence."[109] Following this framework, I read the self-exile of la loca—the main character of "Merengue"—as an act of sexile "motivated by a socio-cultural background that castigates sexual practices and identities that dissent from the heteronormative, hegemonic national discourse."[110] In my reading, I consider how their account alternates with the comments and asides of the narrator, Juliana, who has endeavored to write la loca's biography.[111]

Juliana's narration complements the gaps in the stories la loca recounts from New York about the violence they and their uncle, a gay man, endured due to their sexual preferences and gender identities. However, toward the end of the story, Juliana recognizes that only someone who has experienced abjection can properly and justly recount what they have endured: "I'd like to keep trying to justify this frenetic typing. This excess in living, but the memories live for us. There are memories like there are hearts, you don't remember with a calculated mind, you remember, and to conjugate that verb, the only way to do it is with your body."[112] The uncomfortable memories of la loca become the most reliable source from which to counternarrate official stories that have deemed subjectivities like theirs invisible. Fundamentally, their experiences, their body, and the painful memories inscribed on it are metonymic of a sector of the Dominican (trans)nation that has been historically violated, marginalized, uprooted, and buried by a national discourse that rejects otherness.

Throughout the story, la loca's memories dismantle a series of foundational myths that, according to the perspective of the protagonist, have delineated the essence of lo dominicano. Myth #1: *You have to dance merengue close together or else it's not merengue.* Myth #2: *Every Dominican knows how to dance merengue.* Myth #3: *Dominicans are all crazy about baseball.* Myth #4: *If you think you have something, let it go, if it comes back it was always yours. If not, she was Dominican.* Myth #5: *The Dominican Republic has changed; now we are more tolerant of marginal groups.* Myth #6: *Everyone has a cousin in New York.*[113] The debunking of these myths extends to extrainsular narratives that refuse to acquiesce to or perpetuate dominant narratives of gender and sexuality from the social and spatial borders of the Dominican nation-state. Notably, two of these myths directly related to merengue are challenged within the story to denounce the inherent heterosexist nature of this music genre.

The story begins by dismantling merengue as the primary identity marker for Dominicans. Merengue is presented as the hallmark of a discourse in which queer subjectivities are silenced. From the start, la loca underscores the exclusivist and heterosexist dynamics imbued in merengue as a dance form. La loca's disdain for merengue originates from their need to legitimize themselves as a legible subject within the Dominican imaginary. On several occasions, they refer to their neighborhood—itself a metonym of the island—as a "shithole" and to the DR as "a backward country," as it birthed the musical genre that keeps rejecting them.[114] Although merengue has been linked to national identity since its first appearance on the Dominican cultural scene, it was not until the Trujillo era that it was institutionalized as a symbol of social cohesion. Therefore, I interpret la loca's vitriol toward the genre as not so much about the origins of merengue or the general historical and cultural junctures of its development as a response to the institutionalization of merengue as the ideological tool par excellence of the Trujillato.

Early in the story, la loca recounts memories of the Dominican neighborhood from which they were cast out as "punishment" for their first sexual relationship, at age fourteen, with a man named Gino. These memories are immediately followed by a tirade against the first myth:

As I've explained to you, it was impossible for me to cope with poverty and as an act of adolescent rebellion I abhorred my grandparents, my mother's house, and the neighborhood girl—mainly the neighborhood girl—there was an absurd sexuality in that neighborhood, a fear of the body, that was seeded in me, Juliana, a terrible and definitive bad stench in the body for desiring another body for example, myth number one, a merengue has to be danced tight, or it is not a merengue.[115]

La loca's disdain for the neighborhood—a metaphor for the political structures that engendered uniformity in merengue—extends to the nation that has rejected their queer subjectivity. La loca's social class is evident in this quote, and the phrases "absurd sexuality," "fear of the body," and "bad stench in the body for desiring another body" imply that la loca, aware of the disgust their body provokes, no longer struggles with the material poverty that surrounds them; rather, they struggle with the ideological poverty that invalidates their sexuality and gender identity. The rejection that they have experienced fills them with visceral rancor, prompting them to desecrate the cult of a national identity delimited by a hegemonic discourse that buries living queer masculine subjects.[116]

La loca destabilizes the heterosexual relational model on which the nation-state is built. La loca's intervention also questions the foundations guided by Catholic doctrine and moral principles fostered during the Trujillo era that are imbued in merengue dance.[117] Trujillo's political philosophy was sustained by the moral and religious dogmas of the Catholic Church. When he assumed power, he reinvigorated the role of the Catholic Church in national politics and instituted ecclesiastical marriage, and the Dominican Republic acquired its status as a Catholic nation.[118] This is how heteronormative family values that continue to dominate the nation's official discourses were exalted. The trujillista ideological machine used merengue to solidify and establish the values of the Dominican Republic, including the heteronormative depiction of merengue danced by a man and a woman.[119] So with the denial of the first myth, la loca effaces the ideologies demarcated by Trujillo that consolidated and reinvigorated a heterosexist model of Dominican masculinity.[120]

To dismantle the trujillian ideological machine, la loca also narrates their and their uncle's nightly sexual adventures with boys from the neighborhood. In the recounting of said escapades, a few things stand out: The uncle has an important governmental post, working as Balaguer's bodyguard. He would steal bottles of Johnnie Walker Black Label from the presidential palace to lure the boys from his neighborhood for "bacchanalian nights" during which they would "get drunk, smoke joints, and then jerk off the kids."[121] These references to such despicable acts of sexual violence, as well as abuse of power, are a mockery of the moral foundations that were invigorated during the renewed relationship between church and state in the period of los doce años.[122] They also offer some insight into the deplorable practice of sexual abuse and exploitation of teenage boys and young men so prevalent in the Dominican Republic and the global community at large. La loca fills some of the spaces in the many pages that remained unwritten during the Balaguerato while also, albeit indirectly, reflecting on social realities that go beyond their own experience on the island. Curiously enough, there is an almost terrifying silence in this part of the story, in contrast with other scenes in which merengue plays in the background. This absence of music consciously retreats from sound to center loathsome episodes almost impossible to navigate when narrating and imagining the Dominican nation-state.

In their quest to dismantle heterosexist hegemony, la loca again turns to merengue dancing to contest the second foundational myth, *Every Dominican knows how to dance merengue*. La loca asserts that this is "false as false can be."[123] In one conversation with the narrator, la loca recalls that their grandfather attempted to "cure" their uncle's gayness "by force and by making him dance with women of the night."[124] Here merengue dancing is presented as the pinnacle of heterosexuality and thus a "cure" for gayness. In another conversation with the narrator, la loca points out that dancing in pairs is an outdated custom and has survived only in some Bronx venues frequented by the Dominican community in New York. In their view, these dancers are hanging on to a nostalgic fondness for the merengues of the eighties: "I need to tell you, dear Maestro, that they stopped dancing merengue like that a long time ago, although there are still a few places in the Bronx where they have nights for dancing to music from the '80s. So things change."[125]

La loca attempts to do away with a poetics of dominicanidad that centers and privileges heterosexuality by contesting transnational narratives that center merengue. In contrast to the other stories analyzed in this chapter, Andújar's "Merengue" presents us with a character for whom merengue is no longer "the soundtrack that played in every immigrant's kitchen, whether in Barcelona, in Gallarete, or in New Haven."[126] Further, their sexile is one example of how Dominican emigration post-1965 was not merely economical but also ideological—and in many cases, a matter of survival.

The dismantling of foundational myths by a marginal voice contests the homogenization of the immigrant experience of Dominicans to New York. By enunciating their experience in the borderlands between the Dominican Republic and New York, la loca inscribes queer subjectivities into the sociocultural conception of the transnation and renders them legible in present and future imaginations of Dominican identity. Thus Andújar's "Merengue" is part of a subversive poetics in which marginalized subjectivities are slowly but surely taking center stage in renewed and more encompassing scripts of dominicanidad.

The same sonic archive that Rita Indiana activated to create new discursive narratives of dominicanidad is challenged and rejected in Andújar's "Merengue." Despite being part of the same literary cohort, Rita Indiana and Andújar approach the same musical and cultural archive from the 1970s and 1980s in different ways and use it for different means. This discrepancy, far from being negative, illustrates a shift toward a more encompassing and heterogeneous model of cultural production that does away with the monolithic literary discourse that has prevailed in Dominican narrative. It also illustrates how diverse experiences from the homeland, such as those depicted through the experiences of the narrators and characters in "Cañemo Revival Blues," *Papi*, and "Merengue," shape the way these authors engage with sonic archives and migratory experiences to create multiple narratives of dominicanidad.

From Santo Domingo to New York City: The Sonic Tales of Luis "Terror" Días and Other "Pendejos Anónimos"

In the summer of 2020, I attended a socially distanced gathering with friends and colleagues in Athens, Georgia, where I've lived for the last six years. As a Dominican New Yorker, I suddenly found myself in a situation I never expected: listening to 1980s merengue at an event where I was the only person of Dominican heritage—and in the US South. To my surprise, a whole arsenal of merengues reverberated from microspeakers, and I was suddenly suspended in the memories of my childhood and teenage years between two islands, Hispaniola and Manhattan. In a time marked by much reflection, given the constant isolation from physical contact and inability to travel to my two homelands during the COVID-19 pandemic, I thanked the host for playing a soundtrack with so much importance in both my personal and professional lives and asked about his familiarity with this musical genre. He commented that almost every *miniteca* party (social gathering with dancing and a mobile sound system) of his home-town in Colombia was animated by the sound of these merengues, music that was easy to dance to and set the mood for the other genres that would be played throughout the night.

As described in the previous chapter, the interplay between litera-ture and merengue was the starting point of a discussion that centered a robust archive of sonic narratives that challenge fundamentalist and homogenizing foundations of Dominican identity. In this sense, the host's explanation was key to thinking of this book as a "party" that started with merengue but is now invigorated by other sounds and music icons that have been key players in the transnational Dominican sonic archive.

This chapter records narratives of rupture and continuity with the previous chapter. On the one hand, the texts analyzed here move beyond merengue, centering urban sonic archives that have been repeatedly oblit-erated in the Dominican imaginary. On the other hand, these stories—like those analyzed in the previous chapter—imagine dominicanidad as fluid, in constant movement, not limited to the confines of the island. The shift in Dominican society after Joaquín Balaguer's doce años was characterized by the relative economic revival, the expansion of advertising, and new consumer patterns, among other things. It also marked the return of political dissidents who had left the island during the Balaguerato from the diasporic communities they had established in Europe and the United States. During this time, the Movimiento Renovador de la Universidad Autónoma de Santo Domingo (Reformist Movement of the Autonomous University of Santo Domingo) increased access to postsecondary education, democratizing public higher education. This opened up a space for a wider range of views, shifting the paradigms and focus of the subjects who are centered.

At the same time, a generation of Dominicans on the island, weary of bearing the brunt of the Trujillo and Balaguer curses, converged with a wave of Dominican *émigrés* whose primary language was English, rather than Spanish, and whose lives in the United States influenced the ways they engaged with their dominicanidad. *Desde ambas orillas* (from both shores) emerged a collective effort to find new ways to conceptualize Dominican identity by challenging the structural foundations of the Dominican nation-state. Thus a new process of transnational reconstruction ensued—one in which the borders crossed between music and literature were also crossed geographically. In this process, as I show in this chapter, Dominicans on the island as well as the Dominican diaspora in the United States have a say in the imagination of dominicanidad where geographic and metaphorical borders are being constantly redrawn, pushed, and extended.

Some of the texts I examine in this chapter were written on and about the island. They germinated in an era marked by the distinctive stamp of postmodernity, fluidity, and the very identifiable influence of US American culture on middle-class urban youth from Santo Domingo. This corpus emerges from the disenchantment of younger generations who do not see themselves represented in discursive narratives of dominicanidad. As literary and cultural critics Odalís Pérez and Fernanda Bustamante Escalona have pointed out, these new narratives legitimize the margins, challenge the status quo, and transgress acceptable and homogeneous representations of the Dominican nation-state by expanding the borders of language, geography, gender and sexuality representations, and racial discourses.[1] These more expansive representations of dominicanidad become evident in the way authors such as Rita Indiana, her cohort mates (e.g., Rey Andújar), and her predecessors (e.g., Aurora Arias and Josefina Báez) bridge the separation between high and low culture. Authors such as Rita Indiana and Aurora Arias center stories that have been exiled to the sidelines on the island by a hegemonic standardizing center, whereas works by Josefina Báez and Rey Andújar emerge at the crossroads between Santo Domingo and New York City. The stories of these diasporic Latinx writers centralize interstitial Dominican experiences through the iconic figure of Luis "Terror" Días. In consonance with the focus on Dominican transnational dynamics in the 1990s and early 2000s, these authors record how the diasporic community is reshaping not only identity discourses on the island but also the cultural landscape of the island of Manhattan.

Through a series of texts that center sonic archives from the late 1980s and 1990s in discursive narratives of dominicanidad, this chapter analyzes the role of popular music in the redefinition of the transnational Dominican imaginary from the mid-1980s to the present day. The common thread of these texts is not the dismantling of merengue, per se. Rather, it is their centering of the experiences of marginalized urban subjects in the cities of Santo Domingo and New York. The corpus analyzed here addresses the silences in "official" histories, highlighting the ways subaltern subjects inhabit, negotiate, and reconfigure urban spaces in the transnation. With this in mind, these sonic literary texts can be read as sites where silenced subjects can speak and be heard.

The inclination toward fusion, a characteristic of post-1980s Dominican and Dominican American literature, "evidencia un asedio frontal a los vestigios de ese saber uniformador" (evidences a frontal siege on the remains of that standardizing knowledge)—that is, on the homogeneous and Hispanophilic tendencies that have served as the basis for the construction of (trans)national Dominican cultural identity.[2] In contemporary Dominican narratives, these tendencies are problematized to reframe the same "fundamentalist vision of dominicanidad" discussed in chapter 1.[3] By revisiting musical sites and subjects that were once exiled from the official discourse of the Dominican nation-state, the four authors I analyze in this chapter create knowledge from the fissures in official history through the fusion of music and literature. The sonic memories foregrounded in the five pieces I examine here are useful to contextualize the social conjunctures that have delineated urban, postmodern, transnational subjectivities or, in the words of Rita Indiana herself, "los pendejos anónimos," a metaphor for subjects who have been sidelined by both the imagination of the Dominican nation-state and the diasporic community in the United States.[4]

Such is the case in the short stories "Invi's Paradise" and "Poco Loco" by Aurora Arias, both set in 1980s Santo Domingo. In them, the author revisits an oft-obviated cartography of Santo Domingo and digs into a sonic archive that otherwise exists only in the memories of a generation that is invested in preserving and reproducing them. In both stories, Arias pays tribute to Luis "Terror" Días, an icon of Dominican urban counterculture, roots music, and rock and makes legible the experiences of subjects who, although they inhabited and transited hypervisible spaces in the urban landscape of Santo Domingo, were marginalized. Días's iconicity as a Dominican misfit legitimizes alternative discursive narratives of dominicanidad.

The figure of Luis Días is also rememorialized in two texts authored by Josefina Báez. One was dedicated to his legacy after his death in 2009, and the other includes him as a character in one of the many stories in the text for performance *Levente no. Yolayorkdominicanyork*, about a young woman's encounter with him in New York. Both texts offer a human portrait of the music icon and speak to his life on the margins in the borderlands between the Dominican Republic and New York. Likewise, I interpret the story "Terror" by Rey Andújar as a reflection of the almost ghostly existence of Días during his time in the New York diaspora. This story inscribes the bodies and experiences of Dominicans in the urban landscape of New York beyond the confines of the Dominican enclave in Washington Heights.

In both texts, written after the musical icon's death, these authors were attempting to revive his cultural legacy and criticize the marginalization he had experienced both on the island and in New York. Báez's and Andújar's writings can be read as efforts initiated by artists and friends of the late Días to recover his legacy from oblivion. To do so, they collected scattered and marginal fragments of his life and cultural legacy to insert him into discursive narratives of dominicanidad in New York City. Báez and Andújar refer in their stories to their individual and collective sonic memories of Luis "Terror" Días, re-creating them in the literary space. In doing so, they center his vaivenes between two islands, as a metonym of Dominicans who could not find a place *ni aquí ni allá* (neither here nor there). These Dominican/Latinx authors, who are constantly negotiating their identity and existence in the Nié, present Días's life and legacy as a *rajadura*, what Gloria Anzaldúa describes as a "crack between worlds."[5] Here that rajadura is between the Dominican Republic and New York, an open space where counterknowledge to official narratives of dominicanidad here and there becomes possible.

The last section of this chapter focuses on urban youth during the 1990s and their nocturnal wanderings through the streets of two areas in Santo Domingo: the Zona Colonial, which became the nerve center of counterdiscursive narratives and political resistance in Santo Domingo, especially from 1965 through the 1990s, and El Polígono Central, which became the economic and business center of the capital in the mid-1990s.[6] Disillusioned youth congregated in both spaces amid the nauseating reality of a Santo Domingo looted by politicians, constantly violated by North American and European tourists, besieged by globalization, and abandoned by thousands of its residents who, for economic or political reasons, were forced to immigrate to Europe and the United States. In this section, I analyze Rita Indiana Hernández's book *La estrategia de Chochueca*, which was written within this context, delineated by the social ruin haunted by the specter of the doce años, the attempts at social reform by the Partido Revolucionario Dominicano (1978–1986), and the return to power of Balaguer and the Partido Reformista Social Cristiano (1986–1996). Rather than amplifying the sounds of these conjunctures, Rita Indiana uses them as a point of reference to counternarrate the milestones of urban modernization projects propelled by Balaguer. In this sense, *La estrategia* can be construed as a historiographical attempt to show the cracks in the veneer of a Dominican imaginary that omits subaltern stories, spaces, and subjects. In her attempt to legitimize alternative sounds of the city—more expansive and inclusive ones—Rita Indiana created a sonic novel set at the crossroads between *canción protesta*, Caribbean and Dominican rhythms, and US American music.

AURORA ARIAS, REY ANDÚJAR, AND JOSEFINA BÁEZ: TERROR STILL LIVES IN THE BORDERLANDS

Luis es un mapa de guerra y una batalla,
es un lugar en la memoria y un algo en el
fuego de la dominicanidad.
(Luis is a map of war and a battle,
a place in the memory and a something in the
fire of dominicanidad.)

Luis Días, *¡Échale gas!*

During the 1970s, dominant political sectors and the intellectual elite in the Dominican Republic still conceptualized the nation as a homogeneous "imagined community."[7] In this context, the nation was "imagined" as a beacon of modernity and economic progress in which Hispanocentric values created a false sense of communion among its members. The sense of unity and cultural homogeneity upheld by (neo)trujillista/balaguerista ideologues during Balaguer's doce años was destabilized by members of Dominican society who were thinking about dominicanidad beyond Hispanicity, geography, and essentialisms.[8] This new imagination of the nation emerged as a response to the monolithic and exclusive construction of dominicanidad.

In *La pasión danzaria: Música y baile en el Caribe a través del merengue y la bachata*, Darío Tejeda writes, "Con el proceso de lo que se llamó 'destrujillización' y la democratización política, la sociedad dominicana empezó a forjar un nuevo rostro. Los cambios motorizados principalmente por los sectores urbanos fueron provocando el descubrimiento de su novedoso perfil; la nación empezó a adquirir una mayor conciencia de sí misma."[9] (Dominican society began to forge a new image through a process known as "destrujillización" and political democratization. The changes driven primarily by urban sectors provoked the discovery of its novel profile; the nation began to acquire more self-awareness.) The new consciousness and the process of "destrujillización" (de-trujillization)—as well as "desbalaguerización" (de-balaguerization), or what I describe as the deidentification with the political and social foundations of dominicanidad instituted by Trujillo and perpetuated and promoted by Balaguer—became counterdiscursive cultural movements that assigned new value to popular cultural elements previously disavowed by the (neo)trujillato. In this context, Luis "Terror" Días intervened in official national and cultural discourses of Dominican identity and propelled a renewed self-awareness in the early 1970s, becoming one of the most charismatic and controversial figures for decades as "el más aguerrido revolucionario de la extra-insularidad dominicana"[10] (the most seasoned revolutionary beyond the confines of the Dominican island). With his expansive and relatively inclusive project of nation building, Días made alternative narratives of dominicanidad legible by centering Afro-Dominican traditions, rural cultural expressions, popular music beyond merengue, and cultural interconnections among the Dominican diaspora in the United States.

Días was a member of Convite, a music group mostly composed of young university students who researched, reinterpreted, and revived folk music primarily from rural areas—"toda esa mitología local que la hispanofilia autoritaria del buen dominicano siempre estuvo tratando de ocultar"[11] (all that local mythology that the authoritarian Hispanophilia of the good Dominican was always trying to hide). For Convite, (neo) trujillista ideologies belonged to a past that was in urgent need of renovation. The group's objective was to revisit a collective archive of popular music and traditions to challenge, resist, and renew the unilaterality of antiquated and exclusive discourses of dominicanidad. José Rodríguez, one of the founding members of the collective, confirms this in his paraphrasing of Cuban singer-songwriter Silvio Rodríguez: "Todos sabíamos que aunque la Era *[de Trujillo] estaba pariendo un corazón* y nuestro *cañón de futuro* quería matar canallas, nuestro destino era regresar al origen y aprender de la fuente de lo que es nuestra cultura como totalidad."[12] (We all knew that although the Era *[of Trujillo] was giving birth to a new heart* and that our *ideals of the future* were meant to do away with the rabble, our destiny was to return to the origins and learn from the source what our culture is as a totality.)

While the people in power were concerned with remodeling cities, redistributing rural land, strengthening external investments, and suppressing dissident voices, the youths of this group launched themselves into the rural areas of the nation in search of their roots. Their inquiries and proposals were motivated by centripetal forces that demanded the building of a society exempt from (neo)trujillato remnants. They instead insisted on recovering "las otras voces de la dominicanidad"[13] (the other voices of dominicanidad) to redefine the nation through racial criteria that valued and uplifted Afro-descendant heritage.

After Convite disbanded in 1977, Días did not abandon the project of revisiting collective memories and traditions that had been obliterated and buried by the Trujillato and Balaguerato. His musical production was always imbued with sounds and stories that had remained in the margins during both political periods. His diverse projects culminated in an alternative sonic archive comprising the (hi)stories and spaces that had not made it into the country's official archive. Following Gilles Deleuze and Félix Guattari's notion of the rhizome—connection and heterogeneity, multiplicity, a signifying rupture—Luis "Terror" Días's iconic image and legacy can be construed as rhizomatic in the sense that he navigated in-between spaces, established a logic of unity by becoming a conjunction, and did away with foundations based on exclusivity.[14]

In an interview with Diógenes Céspedes in 2009, Días spoke about the fluid nature of his artistic production, emphasizing how his songs are constantly mutating and never sung with the same harmony and rhythm. For him, the transformation of musical materials was essential to create "un tercer género que es la fusión en sí"[15] (a third genre that is fusion itself). From this and other statements in this interview, we can infer that Días's constant "liberación de la música"[16] (liberation of music) from rigid and repetitive harmonies and rhythms is a site of knowledge production where alternative ways to enunciate and conceptualize Dominican identity can be generated.

Another factor to consider when thinking of Días, his mission, and his cultural production as catalysts of epistemic change is his constant vaivén between la media isla and New York from the 1980s until the years before his death in 2009. During this period, he gained a diasporic collective consciousness that became central to his conceptualization of dominicanidad as borderless, fluid, and relational. His punk rocker aesthetics alongside his sonic fusing of roots Dominican music with US American musical trends evidence the cultural interconnections that have given way to a more hybridized construction of Dominican identity in a context delineated by constant movement between the islands of Manhattan and Hispaniola.

The texts analyzed in the following pages capture this and the aspects of Días's efforts to make alternative scripts of dominicanidad visible. Through the analysis of the literary re-creations of Días and the sociocultural milieus he navigated in the borderlands between the Dominican Republic and New York City, my hope is to make sonic memories and narratives related to the icon visible, legible, and audible as alternative and legitimate epistemological sites of dominicanidad across borders.

LUIS "TERROR" DÍAS AND THE 1980S URBAN SONIC ARCHIVE IN "POCO LOCO" AND "INVI'S PARADISE"

Dominican poet and fiction writer Aurora Arias joined the literary scene in the 1980s. Her first publications appeared in the Dominican magazine *¡Ahora!* Before she began writing fiction, her poetry books *Vivienda de pájaros* (1986) and *Piano lila* (1994) were published, both of which center women's experiences. Her first short-story collection, *Invi's Paradise y otros relatos*, was published in 1998, followed by *Fin de mundo y otros relatos* in 2000. Santo Domingo's subaltern spaces and subjectivities are the primary thematic axes of both books. Her collection *Emoticons* (2007) delves into the uncomfortable and destructive trends of the global economy and their effects on marginalized sectors of Dominican society. *Vida verdadera en el Caribe* (2023), her first novel and most recent publication, challenges the Western imagining of the Dominican Republic as a paradisiacal destination. All in all, her oeuvre offers an underground tour of Santo Domingo that is not meant to appeal to US American, Canadian, or European tourists. Instead, it digs into the open wound of Dominican subjects who have been pushed to the margins and the social realities that have rendered them invisible in the imagination of the Dominican nation. Arias's stories are alternative sites of knowledge production; they offer fictional alternatives to exclusive discourses of dominicanidad.

In *La música caribeña en la literatura de la postmodernidad* (1998),

Héctor López argues that the "Latin American Boom" generated a series of changes in Latin American literature and culture. In the case of the Hispanic Caribbean, popular music took center stage in literature. López writes, "En ese contexto del Caribe hispano, irrumpen unas obras que por la temática, el tratamiento estético y su vinculación con nuestras raíces culturales, ponen de manifiesto los núcleos de un ser, sus angustias, sus sueños y sus máscaras, que nos identifican como una sola entidad cultural."[17] (In the context of the Hispanic Caribbean, some pieces burst onto the scene because their topic, aesthetic treatment, or connections to our cultural roots reveal the nucleus of a being, its anxieties, its dreams, and its masks, identifying us as one cultural entity.) While Arias's texts are illustrative of this trend, shifting our attention to sonic narratives—what López describes as "submundo de la sentimentalidad del Caribe" (the underworld of the sentimentality of the Caribbean)—they also deviate from López's paradigm in the sense that they are not trying to identify Dominicans as "one cultural entity."[18] Rather, her literary universe presents a model of cultural heterogeneity in constant flux, changing with the times.

The soundtrack of the generation of the 1980s and the icons of Dominican counterculture, then, challenge cultural homogeneity and expose the underlying structures that affect collective understandings and approaches to identity. The sonic archive foregrounded in the short stories "Poco Loco" and "Invi's Paradise" destabilize and decenter hegemonic and static constructions of dominicanidad. Arias's choice to center Luis "Terror" Días, whose own creative process went hand in hand with his conception of identity as an anarchist process—a product of "el choque de lo nuevo, el miedo de lo nuevo, el terror a lo nuevo"[19] (the shock of the new, the fear of the new, the terror of the new)—was intentional.

In other words, the identitarian machine is unplugged, and at times destroyed, to make way for new sounds in different contexts. As Arias writes, "La música creada por ellos mismos se alzaba dentro del ambiente urbano dominicano de mediados de los años ochenta como estandarte de lo indecible y tabla de salvación en medio de una sociedad con más tendencia hacia el naufragio que hacia la tierra prometida."[20] (The music they created in the Dominican urban context in the mid-1980s was held up us as a banner of the unspeakable and the last hope in the midst of a society moving more toward shipwreck than to the promised land.) Arias emphasizes the constant presence of music in the individual and collective experiences of the Caribbean and the impact this synergy has on her own creative process. She goes on to say, "Como escritora, me interesa retratar, 'filmar.' Dejar grabado el sonido de la música, en fin darle sonido al texto, como una pretensión omnipotente e ilusoria de abarcarlo todo."[21] (As a writer, I am interested in depicting, in "filming." To leave a recording of the sounds of the music, to make the text aural, like an all-powerful and illusory ambition to take in everything.)

The romance between music and literature in Arias's texts captures the zeitgeist of a generation that would otherwise be written out of the Dominican nation's script. With the reproduction and repetition of a marginal sonic archive of the 1980s, Arias's fiction records the sounds of a past that remain unheard and centers them in the literary space. Literature becomes a jukebox that stores alternative cultural imaginaries.

Arias inserts fragments of Dominican musical memory buried in underground spaces—INVI (a regional urban development project on the farthest western point of Santo Domingo) and a local bar located at the heart of the Zona Colonial—to reconfigure the Dominican cultural imaginary.[22] In some stories in *Invi's Paradise y otros relatos* and *Fin de mundo y otros relatos*, Arias revisits underground and marginal spaces in Santo Domingo frequented by countercultural icon Luis "Terror" Días and his followers. The icon's presence in her stories, beyond "dar vida a un relato basado en un grupo de personajes, en su mayoría artistas, creadores de un fuerte movimiento contracultural"[23] (giving life to a story based on a group of characters, mostly artists, the creators of a strong counterculture movement), gives life to a new approach to dominicanidad that includes the ghosts of Dominican urban life in the 1980s.

"INVI'S PARADISE" AND "POCO LOCO": A FEW STROKES OF "TERROR"

Both "Invi's Paradise" and "Poco Loco" are set in Santo Domingo in the 1980s. During this time, both the Dominican metropolis and the youth who lived in it were experiencing many processes of reconfiguration. At the same time that the state project of restructuring the capital's infrastructure segmented the city, the Zona Colonial, a central space in Arias's stories, became a place of conjunction for young artists who swam against the official current. When approaching these texts, critics such as Néstor Rodríguez and Rita De Maeseneer have focused on the urban underground landscape of Santo Domingo that these stories unveil.[24] Although I am in dialogue with these critics, my reading of "Invi's Paradise" and "Poco Loco" is in direct conversation with literary and cultural studies critic Emily Maguire's attempts to underscore the importance of centering the figure of Luis "Terror" Días in these stories, as well as the context that delineated the cultural and musical inclinations of the lost generation of the 1980s.[25] In this sense, I contend that "Invi's Paradise" and "Poco Loco" revive cultural imaginaries of the 1980s that remained on the sidelines of official discourses of dominicanidad; both stories make legible subaltern subjects, voices, and sounds that resisted dominant authoritarian discourses of the times.

"Poco Loco" is set in a bar of this name in Santo Domingo's Ciudad Nueva neighborhood, in a building across the street from El Parque Independencia. This setting—a heterotopic space where marginalized subjectivities converge—confirms the ways in which Arias's stories validate "illegitimate" places, experiences, and cultural practices banished from the official archives of dominicanidad. Poco Loco, the story's eponymous bar, was open for only a year, but during this time, it was the preferred place for Terror's fans to spend their nights and bask in the charm of marginality while also concocting new ways of being, embodying, and conceptualizing their identities. It was a place where "la ciudad se reconfiguraba. Nuevas propuestas fueron braceando en contra de la corriente de esa dominicanidad oficial"[26] (the city was reconfiguring itself. New proposals were swimming against the current of official dominicanidad). The story emphasizes how the bar Poco Loco became a site of alternative knowledge production where discussions centered on questions of identity as it relates to race and ethnicity, as well as sociopolitical and economic issues that have had an impact on the island:

> En lo que vamos a comenzar, hay temas obligados de amena discusión. Que la idiosincrasia. Que la identidad. Que la negritud. Que la hispanidad. Que si la culpable es la insularidad. Que el colonialismo. Que si las raíces. Que si los indígenas. Que si falta de apoyo gubernamental. Que el subdesarrollo. Que la parte alta, que la represión, que las aguas negras, que los apagones, que los callejones, o el carrito gris. Que si la cultura somos todos o no.[27]

> (When we are about to begin, there are required topics for enjoyable discussion. Whether it's idiosyncrasy. Or identity. Or Blackness. Or Hispanicity. Or if insularity is to blame. Or colonialism. Or the roots. Or indigenous people. Or if government aid is lacking. Or underdevelopment. Or the elite, or repression, or black waters, or blackouts, or alleys, or the gray car. Or if all of us are culture or not.)

In these lines, we see how in spite of their diverse social positions, the gathered patrons—all Terror's acolytes—raise important questions that, as Simon Frith observes, are "central to our sense of identity . . . what we would like to be, not what we are." Raising these questions became a way for this generation to "participate in imagined forms of democracy and desire."[28]

"Poco Loco" also showcases an alternative sonic archive composed of the lyrics of some of Terror's best-known transgressive songs that denounce the diverse forms of violence pervading Dominican society during and after the dictatorship and the doce años. Some of the songs included in the story are "Vickiana," "El carrito gris," and "Anaísa." "Vickiana" is a meditation on the historical violence impinged on women's bodies and sexualities, violence that is very much embedded in the patriarchal foundations of the nation-state. "El carrito gris" refers to the constant terror of being followed or picked up by the national police. "Anaísa" centers Afro-Dominican religiosity, singing to the goddess of love in Dominican voodoo. Terror's sonic archive conjures up a new social consciousness and sense of community and reminds us of the social traumas still latent from the violent, exclusive, and hegemonic foundations of the Dominican nation. In deploying these songs, Arias's story becomes an extension of the defiant and subversive character embodied by Días and reproduced in his music production. It also becomes an invitation to reflect on the ways the past informs identity discourses centered by new generations when rethinking lo que somos (what we are).

"Poco Loco" recounts one of Terror's concerts in the bar, focusing on interactions between the diverse members of the audience and Días's rapport with his followers and congregants. These interchanges reveal what Pablo Vila sees as "alliances between one or multiple identifications of others that strategically coincide in that particular musical performance."[29] In other words, the convergence of fans in the story brings together unfixed and heterogeneous subaltern identities:

> Esta noche acude al Poco Loco la crema y nata de la gente alternativa de Ciudad. Suben las escaleras con frenética desidia: ese chocarse las manos, esa sonrisa de celebridad en ciernes; aquél se dedica a la serigrafía, ésta a la danza afro; "a mí me gusta la sociópata", ¿tú eres cantante de jazz? Ah, qué cool, yo soy cineasta; y yo un estudioso del *Ulises* de James Joyce, que se pronuncia "Yois."[30]

> (That night the cream of the crop of alternative people from the city arrived at Poco Loco. They climbed the stairs with frenetic carelessness: the high fives, the smile of a budding celebrity; that

one does screen printing, this one an Afro-dancer; "I like the sociopath," you're a jazz singer? Oh, that's cool, I'm a filmmaker; and I study *Ulysses* by James Joyce, which is pronounced "Yois.")

People with diverse cultural interests converge in Poco Loco for two reasons: to find a common space where multiple identities, art forms, and trends are in dialogue with each other and to partake in Terror's musical homily, the *"ídolo en común . . . , héroe de lo rural y lo urbano, narrador de noches raídas de represión y bachata"*[31] (idol in common . . . , rural and urban hero, narrator of threadbare nights of repression and bachata). Días is the antidote that, according to the narrator, "logra que nos sintamos menos prisioneros dentro de la habitual prisión"[32] (manages to make us feel less like prisoners of our habitual prison). It is noteworthy that Terror makes the bargoers feel "less like prisoners" in a space that was constructed during the Trujillo dictatorship and reconfigured in the 1980s to try to move beyond its dictatorial past. Paraphrasing Maguire, the presence of Días and his followers in a place that was previously part of the trujillista city—and that later became an emblem of subversion and rebellion—points to the dismantling of the ideological and discursive foundations that originated during the Trujillo dictatorship.[33]

The poetic dismantling of the (neo)trujillista/balaguerista city not only is observed through the physical and ideological reconfiguration of Poco Loco and Terror's central role in the dynamics of the bar but also is evidenced in a particular moment in the story when there is a direct attack on merengue. The narrator makes a comparison between the number of attendees at Terror's concerts and at merengue concerts. She then notes that although the venues differ in terms of geography and visibility—merengue musicians play in the large open space of the Olympic Stadium, whereas Terror's shows happen in closed, clandestine, small spaces—both audiences are equally important in the sense that they represent the diversity of Dominican culture. However, the assault on merengue, which for many is still the cultural emblem of the dictatorship, is clear:[34]

Los conciertos de Terror efectuados aquí y en todas partes, son abarrotados. Esto es tan cierto como que algunas veces no asisten más que cinco gatos, pero esos cinco gatos son tan importantes como los cientos de fanáticos que llenan el Estadio Olímpico para ver cualquier limpiavidrios bailando un merengue de letra repetitiva e insulsa, moviendo en círculos las manos, aupados por empresarios que se ocupan de mantenerlos pegados en la radio a fuerza de payola. Ya Terror lo denunció en una de sus canciones:

"que los vegetales que tengo por hijos, sólo tienen ojos pa' lo limpiavidriiiioooos."[35]

(Terror's concerts held here and everywhere are jam-packed. This is just as true when sometimes no more than five cats come, but those five cats are just as important as the hundreds of fans that fill up the Olympic Stadium to watch some window washer dancing to a merengue with bland, repetitive lyrics, waving their hands in circles, praised by businessmen who make sure they are being constantly played on the radio thanks to *payolas*.[36] Terror condemns this in one of his songs: "The vegetables that are my children only have eyes fo' window waaasherrrrs.")

The pejorative tone with which merengue is described in "Poco Loco" reflects the infiltration of Días's ideology into the voice of the narrator. After 1844, when the Dominican Republic declared its independence as a sovereign state, the national project was strongly tied to merengue, a genre that, although it was an emblem of resistance during the first US intervention in the Dominican Republic (1916–1924), paradoxically became the preferred cultural identifier of the Trujillo era. In many ways, merengue was haunted by the specter of Trujillo until the late 1960s, when its rapid transformation and insertion in diasporic spaces was redemptory. However, merengue was also part of "la lucha sonora," the competition of popular music genres for a spot in the international music marketplace.[37] For Terror, this lucha was twofold. With his defense of music genres that were not mainstream, he sought to resist the commodification of music, which in his view had been detrimental to genres such as merengue and had resulted in the mass production of poor quality and unoriginal themes. To echo this, Arias emphasizes the ways merengue artists' fame was largely a result of payolas. At the same time, I interpret Terror's defense of his own music, in contrast to merengue, as an ideological lucha in which new sounds become a discursive alternative and a form of cultural knowledge production from below. In other words, his music challenged notions of hegemonic dominicanidad still anchored in power structures instituted and perpetuated throughout the twentieth century by the political and cultural elite. In this sense, merengue loses its representational value, unplugging—even if momentarily—the sound machine of the (neo)trujillista city.

"Invi's Paradise" is set between an apartment in the INVI referred to as "Museo del desorden" (Museum of Disarray)—"sede de nuestras alucinaciones, alegrías y desesperanzas"[38] (the headquarters for our hallucinations, joys, and hopelessness)—and a cave, a hidden space, a sort of subaltern world whose congregants are not subject to the established norms of the status quo. By foregrounding these peripheral and underground sites, Arias summons us to rethink dominicanidad from the geographic and cultural margins. Readers engage in a metaphorical walkthrough of the Museo del desorden and the cave, where they are exposed to alternative rhythms, sounds, and ways of embodying dominicanidad. "Invi's Paradise" thus centers cultural and sonic trends that have been dismissed from the dominant script of Dominican identity, including Terror's music and acolytes.

The sonic archive foregrounded in the story is central to destabilize totalizing and uniform understandings of dominicanidad. From the beginning of "Invi's Paradise," we can appreciate the fusion of genres and instruments—clave, maracas, guitar, rock—that creates a more encompassing and inclusive blueprint of Dominican identity. Further, Afrodescendant musical traditions are also acknowledged in the text, with the allusions to *Gagá*, reggae, and *fotuto*. These authorial choices invoke Terror's political commitment to creating new foundational narratives that celebrate diversity and center Afro-Caribbean and Afro-Dominican heritage. Arias draws a cultural blueprint that, in the words of Néstor Rodríguez, overcomes the "discurso europeizante de la nación cuya secuela sigue acaparando hoy el imaginario de la inmensa mayoría de los nacionales dominicanos"[39] (Europeanizing discourse of the nation whose consequences continue to dominate the imaginary of the immense majority of Dominican nationals today).

The strum of Terror's guitar marks the beginning of the story: "Rasga Terror las primeras notas en la guitarra y falta poco para que la vecina del piso de arriba, afanosa en saber qué están haciendo los raros inquilinos de la segunda, baje a pedirles prestado un palito de fósforo."[40] (Terror strums the first notes on his guitar and there isn't much time before the upstairs neighbor, who is dedicated to knowing what the weird tenants on the second floor are doing, comes down to ask for a match.) The story centers "the weird tenants on the second floor," who create their own order in the Museo del desorden. The apparent chaos in which they live, beyond being a mere retaliation against the order imposed by the (neo)trujillista/balaguerista city, can be interpreted as a social reconfiguration in which alternative modes of existence are legible and validated. As such, it is only logical that Terror, a countercultural icon whose musical and social revolution embodied transgressive representations of official Dominican identity, is a pivotal character in "Invi's Paradise." This is clearly illustrated in the description of scruffy and effeminate Terror, who offers a queer alternative to dominant masculinity: "*Él, Terror, exhibe su anatomía fibrosa ahora lampiña, jeans cortos, sucios y apretados, contoneo pedante, pañuelo rojo, atado al cuello.*"[41] (*He, Terror, shows off his fibrous anatomy now hairless, dirty and tight jean shorts, pedantic sway, red scarf tied to his neck.*)

Nonfictional Terror was committed to creating a new order through his sonic and cultural projects. His interview with Diógenes Céspedes conflates his identity and his own understanding of dominicanidad as fluid and ever-changing, the result of asynchronous and synchronous sociohistorical and cultural conjunctures:

> Si creas tu propio orden, creas tu propia forma de ver el mundo, y la extrapolas a la música, vas a tener tu autenticidad. Claro que vas a crear una anarquía primero, y la creatividad primero tiene que ser anárquica, hay que crear el choque de lo nuevo, el miedo de lo nuevo, el terror a lo nuevo, hay que lograr que un grupo te odie y otro te ame.[42]

> (If you create your own order, you create your own way of seeing the world, and you extrapolate it to your music, you are going to be authentic. Surely you will create an anarchy first, and creativity must be firstly anarchist, you have to create the clash between the new, the fear of the new, the terror of the new, you have to make one group hate you and another group love you.)

In addition to his chameleonlike, cutting-edge, and boundary-breaking image, Días's experimentation with sound fusion and constant centering of marginalized cultural traditions function as discursive strategies to introduce subjectivities and musical expressions that were relegated to the sidelines in the cultural and social cartographies of the (neo)trujillista/balaguerista city. The affirmation of the "I" by Terror in the symbolic space of the story is not surprising. During a concert, the audience asks him to play a Bob Marley song. He rejects the request and decides to play one of his own songs—one that centers a subjectivity that mirrors the social reality of many rural and urban Dominican men:

> Entonces todos le piden a Terror que interprete a Marley; Marley les recuerda a los días que pasaron juntos en la playa; hay toda una añoranza, Bob Marley y la felicidad total. Terror se niega, one, two, three, four, Andresito Reyna, ordena, porque yo, yo, yo, en este país, ja, ja, yo, yo, yo. La vida para él es un gran escenario con una sola estrella. Él.[43]

(Then everyone asks Terror to play a Marley song; Marley reminds them of the days they spent at the beach; there's a sense of longing, Bob Marley and total happiness. Terror refuses, one, two, three, four, "Andresito Reyna," he orders, because I, I, I, in this country, ha ha, I, I, I. For him, life is like a big stage with only one star. Him.)

Maguire interprets this declaration as "un gesto tal vez egoísta pero también indicativo del ambiente particular del momento"[44] (a selfish gesture, perhaps, but also indicative of the particular atmosphere of the moment). I take this even further and argue that the "I" is an ontological shift from the individual to a collective consciousness. The assertion and repetition of the "I" six times points to a multiplication of the subject; the act of naming oneself multiple times can generate a collective "we." The declaration of the "I" in this passage is a call for creating community beyond immediate social circles, summoning the audience to consider the tribulations of working-class Dominican men and women such as the ones presented in "Andresito Reyna," the song Terror chooses to perform instead. In this well-known song, Terror speaks of the effects of violence, alcohol, and cockfighting on the lives of a local antihero and his romantic partner. By mentioning this song, Arias evinces Terror's mission to elevate the collective consciousness toward an inclusivity of local narratives that do not necessarily take place in urban spaces populated by middle-class youth. In this sense, it amplifies his efforts to legitimize oft-ignored aspects of dominicanidad.

"Invi's Paradise" is imbued with Terror's essence; it personifies the rebellious, insubordinate, and defiant character of his music. Like Terror, the story is a type of "terror" that confronts the reader with national scripts founded on principles of othering, excluding, and silencing. Arias's utilization of Terror conjures more inclusive narratives of dominicanidad that foreground subaltern subjects, as well as cultural and sonic archives that had been exiled from official discourses on Dominican identity. "Invi's Paradise" is a celebration of a subculture that, though brief in trajectory, managed to remain in the memory of those who, through literature, pay tribute to the subversive spirit of a musical icon and his legacy.

Dominican artist Álex Guerrero describes Terror as "la banda sonora de nuestra generación"[45] (the sound box of our generation [the 1980s]). Arias's centering of this sound box in "Poco Loco" and "Invi's Paradise" amplifies the sounds of a decade, a generation, and a cultural-musical icon that have been seminal to cementing, promoting, and validating alternative ways of experiencing and embodying dominicanidad. Through her representation of this decade and Terror, Arias reimagines lo dominicano. She writes about cultural transformations that were taking place in a sort of borderland between rigid and fluid ways of imagining Dominican identity. Thus both stories reference fluid identity discourses that interrupt the stagnancy of a literary canon still shaped by the ideological foundations of a dictatorial past. Arias's stories narrate the countercultural proliferation of the 1980s in alternative urban spaces. By centering the propensities and anxieties of subaltern subjectivities and the countercultural icon of Luis "Terror" Días, "Invi's Paradise" and "Poco Loco" fracture the genealogy of a literary canon tied to the ideological (neo)trujillista apparatus. Arias's work is therefore a political project aimed at disassembling the rigid identitarian structures imposed by the (neo)trujillista/balaguerista city.

CENTERING SILENCED BODIES IN TRANSNATIONAL DOMINICANIDAD: "TERROR" LIVES IN ALL OF US

Centering marginalized experiences continues to be crucial to conceptualizing emergent discourses that negotiate and complicate the hegemonic project of dominicanidad. New discursive narratives about Dominican identity at the intersection of the Dominican Republic and New York are articulated in Rey Andújar's short story "Terror." In this piece, as with Aurora Arias, the author centers Terror, portraying him as a figure who, despite being consistently repudiated, injured, and violated by an island that is repeating itself in the diasporic Caribbean,[46] manages to survive in the individual and collective memories of those who knew him and those influenced by his legacy. His presence in Andújar's story, and the ways Terror is a foil to the narrator and some of the characters in the story, opens a series of wounds that may be familiar to Dominican migrants in New York City, whose bodies bear evidence of the social and historical conjunctures that have forced them to auto-exile in Manhattan. Thus my reading of "Terror" focuses on how it disrupts the silencing of voices in the Dominican literary imaginary aquí y allá by centering marginalized bodies.

Andújar's "Terror" is narrated in the first and third person by an unnamed man who self-exiles in New York for reasons that are never explicitly delineated, though over the course of the story, it becomes clear that he has fled as a result of othering, feelings of abandonment, and the violence he experienced and witnessed on the island. With the goal of reinventing himself and moving beyond the limitations of the island space, the narrator lands in New York "with dreams that were shattered immediately."[47] Upon his arrival in New York City, his body, an open wound between two countries, becomes vulnerable to additional injuries and pain in this new geographic space.

The story begins with the description of his arrival at the John F. Kennedy Airport in New York. Some of the violent images used to describe this first encounter with New York's winter presage his looming exposure to other forms of violence in the diasporic space: "After leaving JFK without a fucking coat, and a slice of January cut open my chest and filled it with pain urging me to return. But to where?"[48] This vulnerability is shared by the two Dominican women with whom the narrator shares an apartment in Queens and the literary representation of Terror—the only named character in the story. In the case of the women and the narrator, they are unable to escape the terrors experienced on the home island and overcome their transnational anonymity. As to Terror, he faces constant dismissal and ostracizing in the insular space and anonymity in the extra-insular space.

The presence of these bodies in the symbolic space is key to understanding the diasporic space as nonemancipatory; it is a continuation of the home island, and those who migrate because they could not stay, to paraphrase Torres-Saillant, bring with them the good and bad from the island.[49] All four characters—the two women, the narrator, and Terror—inhabit wounded bodies that, despite geographic distance, cannot overcome the diverse forms of trauma inflicted on them by the hegemonic powers on the island.

The story foregrounds subjectivities that have been affected by the structural violence of the nation-state. Even if the diasporic space does not assuage the pain inflicted on the characters of "Terror," Andújar presents narratives of Dominican migration that complicate the relationship between homeland and hostland by highlighting the impossibility of total detachment from the memories, experiences, and life on the island in the diasporic space.

Early in the story, the narrator discovers that the sadness of the older woman with whom he shares an apartment in Queens is due to the "accidental" murder of her daughter in a shootout between a policeman and a bank robber on the island. In his recounting of the story, the narrator emphasizes the mishandling of the situation by the Dominican police that resulted in the young woman's unfortunate death and the subsequent auto-exile of her grieving mother to New York. He goes as far as to say, "They [the police] were supposed to rescue survivors, and instead they ended up bombarding them in their ineptitude."[50] With this assertion, the narrator unearths "one of the more famous heists in recent Dominican history"[51] to show how bodies, in this case those of the deceased daughter and auto-exiled mother, remain illegible in official accounts of the event. In this way, the story presents Dominican migration to New York in the 1980s as a multilayered experience, the product of diverse junctures that are not necessarily tied to macropolitics and financial needs. Migration, as shown in the case of the grieving mother, is also an unsuccessful attempt to forget, to run away from the memories of violence that affected her personally. As the narrator states, "She did not want to know anymore and took refuge in that apartment with a collection of trashy romance novels and the comfort of chicken and rice on Saturdays of a drunken stupor."[52]

His other roommate is a woman in her thirties who, despite her youth, is already worn down, decaying, consumed by her nostalgia for the 1980s and Días's song "Vickiana." Her body, a ghostly image of the star that inspired the song, is the medium through which the narrator discovers the music of Terror, another ghost who, like the narrator and his two roommates, lives anonymously in the city of New York:

> We didn't have to turn on the lights, but the sense of touch doesn't lie and there was her ass all fallen with the misery of all those kilometers of cellulite. After coming twice, we drank coffee baptized with Panamanian rum, the lights still off. She invited me to listen to music in her room. It was one of Terror's pirated albums, a song dedicated to Vickiana, a cabaret star of decadence that had her fifteen minutes in the brevity of the '80s.[53]

When he hears the song, the narrator says, "except for the guitar and the voice, everything else was dispensable. The brutality of the phrasing followed me past dawn; seldom had I heard an instrument played using so much force."[54] From this fragment, we can deduce that Terror's undeniable talent, grit, and "force" travel with diasporic subjects and produce an alternate cultural and musical "Archive of Dominicanidad," to borrow from García-Peña, beyond the confines of the island space.[55] The narrator's description of the way Terror's music and voice were imprinted in his memory as the only things that were not "dispensable" also reveals the unique relationship between music and identity in Caribbean and diasporic Caribbean subjectivities. The reference to Terror in this instance, and the way he haunts the sonic memories of the narrator and roommate, is an unfortunate reminder of the wounds inscribed on migrant bodies that are constantly rejected, marginalized, and dehumanized on the island and its extension in the diasporic space. The mythical figure of Terror thus emerges in the literary space to show the wounds that migration cannot heal or undo.

In this story, Andújar re-creates a decaying version of Terror—the remains of an icon yearning to replicate his 1980s Santo Domingo fame on small bar stages in New York. During the narrator's nightly barhopping, he sees Terror in a bar called Caña. When the narrator enters the bar, he suddenly realizes that he is anonymous in New York: "As far as this city was concerned, I was a stranger to this city." A member of a Latino theater company in Corona, Queens, where he plays futile roles in "theater for aficionados, using hours that [he] stole from sleep: mediocre theater, often pathetic," the narrator writes novels that nobody reads. During this first encounter with Terror, the narrator realizes that both are actually strangers in New York City, as Terror isn't well known in New York. Terror has a small following of "hip chicks in Brooklyn" who idolize him and are his usual audience on small stages, but they don't compare to his 1980s crowds or acolytes.[56]

After this encounter, the narrator no longer sees Terror as an icon, but as an immigrant whose dreams of removing himself from the painful memories and rejection sustained on the home island are truncated by his desire to return to a few corners of the Dominican capital where he was not a stranger: "to that shithole in Güibia, to the garbage on the beach of Montesinos, to the philosophy of Barra Payán at four in the morning, to the corner stores of Ciudad Nueva, to the possibility of robbery on Charles de Gaulle, or the motels with their flashy signs: Santo Domingo, a bite on the black kiss."[57] Disappointed by this, the narrator regrets having seen the musician's misery in New York that night at Caña because Terror's ghostly image and longing to return reflected the narrator's own relationship with the clashing memories of an island that keep repeating themselves in New York:

> It took the whole summer to understand that the only thing immigrants drag here, in addition to their plans and the blind promise of progress, is basic anthropology. The affable sounds that connect our bones to the earth, our tears to our nerves, the distance between what is said and what is done, the degrees of separation of the blood.[58]

With the realization that these realities unite him with Terror, the narrator begins taking zombielike walks through the streets of New York City. During his daily meandering, he reflects on his abandonment by his mother, who had moved to Holland to prostitute herself for economic reasons. In what could be perceived as an act of vengeance toward his mother, while she is visiting New York, he invites her to a play in which he dresses as a woman in a ménage à trois with two men. The performance makes him truly visible to his mother—a metonym for the nation that rejected and abandoned him—and she thinks of him as having been corrupted by New York's anti-values. She assumes he is an addict, consumed by the drug epidemic that plagued Dominican youth in the 1980s and 1990s. Since the stage becomes a space of validation and legitimization of his gender identity and sexuality in front of the audience and his mother, this performance of his identity can be interpreted in two ways. One is as an emotional reaction to his mother's disavowal of him and his gender identity and sexuality, noted in her preference to think of him as a drug user rather than as queer. The other is as a direct contestation of the hegemonic and heterosexist foundations of the Dominican nation-state.

The contestation of the inherent heterosexism of the Dominican nation-state becomes more evident when the narrator returns to the island wearing the black-and-white dress, wig, and makeup he used in his performances in New York. Upon his arrival, the narrator transforms in the privacy of a rented apartment in Santo Domingo. There he is both actor and spectator. His transformative ritual is initiated with a long shower, followed by putting on the dress and wig. He applies makeup, then lights candles and reads aloud stories by Manuel Ramos Otero. His choice of reading is of particular significance, as Ramos Otero, like the narrator, was a "sexile" who left Puerto Rico and fled to New York to have the freedom to express his gender identity and sexuality openly without fear of persecution.[59] In this way, the narrator situates his reality within a Pan-Caribbean poetics of queer and trans abjection. It should be noted that while the narrator's migration to New York City did not exactly free him from judgment and reprisal, it was in New York that he was able to "come out" to his mother during his theatrical performance, and we can even infer that this propelled him to return to the island and expose himself publicly as a queer, gender-nonconforming subject.

On the third night of this ritual, the narrator decides to stroll the streets of Santo Domingo sporting his black-and-white dress and wig in a context where it is "still strange to see a man walking around dressed as a woman on the streets, even today when it's been so exposed and declared openly."[60] This walk opens doors to new scripts of dominicanidad in which alternative forms of gender identity and sexuality are possible, an attempt, in the words of Mayra Santos Febres, to "cease the logic of the real, replacing it with the logical of the probable."[61] On the streets, the cross-dressing body destabilizes the heteronormative order deemed as "real," introducing and validating other gender identities. This enunciation is interrupted, however, when a group of men insult and assault the narrator. Following this unfortunate event, the narrator walks slouched over on the darker side of the street, hiding himself. The disruption of the narrator dressed as a woman in public is a sporadic yet significant social and cultural intervention that, even if only for an instant, inscribes the abject body into the collective consciousness of all who witness this "embodied transgender expression."[62]

At the end of the story, we learn that the narrator's return to the island coincided with Terror's homecoming. Terror is now a specter of the person he used to be—the scarred and exhausted body of a returnee whose attempt to escape the constant rejections of his home island in New York City had been unsuccessful. Both characters "exhibited themselves" upon their return to the island—the narrator as a cross-dresser and Terror as the specter of the icon he once was—and both were annihilated by dominant discourses on the island that still delineate which bodies fit into the rubric of dominicanidad. Ultimately, the narrator is beaten down by the men who insulted him; he says they "had beaten the transvestite out of me." Before his assault, the narrator had gone to see Terror play a show, but instead of seeing the "force" Terror was, he saw the specter of Luis Días, returned to the stage in the Zona Colonial, but even more deteriorated than he had appeared in the narrator's first encounter with him in New York. The narrator describes what he sees: Terror is "on an improvised stage pouring rum on his head and spitting a mouthful of it onto his guitar as if it were a cock under one blue light and one green one that created a silhouette of how I would remember him long after that concert for a girl in a little black and white dress, the object of all the criticism and all his songs."[63]

While bedridden in a hospital following his near-fatal assault the night he witnessed Terror's physical deterioration in the Zona Colonial, the narrator decides to move to Cabarete, a tourist area in the northern part of the island. After he saves some money, he migrates to California and later Puerto Rico. He then publishes two books, "if only to experience another form of failure." Settled in Old San Juan, he learns of Terror's death. Toward the end of the story, the narrator suggests that to vindicate Terror's memory and retaliate against a nation that is constantly ostracizing bodies like his and Terror's, he ought to return to the Dominican Republic and revisit painful memories. Upon his return, he stops in a bookstore and sees a book titled *La narrativa yugulada* (The strangled narrative). At the bookseller's insistence, he buys it, but at that moment he notices something that catches his eye much more: a blue-green handbound book, *¡Échale gas!* (Step on the gas!), a collection of interviews, testimonials, and works by and about Terror. In a romantic outburst, he buys the book and realizes that "coincidences don't end" and that they "feed the game that this city is. So many planes and so much sadness; so much wreckage; so much of myself run aground, just to prove that Terror never dies."[64]

The narrator's pilgrimage thus brings him back to an island that is constantly repeating itself at home and abroad. His return is an attempt to avenge the bodies gnawed on and strangled by violence and constant marginalization, and it brings forth an intriguing—and optimistic—outlook on how the circularity of diaspora offers an opportunity to rethink ourselves and rewrite our stories outside the confines of nation-states. One such example is the narrator's encounter with the collection *Luis Días, ¡Échale gas!*, a book initially published in 1999 (with a second edition in 2012) to preserve the legacy of Terror, an homage to a countercultural musical icon who, in spite of many metaphorical and physical deaths, persists in the memory of generations of Dominicans on and off the island. The narrator's act of retaliation and self-assertion is, then, the recounting of his story—one that is undeniably interconnected with other diasporic subjects such as his roommates and Terror. It is a story of many stories that bridge the borderlands between time and space. If anything, this story and the texts by Josefina Báez that I analyze in the next section remind us that there is something to learn from repetition and that the wounds inscribed in our migrant bodies, rather than being construed as fatality, can allow us to rethink ourselves and rewrite our stories beyond borders.

LEVENTE NO. YOLAYORKDOMINICANYORK AND "LA LISTA DEL TERROR": LUIS "TERROR" DÍAS BETWEEN HERE AND THERE

Esta historia es la historia de los que estamos siempre fuera de La Historia. (This story is the history of those of us who are always outside of History.)

JOSEFINA BÁEZ, *Levente no. Yolayorkdominicanyork*

The references to Terror in Josefina Báez's writing occur organically, a product of the many interactions, encounters, and shared experiences between the two artists—both translocated subjects, always in motion, constantly crossing physical, disciplinary, and linguistic borders. It is only natural that the echoes of Terror's song "Liborio" are part of the sonic archive that enlivens Báez's performance piece *Dominicanish* (2000), which I analyze in chapter 4. Even more natural and, dare I say, genuine is the space Báez carves out to honor Terror in *Levente no. Yolayorkdomin-*

icanyork (2011), a text for performance, and "Lista del Terror," the poem she wrote the month of his death, December 2009, and first published on the Cielo Naranja website. In both the excerpt of *Levente no. Yolayorkdominicanyork* and the poem, Terror's image and legacy extend and multiply themselves in the literary space. Báez's literary re-creations of Terror foreground the history and itinerary of a translocated subject who, in spite of being visible in the spaces he inhabited (New York and Hispaniola), was perpetually marginalized and excluded in both. I read Báez's depiction of Terror through the lens of Lorgia García-Peña's conceptualization of the symbolic space of El Nié as "the body that carries the violent borders that deter them from entering the nation, from access to full citizenship and from public, cultural, historical, and political representations."[65] His figure, then, is a bridge between the systems of oppression and exclusion that have deemed him and other inhabitants of El Nié invisible. His existence shows the cracks between two worlds, what Anzaldúa calls the "rajaduras," where alternative knowledges are produced.

"Lista del Terror" is a eulogy to Terror in the form of a list that can be read as the compendium of his life—a comprehensive and detailed account of his trajectory from his birth in Bonao to his death in Santo Domingo, when his heart gave out and there was no more fight left in his physical body. The list emphasizes Terror's immortality in the Dominican imaginary. Terror is the heart of a space that transcends the border between *here* and *there*, "el resultado de un proceso complejo" (the result of a complex process). In the poem, Terror is portrayed as ubiquitous and able to be in two places at once: "Terror en Quisqueya en el Hudson. / Terror en Erre De." (Terror in Quisqueya in the Hudson River. / ... Terror in the DR.) He is also the main referent of Dominican cultural history, filling the silences left by official histories: "Terror se convierte en fuente. / ... El Terror es la música de Erre De por dentro. Y por fuera." (Terror becomes a source. / ... Terror is the music inside the DR. And outside.) Báez centers Terror as the "source," rectifying his erasure from official cultural archives in both the US and the DR and creating an alternative to dominant sonic archives.[66]

Although Báez accentuates some of the nuances we saw in Arias's stories, such as rebellion, insubordination, and irreverence, both of Báez's texts also emphasize some facets of Terror's life that speak to his positionality as a Dominican immigrant artist in New York. In her first encounter with Terror, the narrator of *Levente no. Yolayorkdominicanyork* describes several aspects of his behavior that make him more relatable—less godlike—to his fans. In New York, Terror is not the same 1980s star who took off his sweat-covered shirt on stage and blessed his fans with every drop that exuded from his pores. Rather, Báez says, "Era como nosotros. Tú sabes. Cojonú. Enrredao. Boca suelta. Con el corazón y la cabeza en chercha."[67] (He was like us. You know. Awesome. Messed up. A loose cannon. With his heart and his head in having a good time.) Báez shows us a more intimate, less iconic Terror who doesn't keep his distance from his followers. Her version of Terror is an inhabitant of El Nié, another interstitial body confronting a second erasure in New York. Nonetheless, the erasures of Terror from both the island and the diasporic space are overcome by his omnipresence—"pero el Terror está en todas partes"[68] (but Terror is everywhere)—that is the result of the in-betweenness of his existence, rendering his condition redemptory as well as an opportunity to create a larger and more encompassing borderless community.

In "Transnational Music and Dance in Dominican New York," ethnomusicologist Thomas van Buren and folklorist Leonardo Iván Domínguez explore the transmigrant experiences of Dominicans by focusing on the transnational dynamics between the Dominican Republic and New York City through expressive forms of culture such as music, dance, poetry, and folk religious practices.[69] Their study situates these dynamics as paramount to understanding the intricate political, economic, and cultural flows between eastern Hispaniola and New York City.[70] Van Buren and Domínguez argue that "beyond the mere reinforcement of cultural patterns, transnationalism also entails the maintenance of national identity, either through the re-creation of a home culture, or by the expression of a variation of it within the construct of the new environment."[71] I would argue that the literary re-creation of Terror in Báez's texts also re-creates alternative sounds of dominicanidad from the diasporic space.

The passage of *Levente no. Yolayorkdominicanyork* dedicated to Terror instantiates this idea as it activates a sonic and cultural archive the Dominican nation-state otherwise suppresses. In it, the narrator describes her experience seeing and hearing Terror play live at the annual folk music festival Quisqueya en el Hudson.[72] By recording fragments of a seminal cultural event that took place in the Dominican community of Washington Heights, Báez, in dialogue with the authors of this chapter, auscultate sounds otherwise ignored in the arrhythmic heartbeat of hegemonic dominicanidad.

The young narrator's sonic memory of Terror at the 1997 iteration of Quisqueya en el Hudson evinces the ways Terror's physical presence (even after his death) and music can be useful to conceptualize dominicanidad as a tapestry made from a collection of threads and pieces that transcend official memories and geographic boundaries. Rather, as seen in the words of the narrator, Terror's music, a sound that is constantly skipped in the rhythm of the Dominican heart, takes her to many places and memories that are also part of her identity. She says, "Pero cuando él tocó . . . diantre la música me llevó pa' to lo sitio."[73] (But when he played . . . heck, his music took me to all kinds of places.) Terror's live performance adds new life to a sonic archive she had previously accessed only through her mother's old records, offering her a real experience of an alternative understanding of Dominican cultural identity.[74] Hearing and seeing the embodiment of an alternative music archive that marked her mother's generation is a metaphorical homecoming to a past that is very much latent, unspoken, in her family history. Pablo Vila argues that when we submit ourselves to the bodily pleasure of a performance or listening to music, we understand part of our identity. In this sense, being part of the musical performativity becomes an identity discourse that "through repetition and its inscription on the body, [has] the capacity to [re]produce what [it] name[s]."[75]

The repetition and inscription of Terror's signature in the text become another way to reproduce him in the literary space. In both of Báez's pieces, Terror signs his autograph by writing his name as a drawing of a guitar. In doing so, he represents sound through the visual. Thus the reader is able to look at what we can't listen to, creating a trans-sensory experience where the audible and nonaudible complement one another.[76] Additionally, by foregrounding the repetitive act of Terror's signature, the visual imprinting of his unique signature in both texts makes his footprint in transnational Dominican cultural history legible, visible, and audible.

Báez and Andújar both reclaimed Luis "Terror" Días after his death in 2009. Terror's physical death, then, was a gateway to recovering and centering his legacy from below—from the peripheries of the Dominican diaspora in the United States. In Báez's works, Terror's death invites us to think about his life and death not as loss, but as an opportunity to create new narratives and knowledge. Further, Terror's life and death as conceptualized by Báez were "el resultado de un proceso complejo" (the result of a complicated process) that ultimately is the process of all inhabitants of El Nié: "El Terror en todos nosotros. / El Terror de todos. / Todos somos Terror."[77] (Terror is in all of us. / Everyone's Terror. / We are all Terror.) Beyond celebrating the rebellious spirit of youth in the 1980s, as Arias does, Báez celebrates the permanence of Terror's cultural legacy both on the island and in the Dominican immigrant community in New York, legitimizing the rajadura Terror was and continues to be as a form of knowledge production for alternative and fluid narratives of dominicanidad.

These new approaches to scripts of dominicanidad also took center stage for the urban youth of the 1990s, with their almost anonymous existence in urban Santo Domingo and the musical proclivities that marked their generation, as portrayed in Rita Indiana's *La estrategia de Chochueca*. In this section, I read the phantomlike existence of these youth as a continuation of the structural and foundational intransigence of the same hegemonic narratives that made Terror illegible in official discourses of dominicanidad. In doing so, I amplify the intersections between popular music and the written word that proliferate in Dominican fiction narrative as sonic literary texts.

In the prologue to the third edition of Rita Indiana's *La estrategia de Chochueca*, Juan Duchesne-Winter quotes the words of Néstor Rodríguez, who deemed the novella "la contribución más importante a la novelística dominicana de los últimos 20 años"[78] (the most important contribution to the Dominican novel in the past twenty years). Two decades after this statement, I reread it today as a seminal illustration of a literary wave that has moved beyond one-dimensional and nationalistic discourses of dominicanidad.[79] Further, I approach the novella as a space where sound enters the domain of language and the sonic and nonsonic converge to provide a more holistic and encompassing script of dominicanidad. Within this framework, I consider how *La estrategia de Chochueca* legitimizes new spaces, experiences, and subjects in the Dominican imaginary and how Rita Indiana creates knowledge from the cracks of history and official discourses of dominicanidad through conflating the sonic and nonsonic.

In *The Practice of Everyday Life*, Michel de Certeau asserts that the "concept city" is a place of distributions, differentiations, rejections, transformations, and appropriations. Urban life, in de Certeau's view, "increasingly permits the re-emergence of the element that the urbanistic project excluded." Thus "the city is left prey to contradictory movements that counterbalance and combine themselves outside the reach of panoptic power," where "the ruses and combination of powers that have no readable identity proliferate."[80] In this sense, the urban cartography re-created in *La estrategia de Chochueca* centers the practices that resist and survive the decaying and stagnant sociopolitical and geographic demarcations of the (neo)trujillista/balaguerista city.

Rita Indiana's portrayal of Dominican urban life is mostly anchored in what used to be the center of the Dominican capital, the Zona Colonial, and neighborhoods in the western part of the capital, which became the new *centro* in the 1980s.[81] She privileges geographic spaces rejected and eliminated by the (neo)trujillista/balaguerista city, centering illegitimate and unreadable spaces, bodies, and experiences. The novella validates the existence of subaltern subjects in an urban center that, as Fernanda Bustamante points out, "da cuenta de la transformación de las dinámicas sociales después de la represión del último gobierno de Balaguer, al mismo tiempo que desmantela los discursos hegemónicos en los que se ha envuelto la 'dominicanidad'"[82] (accounts for the transformation of social dynamics after the repression of the Balaguer government, while at the same time dismantling the hegemonic discourses in which "dominicanidad" is enveloped).

La estrategia de Chochueca is the story of the nighttime escapades of a generation yearning for a social and spatial structure unlike that of their past and present, one where their differences are no longer squashed or eliminated. Rita Indiana weaves a story that follows a group of young people through a series of mishaps, delineating what Néstor Rodríguez calls a "subversive cartography" of Santo Domingo.[83] The novella revolves around the theft of a set of speakers and the various attempts by Silvia, the narrator, and some of her friends to find and return them without being caught by the police. The speakers signify the sounds of a city buried in the physical and metaphorical ruins of the aftermath of thirty-one years of dictatorship, political instability, and political unrest: the second US occupation, La Guerra de Abril, Balaguer's doce años and his return to the presidency in 1986 after two terms of the Partido Revolucionario Dominicano, and the International Monetary Fund's austerity measures of 1985. With this context in the background, Silvia and her friends draw new geographic and cultural cartographies of the city and privilege new sounds as means of counteracting the political and economic ruin that surrounds them.

The novella bridges local and global music to establish an urban spatial and ideological reordering in which subjects and expressions that have remained marginal in hegemonic dominicanidad become legible and visible, even if only in the symbolic space of literature. The sonic archive and musical artifacts (speakers, CDs, music boxes, cassettes) that populate the text create what Lorna Torrado calls a *ciudad musical*: "una realidad alterna que apunta hacia un nuevo sujeto urbano globalizado que no tiene que limitarse al imaginario cultural caribeño"[84] (an alternate reality that points toward a new globalized subject that does not have to be limited to the Caribbean cultural imaginary).

It is no coincidence that this ciudad musical in which the sonic (music) and nonsonic (literature) conflate provides the rhythm and structure of *La estrategia de Chochueca*; it is a narrative mechanism, a rhetorical technique, and an ideological tool. Music is a constant throughout the seven chapters of the book, where three music-centered spaces—a record store, a concert, and a rave—converge. Further, music idols are referenced to contextualize the popular culture trends of a particular era, including Madonna, Kurt Cobain, the Meat Puppets, David Byrne, and the Talking Heads. At other times, as intertexts, lyrics of recognizable popular songs appear in the story: "Alguien ha cometido la temeridad de poner a Talking Heads en el equipo de música. 'Memories can't wait,' la guitarra que tiembla y habla por una boca seca, pa, pa, . . . never woke up had no regrets . . ."[85] (Someone has committed the recklessness of putting Talking Heads on the stereo. "Memories can't wait," the guitar that trembles and speaks with a dry mouth, pa, pa, . . . never woke up had no regrets . . .)

Music also takes center stage through the speakers. At the beginning of the story, the stolen speakers, dusted off and extracted from the ruins of a pawn shop, fall into the hands of "una generación de dominicanos que no aparecen en la publicidad, que no es pensada por la política y que podría pertenecer a cualquier otra ciudad, porque sus realidades sobrepasan el territorio insular para reflejarse en la realidad urbana de ciudades como Nueva York, Barcelona o Ciudad de México"[86] (a new generation of Dominicans that don't appear in advertising, are not thought about in politics, and could belong to any other city because their realities exceed the island territory to reflect the urban reality of cities like New York, Barcelona, and Mexico City).

The reappropriation of the speakers by the youth portrayed in the novel, especially the narrator, a young modern-day flaneuse who reinvents the city and its sounds with every night stroll, is an attempt to reset—at least in the symbolic plane—the ideological foundations that have marked the rhythm of the city. In the words of Torrado, "La importancia de las bocinas reitera el valor literal y simbólico que tiene la música a través de la novela, y simultáneamente el robo funciona como rechazo metafórico del *status quo* y de la Ciudad Trujillo"[87] (the importance of the loudspeakers reiterates the literal and symbolic value the music has throughout the novel, and simultaneously the robbery functions as a metaphorical rejection of the status quo and of the trujillista city).

In their quest to find the speakers, Silvia and her friend Saturnino end up in a pawn shop, a repository of unredeemed items that may never return to their original owners. Silvia describes the shop's warehouse as a chaotic space filled with eclectic objects:

Huacales llenos de armas blancas, grandes y pequeñas dagas al servicio de la población, televisores, tres o cuatro bicicletas, enciclopedias, planchas y tostadoras, bates de baseball, un espejo con el marco labrado feísimo, un lío de ropa en una funda, cajitas de música, muebles que olían a mocato, cajas fuertes, discos compactos usados y nuevos, todo en un supremo desorden, cada cosa encima o al lado de la otra, en una sinfonía barroca de metal, mierda y fibra de vidrio; y al fondo una gran cosa cubierta con una lona azul: las bocinas.[88]

(Crates full of blades, small and large daggers at the service of the population, televisions, three or four bicycles, encyclopedias, irons and toasters, baseball bats, a mirror in a very ugly carved frame, a mess of clothes in a plastic bag, music boxes, furniture that smelled of mold, safes, used and new CDs, everything in supreme disorder, each item on top of or next to another, in a baroque symphony of metal, shit, and fiberglass; and at the back, something big covered in a blue tarp: the loudspeakers.)

The pawn shop is a metonymic representation of the Dominican nation: a chaotic, disjointed space in which incongruent objects are juxtaposed, creating an excessive and disordered array of elements that describe the eastern side of Hispaniola. At first Rita Indiana's choice to confront her characters with this chaos may be perceived as fatalist, as if they are doomed to live in the ruins of the historical mess they inherited, unable to create sense and order out of it. Yet the presence of musical objects in the pawn shop (the music boxes, CDs, and speakers) marks an opportunity to create some sort of order in their immediate and current historical context. CDs, for instance, had a revolutionary explosion in the 1980s, during the age of global changes in digital recording, and were the optimal medium for recorded music throughout the 1980s and 1990s. References to CDs throughout the novella, both directly and through the various mentions of the music of punk, rock, pop, and reggae bands and icons, situate the characters in a context heavily influenced by global music trends (particularly from the US). In this sense, by centering the sounds that defined a generation of Dominican youth, *La estrategia de Chochueca* can be understood as an attempt to depart from the chaotic past that keeps invading and obstructing the present of the youth represented in its pages.

In a similar, yet somewhat divergent, vein, the author's choice to center the speakers in the story could also be an attempt to confront the reader with the frustrations of a generation of youth who, in spite of having a visible device that can amplify their voices and project their concerns, are unable to use it in the public eye of a Santo Domingo that is still influenced and defined by the ideological apparatus of the (neo)trujillista/balaguerista city. Silvia and her friends must keep hiding the speakers, making use of the nights to move them around the city until they reach their unknown final destination. Torrado suggests that Silvia's efforts to transport the speakers through the margins of the city can be read as a "crítica de la realidad dominicana atrapada entre un sistema ideológico-político fallido y un presente estéril que no ofrece opciones viables"[89] (criticism of the Dominican reality trapped between a failed ideological-political system and a sterile present that does not offer any viable options). To this I would add that the constant movement and transiting of the speakers through the capital's underground serve as a metaphor for the impetus of these youth to keep moving until they find a way to (re)produce new sounds that would counter, and perhaps annihilate, the noise of a city that refuses to hear them.

To reframe the foundations of the Dominican imaginary through music, the novella also highlights an event that has been kept at the margins of official narratives of the Dominican nation-state: the Siete Días con el Pueblo music festival, the first international meeting of the Nueva Canción organized by the Central General de Trabajadores in 1974. The festival was a collective act designed to mark music as political—a tool to resist and denounce repressive and authoritarian regimes in Latin America and the Caribbean during the 1970s.[90] Those who opposed the authoritarian regime of Balaguer gathered during the seven days of the series of concerts with music icons of canción protesta from Latin America and the Caribbean to denounce the repression, constant harassment, and violence that prevailed during the doce años, as well as the unjust imprisonment of political dissidents in the Dominican Republic, Latin America, and the Caribbean. From the brief yet concise manifesto of the event, we can appreciate how the political climate in Latin America and the Caribbean culminated in a collaborative solidarity project that championed popular resistance as means to combat political repression.[91]

By foregrounding Siete Días con el Pueblo, Rita Indiana underscores the role of music in dissident politics as an avenue for unity and grassroots change. In the novella, Salim, one of Silvia's friends, recounts his unforgettable childhood encounter with Silvio Rodríguez and his own father, Don xxxxx, a vocal critic of the Balaguerato:

Pasaba Silvio Rodríguez con una camisita de rayas y me cargaba un hombre altísimo y les decía a unos jóvenes que yo era el hijo, que yo era el hijo, que yo era el hijo . . . y los presos, los presos, los presos, mi mamá desgañitándose con una consigna y yo con los bracitos alrededor de su cuello.[92]

(Silvio Rodríguez was walking by in a striped T-shirt and a very tall man was carrying me and I told some young people that I was the son, that I was the son, that I was the son . . . and the prisoners, the prisoners, the prisoners, my mother scolding herself with an idiom while I had my little arms around her neck.)

The reference to this event in the novella situates Dominican political struggles against authoritarianism in a pan–Latin American/Caribbean context, while it also demonstrates the incongruence and lack of historical and social continuity of the ideological footing of the Siete Días con el Pueblo music festival over time and under the influence of the Balaguerato. We see this through the character Don xxxxx, who resurfaces in the story when Silvia and one of her friends are unloading the speakers from a truck with the help of a security guard and a shoe store clerk. Silvia describes Don xxxxx in an ironic tone, revealing her disappointment that Salim's father isn't the revolutionary man of his son's stories: "Don xxxxx ahora trabaja en el gobierno y tiene en la mirada esa cosa rara de los que fueron torturados en los doce años y ahora trabajan junto a sus torturadores."[93] (Don xxxxx now works a government job and has that strange look in his eyes of those who were tortured during los doce años and now work alongside their torturers.) Despite having been tortured during the period of the doce años and having protested the imprisonment of the political opposition alongside his wife during Siete Días con el Pueblo, Don xxxxx then became an ally of the system that had oppressed him. Salim recounts:

Mis papás, Silvia, eran como anormales, sus fiestas eran para elaborar estrategias; aquí van los afiches, aquí los panfletos, aquí las bombas, y ponían sus bombitas sí, tú tenía que ver a mi vieja cuando el viejo estaba preso, tenía un tiro en la rodilla que le dieron en la loma, y con to eso aguantó, un pesao el viejo, un héroe, y en el concierto de siete días con el pueblo, tú tenía que ver eso, pidiendo libertad para los presos políticos y mi mamá me levantaba del piso del estadio olímpico y yo le veía los ojos morados de llorar y me decía en secreto: tu papá, tu papá.[94]

(My parents, Silvia, were not normal, their parties were for strategizing, here are the posters, here are the pamphlets, here are the bombs, and they put their little bombs, yes, you had to see my old woman when the old man was in prison, they shot him in the knee on the hill, and even with that, he endured, stubborn the old man, a hero and in the siete días con el pueblo concert, you shoulda seen that, asking for freedom for the political prisoners and my mom was picking me up from the floor of the Olympic Stadium and I saw her brown teary eyes and she told me in secret: "Your father, your father.")

Reflecting on the shift in Salim's father's ideologies, Silvia concludes, hopelessly, that in the end ideals lead to nothing because ultimately everyone prefers comfort over the fight: "Y cuando Salim me contaba todo eso yo no podía evitar sentir una ligera envidia, hasta que veía a su papá y me daba cuenta de que todo da igual, al final todo es mentira, todos queremos un carrito japonés y una piscina."[95] (And when Salim told me all that I couldn't help feeling a slight envy, until I saw his father and realized that nothing matters, in the end everything is a lie, we all want a Japanese car and a swimming pool.) *La estrategia de Chochueca* is part of a Caribbean literary tradition that consists of "not only projects for ironizing a set of values taken as universal [but] also, projects that communicate their own turbulence, their own clash, and their own void."[96] By situating Don xxxxx in clashing ideological contexts, Rita Indiana reflects on her "own turbulence" and "own void" that are constantly haunting her literary, sonic, and performance projects. Don xxxxx represents the moral emptiness that remains when ideals and revolutionary movements are short-lived—a constant theme in Rita Indiana's artistic and literary works. In his final intervention in the story, Don xxxxx, now a metonymic extension of the Balaguerato, no longer sees music as a metaphorical weapon to fight political repression; rather, his new inclination to reduce music, here in the form of speakers, to useless, substandard, vain objects suggests a deliberate attempt on his part to invalidate "disruptive" sounds.

Another of the novella's settings, in this case a bar on El Conde Street called Century, which is frequented by young people who listen to music from the United States, is also a site of ideological dissonance. Silvia describes Century as a place that "tenía fama de antro de raros"[97] (had a reputation of being a club for weirdos). When the owner closes the doors on Silvia and her friends, they sit outside the bar drinking beer and talking about "Cobain y Meat Puppets y bla bla bla nos vemos el sábado"[98] (Cobain and the Meat Puppets and blah, blah, blah, we'll see you on Saturday). The bands and musical icons that were integrated into the daily lives of these subaltern youths reveal the impact of US culture on middle-class Dominican urban youth in the 1990s. Their proclivity toward US American music often clashes with *son*, merengue, and salsa from the Spanish-speaking Caribbean in the novel. The juxtaposition between these music styles is an extension of la lucha sonora—Caribbean music competing with US American popular music in local and global marketplaces.[99]

Ironically, this proliferation of foreign music and trends culminated in an explosion of global cultural streams through the Mac Universe and cable TV accessed by middle- and upper-class youth in the DR. At least in the symbolic space, such access was a step toward breaking the dam of cultural homogeneity and Hispanophilia that was promoted and instituted by the (neo)trujillista/balaguerista city. With the insertion of foreign trends into the Dominican sonic and geographic cartography, new spaces and experiences are validated, and Century becomes a sacred space. In Century, the DJ is the priest who presides over the congregation, delivering music as homily: "La música estaba brutal. El dj diminuto detrás de sus platos tenía una cabeza afeitada perfecta, el dj y su zug zigui zug, el dj como el sacerdote de alguna secta de titanio ante los monigotes que bailaban en la pista, un óvalo pintado de rosado pepto-bismol."[100] (The music was brutal. The tiny DJ behind his turntables had a perfectly shaved head, the DJ and his zug zigui zug, the DJ like the priest of some titanium sect before the puppets that danced on the floor, an oval painted in Pepto-Bismol pink.) Church organs are replaced by a record player and vinyl, which project strident sounds in English.

The intertextual dialogue between music and literature established in *La estrategia de Chochueca* foregrounds a central concern of Rita Indiana's own musical and literary production: making alternative narratives of dominicanidad legible. From her work as a musician and fiction writer to her column in the Spanish newspaper *El País* to her performance pieces, Rita Indiana blurs dominant demarcations of Dominican identity such as Eurocentrism, heteronormativity, and language purity. She often integrates dimensions that the lettered city has tried to annihilate through its creation of national fictions that are manipulated and outlined according to the political interests of their creators.[101] One example is centering Afro-descendant cultural elements in her works, a discursive tool in "la lucha contra los fantasmas ideológicos de la Ciudad Trujillo"[102] (the fight against the ideological ghosts of the trujillista city).

In *La estrategia de Chochueca*, for example, some of Silvia's childhood memories acknowledge the historical marginalization of Afro-Dominican traditions. She recalls her walks with her uncle Manolo, who made up fabulous stories in which they were always victorious and returned home with "la mochila llena de esmeraldas para la abuela" (a backpack full of emeralds for grandma), which Silvia later puts in order by size and color.[103] While she completes her taxonomic duties, Silvia experiences a moment of magical realism in which coins fall from the sky: "Me las tiraba el dios al que le rezaba todas las noches, o era uno de los que la vecina tenía en un cuartucho, unos sobre otros, vela sobre vela, uno pisando a un monstruo, uno en un caballo, cualquiera podía ser."[104] (The God I pray to every night was throwing them at me, or it was one of those [saints] the neighbor had in her dingy room, one on top of the other, candle after candle, one stepping on a monster, one on a horse, it could've been anyone.) Paraphrasing Torres-Saillant, I interpret this passage as one of many possible avenues to overcome the pro-Hispanic disposition that has dominated the debate of Dominican identity through the representation of the nation as Catholic, for instance.[105] This passage directly references Afro-Dominican religious practices, mentioning two of the lúas (deities) of the 21 Divisions, piled up in the neighbor's "dingy room": Belie Belcan (Saint Michael), defender of truth and justice, and Ogun Balendyo (Saint James), the great protector, fighter, and healer.

Reading La estrategia de Chochueca following the interrogations García-Peña poses in The Borders of Dominicanidad "bring[s] attention to the contradictions that surge within history and literature, showing how literature works, at times, to sustain hegemony, while at others, it serves to contest it."[106] As a light-skinned Dominican with a middle-class background, Rita Indiana summons other light-skinned, middle-class Dominican readers who may see themselves in Silvia to reflect on their contribution to the constant repetitions of foundational "truths" that marginalize Afro-descendance and elevate hispanismo. Following this logic, it would be appropriate to say that by invoking Afro-dominicanidad in the novella, Rita Indiana is contesting dominant pro-Hispanic discourses via Silvia, who, although a subaltern subject herself, at times resembles those who have enacted the rejection, marginalization, and silencing of Afro-derived cultural elements, subjects, and experiences. With this intervention, La estrategia de Chochueca goes beyond interrupting the monopolization of dominicanidad by intellectual elites who have privileged Hispanic elements in their imagination of Dominican history and the Dominican people.[107]

La estrategia de Chochueca also brings attention to another contradiction through a brief yet meaningful reference to Silvia's perceptions of and feelings toward the presence of Haitians in Santo Domingo. During her many walks through the tourist-laden Zona Colonial, Silvia fixes her attention on a Haitian street vendor, who mistakes her for a tourist and tries to sell her "una estatuica de madera"[108] (a miniature wooden statue).

In her description of the encounter with the man, she focuses on his gaze and the fear it provokes in her, "esa mirada de niño que odia y que le llena a uno como de miedos el pecho"[109] (that gaze of a hateful child that fills one's chest with fears). Later, she confesses that her fears have nothing to do with the fact that a neighbor told her that Haitians eat children, because she overcame those fears "después de que los vi construir [los haitianos] la mitad de la ciudad con sus brazos"[110] (after she saw them [Haitians] build half of the city with their arms). Highlighting Haitians' roles in the construction of Santo Domingo evinces how the city itself is an ontological site that generates more inclusive discourses of identity—in this case, countering a discourse that holds Haitians as corollary. For a moment, the novella becomes a metaphor of the stolen speakers, amplifying the role of Haitians in the edification of a city that is constantly rejecting them.

The incorporation of music in *La estrategia de Chochueca* allows real problems to be solved on a symbolic level, presented as an alternative reality—a form of "negotiated" consciousness.[111] In this sense, the novella reveals "el claro desfase entre el paradigma de identidad cultural surgido de la ciudad trujillista—ese que sigue vigente como santo y seña de la cultura política dominicana—, y una cultura distinta, marcada por el entrecruzamiento de conductas, discursos y niveles de comunicación heterogéneos"[112] (the clear gap between the cultural identity paradigm that sprang from the trujillista city—still valid as a marked sign of Dominican political culture—and a different culture, characterized by the intertwining of heterogeneous behaviors, discourses, and levels of communication). Further, the sonic events and archives centered in *La estrategia de Chochueca*'s urban liminality demonstrate the points of rupture between the paradigms established between the (neo)trujillista/balaguerista ideological apparatus and alternative understanding of dominicanidad.

La estrategia de Chochueca opens and closes with references to music. In the beginning of the novel, "la sola acción de andar" (the act of walking) bridges sound and movement: "La sola acción de andar ofrece posibilidades inevitables, se camina sin pensar que se camina, más bien tintineamos las caderas acompasando las piernas a la cadencia autómata."[113] (The mere act of walking offers inevitable possibilities, one walks without thinking that they are walking, it's more like clinking our hips, our legs in step with the robotic cadence.) The act of walking—of navigating space with new sensibilities and a new attitude—moves the body left, right, backward, and forward; it resembles a dance in which one is moving without thinking, letting sound be the guide. In *Cuerpo y cultura: Las músicas "mulatas" y la subversión del baile*, Ángel Quintero Rivera explains how dance practices for enslaved subjects "constituían una expresión ritual de memorias colectivas, una estética de la seducción . . . o una vía de comunicación e incitación libertaria"[114] (constituted a ritual expression of collective memories, an aesthetic of seduction . . . or a way of communication and libertarian incitement). Following this line of argumentation, conscious of the sociohistorical differences between the horrors of chattel slavery and modern-day readings of social structures and dynamics as forms of slavery, I interpret the "act of walking" as a "ritual expression of collective memories" that seduces us, the readers, to liberate dominicanidad from the chains of (neo)trujillista/balaguerista ideologies.

The verbal threads woven into the novella's final paragraphs invoke the universe of sound: "oigo los gritos" (I hear the screams), "dando voces de auxilio" (crying out for help), "los gritos de las mujeres" (the screams of women). In the penultimate paragraph, "los gritos desaparecen dibujando virutas diminutas en el silencio" (the screams disappear, drawing tiny shavings in the silence). By the end of the novella, the sound fades, words come to their end, and only a sonic image prevails, "el zumbido de las lámparas llenas de moscas" (the buzzing of the lamps full of flies), to keep buzzing in the ears of (neo)trujillista/balaguerista ideologues.[115] The sonic and nonsonic events centered in La estrategia de Chochueca's urban liminality become useful to see and reflect on the cracks in the veneer of the (neo)trujillista/balaguerista ideological apparatus. Like the other three texts analyzed in this chapter, La estrategia becomes a space of reflection where the stories of those marginalized by the (neo)trujillista/balaguerista city make sense of their present by revisiting specific events, stories, and icons of the past. Their narrative takes center stage to unearth urban stories that would otherwise remain covered in dust.

Reframing Afro-Latina Narratives of Girlhood and Womanhood: Bridging the Borders between Fiction, Nonfiction, and Hip-Hop

It took me a couple of years and a major move (from New York to Athens, Georgia) to think of how almost every part and intersection of the map of my coming of age in New York City was connected to hip-hop culture. While away from my dear city, I often re-created mental maps of essential places, experiences, and memories that make up the fabric of who I have been for the past three decades. I recall the many nights when my hands were raised at nightclubs, singing along with the infamous line of the Notorious B.I.G.'s hit single "Big Poppa": "I love it when you call me big poppa / Throw your hands in the air if you's a true player."[1] I also remember being super excited when I rang up Biggie's widow, Faith Evans, while I was a cashier at what used to be a Gap store on Fifty-Fourth Street and Madison Avenue in the early 2000s. Even more striking to me, I used to pass by 1520 Sedgwick Avenue, the birthplace of hip-hop in the 1970s, almost every day on my way to Lehman College, and just a few corners away from my grandmother's apartment on Prospect Avenue in the Bronx was the oldest Latinx music store in New York City, Casa Amadeo.

My ruminations take me back to La Casita de Chema (now known as Centro Cultural Rincón Criollo), a vibrant cultural space where Puerto Rican and Latinx communities gather to celebrate their heritage, as well as my years living in Harlem and my constant trips to the Dominican Studies Institute (also in Harlem). My move to Georgia was crucial in making these connections; being away from New York City delineated the contours that make up my personal map and allowed me to see with fresh eyes, and a pinch of nostalgia, that which has informed my identity.

This chapter and the next one bring me closer to my understanding of home, which at times is a bridge between Santo Domingo and New York (as discussed in the previous two chapters), an in-between space that Josefina Báez calls El Nié. At other times, it is my beloved New York City, the place that imprinted on me, shaped the many layers of my identity, and made me the scholar I am today (see fig. 3.1). This chapter, and to some extent the next chapter, pay homage to my hometown of New York City—its good, its bad, and its ugly—and all the cultural greatness that sprang out of this concrete jungle. New York City showed me that concrete is at times much more fertile than green spaces. Even in my darkest of moments, after a surgery that made me biologically infertile, New York City keeps teaching me that there are many ways to be fertile. In New York, this good Catholic girl became rad. Much like the subjects of this chapter, Raquel Cepeda and Elizabeth Acevedo, this dominicanyork Latina from Santo Domingo found her voice by listening to others in a place where dreams come true and get crushed, where the lights never stop shining and the music never stops playing.

Given the relevance of popular music and literature in my personal and professional lives, the dialogue between both disciplines is essential to my reading of the texts I analyze in this and the other chapters. Latina scholar and anthropologist Frances Aparicio reflects in *Listening to Salsa: Gender, Latin Popular Music, and Puerto Rican Cultures* on the relevance of popular music as a literary subtext and intertext:

> Musical subtexts and intertexts suggest, first of all, a new definition and location of the literary text that questions and displaces the privileged site of literature as an art for and by the elite. The postmodern politics of integrating popular music—neither classical nor art music—within fiction destabilizes the modern(ist) notion of art as a space exempt from the "vulgar" reality of the masses: it questions the idea of literature as a new reality that can substitute for and transcend the social spaces of the masses.[2]

In this chapter, I highlight the points of interaction between the literature produced by two Afro-Latina writers and hip-hop. In my analysis of Cepeda's memoir, *Bird of Paradise: How I Became Latina*, and Elizabeth Acevedo's novel in verse, *The Poet X*, I argue that both writers establish connections between "atypical" sonic archives, poetry, and memoir in the articulation of Latinx cultural identity. I center Cepeda's and Acevedo's portrayals of the experiences of Afro-diasporic Latina subjects as well as foreground the obviated and often forgotten historical, political, and cultural ties between New York Dominicans and hip-hop culture. Further, given that Spanish-speaking migrants and second-generationers such as Raquel Cepeda and Elizabeth Acevedo occupy a disadvantaged position that has obvious implications on their notions of identity, their

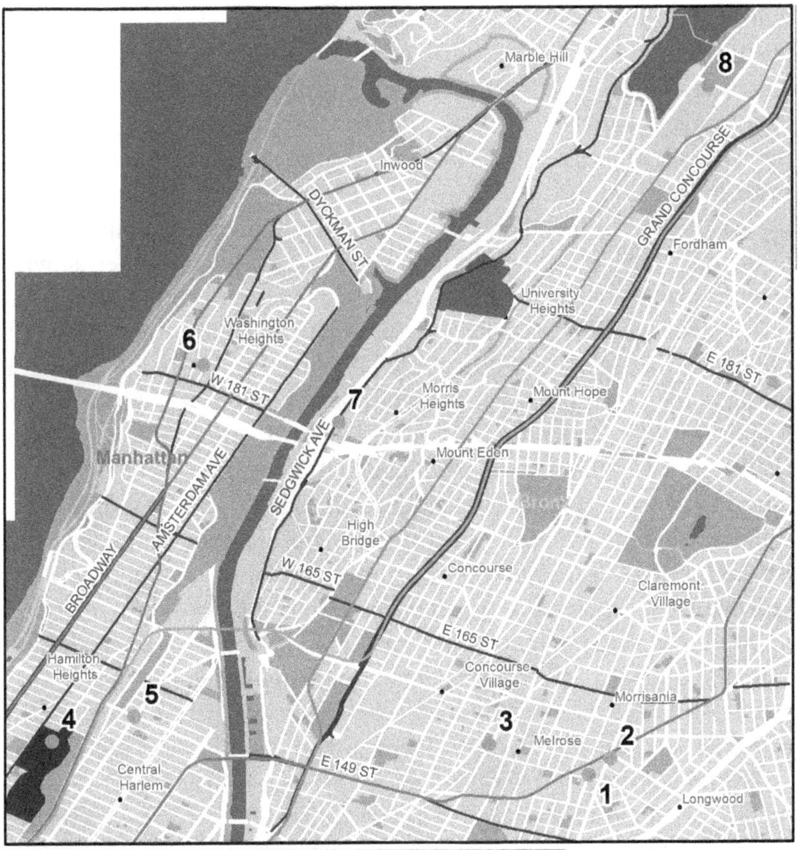

1. 750 Union Avenue, Bronx, NY 10459
2. Casa Amadeo, 786 Prospect Avenue, Bronx, NY 10455
3. La Casita de Chema, 749 Brook Avenue, Bronx, NY 10451
4. CUNY Dominican Studies Institute,
   The City University of New York,
   1860 Convent Avenue New York, NY 10031
5. 300 West 145th Street, New York, NY 10039
6. 44 Bennett Avenue, New York, NY 10033
7. 1520 Sedgwick Avenue, Bronx, NY 10453
8. Lehman College of the City University of New York,
   250 Bedford Park Boulevard, Bronx, NY 10468

Legend

Rail Lines

- 1-2
- 4
- A-C
- D

Bronx Community College

City University of New York

FIGURE 3.1. *Digital map of Upper Manhattan and the Bronx by Meagan Duever.*

marginal positionality situates them in a condition of "otherness" vis-à-vis the dominant social, political, economic, ethnic, racial, and cultural structures. In this regard, Silvio Torres-Saillant emphasizes that the sense of awareness of their otherness and their diasporic uprooting "penetrate the core of Latino identity," and "the language of unity functions as an instrument of survival."[3]

In "Black Feminist Formations in the Dominican Republic since *La Sentencia*," April Mayes reflects on how Afro-descendant women activists from Hispaniola have produced new articulations of Dominican identity that include and make legible, visible, and audible the bodies and voices of women through the affirmation of Blackness and reimagines what it means to be Dominican, women, and Black beyond the confines of the island.[4] Mayes's cogent articulation of how "Dominican black feminism challenges the construction of differential citizenship through its sustained support of immigrant's and human rights" is a useful framework through which to approach the works of Afro-diasporic multimedia artists and writers, including Cepeda and Acevedo, as "an opportunity to redefine Dominicanness around an affirmation of Blackness."[5]

This chapter navigates two hybrid literary genres that break away from the notion of cohesiveness. One is a memoir that is divided into a more traditional autobiographical account and an experimental narrative of a scientific genetic search for identity, and the other is a novel structured and narrated in freestyle slam poetry verses. They mirror the fragmented identities of their subjects through hybrid fiction and nonfiction narratives. In both, a multigenerational hip-hop sonic archive becomes the glue, a "lingua franca," in the words of Cepeda, that breaks down the barriers and bridges the gaps between readers and authors.[6] In this sense, both authors celebrate the "impure" and carve out new discursive spaces that center Black Latina girls' and women's experiences through their engagement with hip-hop culture. Although *The Poet X* is not a memoir, the comparison between the genres is useful for seeing the various current literary mediums that focus on issues pertaining to the experiences of Afro-Latinas of Dominican heritage. Luisa María González observes of Cepeda's memoir that it serves as a counternarrative "to colonizing hegemonic discourses" and "explore[s] the impact of cultural memory and consciousness on the construction of a new Latinx narrative, thus shaping a collective identity. For this young female generation, individual and cultural memory is a subversive weapon, used to challenge the stereotyping and criminalization of Latinx by the dominant culture in US society."[7] The same can be said of Acevedo's novel.

I propose that what is at stake in these works by Cepeda and Acevedo can be illuminated by reading them with an eye toward studies of hip-hop by African American feminist critics. Brittney Cooper argues that women of color of her generation "identify as hip-hop because the music, the culture, the fashion, and the figures provide the soundtrack to our girlhood and our young womanhood." She continues, "Our coming of age happened in the linguistically and rhetorically rich cultural milieu and transformation that was the 1990s. The decade of the woman but also the decade of the female MC: Queen Latifah, MC Lyte, The Rat, Left Eye and TLC, Foxy Brown, Lil' Kim and Lauryn Hill."[8]

Although Raquel Cepeda, a self-proclaimed cultural activist who has been immersed in the world of hip-hop since her youth, does not consider herself a feminist, her memoir depicts her embodied experiences and struggles, as well as her resistance to the patriarchal impositions of her parents and immediate community. Portions of her memoir go as far back as the late 1970s and 1980s, decades when hip-hop existed on the margins of New York's cultural scene. Yet, as Cooper notes, it influenced her girlhood and womanhood as a Black dominiyorkian Latina coming of age during the birth and solidification of hip-hop culture in New York City.[9] The same argument can be made for Acevedo and her novel despite the difference in eras. Set in the second decade of the 2000s, it also delves into the interlocking oppressions that affect Black Latina girls coming of age in New York City. I frame both texts that I analyze in this chapter using the definition of hip-hop feminism proposed by Aisha Durham, Brittney Cooper, and Susana Morris, "as a generationally specific articulation of feminist consciousness, epistemology, and politics rooted in the pioneering work of multiple generations of black feminists based in the United States and elsewhere in the diaspora but focused on questions and issues that grow out of the aesthetic and political prerogatives of hip-hop."[10]

Both texts highlight the often-ignored role of girls and women as producers and carriers of Afro-diasporic and US American cultures. Borrowing from Afro-Latina feminist scholar Omaris Zamora's reflections on Afro-Latinas as knowledge creators, this chapter evinces how Cepeda and Acevedo "possess multiple understandings of blackness (i.e., Caribbean, transnational, diasporic), womanhood, and feminist epistemologies" that disrupt essential and hegemonic notions of Blackness, Dominicanidad, Latinidad, and Americanness in both the United States and the Dominican Republic.[11]

In writing about one's life, one often has to rely on a combination of memory, imagination and strong emotion that may result in "poetic truth."

JUDITH ORTIZ COFER, *Silent Dancing: A Partial Remembrance of a Puerto Rican Childhood*

When I first read *Bird of Paradise: How I Became Latina* in 2013, I immediately felt a strong sense of connection with Raquel Cepeda's story. Not because I shared the same lived experiences as a daughter (in my case, a granddaughter) of Dominican immigrants. Rather, in the distinct layers of our personal stories, I discovered a distant yet relatable story of coming of age as a Dominican between New York City and Santo Domingo. Though I did not, as she did, grow up in Inwood, nor live on the West Coast for a brief period of my young adult life, nor survive the "crack era" in New York City, nor have firsthand experiences of the early years of hip-hop culture, I did (and still do) endure intergenerational tensions with family members about ethnicity, race, respectability, and politics, and I share the undeniable influences of cultural expressions such as hip-hop in my understanding of my migrant Dominican and New Yorker identities. Like Cepeda, I also found parts of the fabric that keeps shaping my identity in hip-hop lyrics.

Two names mentioned in Josefina Báez's "Washington Heights List" became a constant reminder of the recurring circles of violence that haunted those of us who grew up between the ghosts of a balaguerista past that were ever present, even when we were away from the island, and the historical and present violence asphyxiating minoritized inner-city folks in New York City: Sagrario Díaz, a student leader and activist killed by the Dominican police during the repressive period of the doce años de Balaguer in 1972 at the Universidad Autónoma de Santo Domingo, and José "Kiko" García, a twenty-three-year-old Dominican man killed by the police in 1992.[12] García's death was a catalyst for riots against police brutality in the Washington Heights neighborhood of Manhattan.[13] A mix of fear toward and frustration over state-imposed authority drove me to tap into a sonic archive that was not permitted in my two homes, an archive that spoke about other truths that went against the current of the ideological foundations of my households and immediate communities: hip-hop. One album in particular, N.W.A's *Straight Outta Compton*, shaped my political consciousness. After listening to songs such as "Fuck tha Police," I could see the links between Kiko García's tragic death at the hands of the police and the lyrics, which reverberated into a multiplicity of links with other violent deaths at the hands of state-imposed authority within and beyond New York.

Today I think back, as Cepeda did, on how hip-hop culture is an invaluable avenue to reflect on the tensions between Black and Brown youth and law enforcement. At age twenty-one, I gained the right to vote in the US, but I also gained a political consciousness that was—and continues to be—shaped by the Afro-diasporic cultural movement of hip-hop. As I write this chapter, two things come to mind: the shared social injustices and discrimination against Black and Brown bodies across and beyond the US and the social value of hip-hop as a site to express the social frustrations of minoritized and marginalized urban youth across geographic and temporal lines. George Lipsitz writes in *Time Passages: Collective Memory and American Popular Culture*, "By looking at the music itself, we can find dialogic traces of the past and discern their enduring utility in the present."[14] Thus centering the role of mid-1970s, 1980s, and early 1990s hip-hop culture in Cepeda's *Bird of Paradise: How I Became Latina*, especially in our current sociopolitical climate, is useful to appreciate the "enduring utility" of the early decades of hip-hop in our historical present.

As a Dominican Latina who self-identifies as a dominicanyork, lives in the US South, and focuses on the impact of the early decades of hip-hop in the identity formation of a fellow dominicana from New York City, I would be remiss not to mention the impact Cepeda's memoir has had in various iterations in my course called Coming-of-Age Latinx in the US. In my third iteration of teaching on *Bird of Paradise* in this course, in the spring of 2022, the discussions in class about the memoir confirmed once again the atemporality and "borderlessness" of hip-hop and the appeal, impact, and "enduring utility" that N.W.A's seminal album *Straight Outta Compton* still has on youth from diverse backgrounds. In the class, students not only dug deeper into the social, cultural, and aesthetic value of 1970s and 1980s hip-hop but also created and curated a playlist of the songs and artists that make up part of the fabric of Raquel Cepeda's story and linked them to current struggles affecting Latinx, Afro-Latinx, and African American youth in Georgia today. They went way beyond the expectations of the class in creating links between their personal and public narratives, and the struggles of their communities and old-school hip-hop were yet another reminder of why there is an "enduring utility" in revisiting the past to continue building spaces of resistance in our historical present.

Suzanne Bost maintains that memoir has "helped to shape what it means to come to consciousness as a Chicana, Chicano, Chicanx, Latina, Latino, Latinx subject"—"to create a heroic, racially and sexually conscious self." Rather than highlighting "successful narratives of selfhood," Bost's approach considers how structures of discrimination, including racism, sexism, misogyny, homophobia, and colonial legacies, influence how Latinx authors narrate "the continued compromises, contradictions, and collusions that shape their lives."[15]

Bird of Paradise, the first coming-of-age memoir published by a second-generation Dominican American author, and set in New York City, presents a narrative of selfhood in which the messy and murky lines that make up Raquel Cepeda's identity intersect to give meaning to her existence. In other words, writing her life results from her "almost instinctive urge to communicate, speak, to write about life on the borders, life in the shadows."[16] In the book, Harlem-born spoken-word artist, documentary filmmaker, hip-hop journalist, and writer Cepeda tells an agonizing story about her private and public struggles to discover, shape, and reconcile her many identities. The book makes clear how growing up amid hip-hop culture and her work in hip-hop journalism were pivotal in creating her ethnic, racial, gender, and sexual consciousness as a Latina/dominicana in New York City. *Bird of Paradise* is an attempt to contest and challenge the notions of the various layers of Cepeda's identity while also reimagining the physical and imaginary borders of her latinidad and dominicanidad.[17]

Cepeda blends her life story with those of others within her family unit and immediate communities as the book journeys through memories connected to her parents' lives, her intermittent stays in the Dominican Republic after her birth, her life and struggles, and being an urban inner-city youth in New York City from the 1980s through the first decade of the 2000s. Connected to these memories is also a clear intention to insert her story within the context of hip-hop and highlight its impact on her identity formation. Doing so offsets the historical absence of narratives linking Spanish-speaking Afro-Caribbeans to hip-hop culture in New York City. She thus engages in a collaborative process of identity negotiation and survival in which hip-hop is at the center.

Following Gaye Theresa Johnson's approach to hip-hop culture in *Spaces of Conflict, Sounds of Solidarity: Music, Race, and Spatial Entitlement in Los Angeles*, my analysis of *Bird of Paradise* highlights Cepeda's memoir as a historiographical site in which to reflect on Black and Brown spatial struggle and cultural expression in New York City, carving a space within hip-hop culture history for Dominicans.[18] It also makes sense to think of this memoir as a site of dissension, of visibility, of contestation, and of awareness of Black feminist epistemologies that reframe conceptualization of dominicanidad from the flesh of an Afro-Latina dominiyorkian.

In "The Construction of the Self in U.S. Latina Autobiographies," Lourdes Torres analyzes three canonical Latina autobiographies and deems them "revolutionary and subversive at many levels."[19] These works challenge traditional conventions of autobiographies in their structure and content, subvert patriarchal understandings of culture—both Anglo and Latino—and often destabilize linguistic norms by mixing English and Spanish. Torres also contends that the autobiographies she analyzes "address the question of the politics of multiple identities from a position which seeks to integrate ethnicity, class, gender, sexuality, and language."[20] Cepeda's memoir addresses similar questions to those of her predecessors by creating seamless connections between the construction of her Latina/dominiyorkian identities, hip-hop culture, and mitochondrial DNA analysis. In a context where her ethnic backgrounds and race are being constantly probed, challenged, denied, or silenced by mainstream society, her communities, and members of her family, Cepeda's memoir is, as Christina Lam suggests, "a task of recovery," "an alternate archive to official histories of Dominicanidad," and "acts of 'contradiction.'"[21]

Since the memoir inscribes erasures of Dominican immigrant narratives in transnational archives between the Dominican Republic and New York, reading it with Lorgia García-Peña's conceptual framework of contradiction in mind becomes useful to challenge mainstream and dominant understandings of Dominican and US Latinx identities. Cepeda's memoir is a counternarrative, and it is a conscious move to foreground Afro-latinidad to "reveal and recognize hidden histories and subalternized knowledges, while unsettling and challenging dominant (essentialist, nationalist, imperial, patriarchal) notions of African-ness, American-ness, and Latinidad, along with the forms of power/knowledge that are embedded in these categories."[22]

Bird of Paradise is divided into two sections: a coming-of-age story in part 1 and a genealogical exploration in part 2. Trent Masiki argues that this "stylistic hybridity mirrors Cepeda's ethnoracial hybridity, her claim to Spanish, Taíno and West African ancestry."[23] The first ten chapters making up the coming-of-age section of the text narrate Cepeda's family's migration and their connections and disconnections with their homeland. They also recount key moments of Cepeda's intra- and extra-familial life in the Dominican Republic and the United States. In this part, the author unveils some of the most traumatic events of her life, her relationship with her parents, and her many strategies to negotiate and survive the family dynamics and the violence that prevailed during the "crack era" in Upper

Manhattan, a period in New York history marred by the crime and violence that surrounded the drug trade.[24]

It is against this background that Cepeda is attracted to the effervescence of hip-hop culture, which becomes an integral part of her identity. Through the portrayal of Cepeda's relationship with her parents, neighbors, and peers, the first part of the book exposes the entangled process of the identity formation of second-generation Dominican Americans in New York City and how they confront, negotiate, and cope with the differences between them and their first-generation immigrant parents and community. To that effect, Lam notes that the memoir "is an alternate archive to official histories of Dominicanidad," "takes on the ask of giving a voice to the complexity of Latinx identity," and "is, arguably, driven by the need to work through and past the silences that are the hallmark of trauma, and Cepeda does so while simultaneously bearing witness to her own becoming."[25] By revisiting the silences, Cepeda excavates the rajaduras to find, (re)write, bridge, and integrate new ways of knowing herself and her communities.

In the book's second part, Cepeda revisits and excavates the biological basis of her identity. Although I do not focus on this part of the book, it is worth mentioning that through the exploration of ancestral DNA, she uses her personal story as an example of the racial complexities of Latinxs by bridging the divide between the scientific past and the cultural politics of latinidad. She highlights the multifaceted process of identity formation through the conflation of science, mysticism, and the cultural richness of her hyphenated upbringing in her path to self-discovery. As she explains:

My transnational identity may have been formed when I was a child growing up in New York City and Santo Domingo, but it was enhanced because of the synthesis between *logos* and *mythos*, science and mysticism. The science of ancestral DNA testing, combined with the mostly unsolicited spiritual information I've received in North and West Africa, Europe and the Caribbean, South America, and the United States, from all sorts of people from every imaginable walk of life, has been reaffirming.[26]

Lam interprets the title of Raquel Cepeda's memoir as the author's process of "becoming" and identity formation, a constant negotiation, and continuous fluctuations between places.[27] Like Lam, my reading of the title evokes the idea of mobility, yet rather than "becoming," I focus on the material and metaphorical meaning of paradise/*paraíso*. At first glance, the title of the memoir situates Cepeda's paraíso in Africa, the origin of the bird of paradise, a sub-Saharan flower that found homes in the Americas and parts of Europe. In a metaphorical sense, the many travels of the flower and its appropriation in Los Angeles and Madeira as the official and national flower, respectively, point to how symbols derived from African cultures are inscribed in the national and cultural identities of the West. Cepeda reaffirms the inscription of Afro-diasporic subjects such as herself in the places where she was born, lived, traveled, or adopted as home. Paraíso is also a literal physical place, a neighborhood in Santo Domingo, the capital of the Dominican Republic. In the opening lines of the book, we learn that Paraíso is where Cepeda's parents, Rocío and Eduardo, met. This encounter in Paraíso led to her parents' marriage and her mother's subsequent translocation to Harlem, New York. Amid the violence of the 1980s and 1990s, New York became the cradle of hip-hop, one of urban youth's most influential cultural expressions. For Cepeda, it became another form of paraíso. These various definitions of paradise represent the multiple places and spaces that play critical roles in her self-definition as a Black dominiyorkian Latina. Ultimately, they all conflate as the story progresses, and it becomes clear that paraíso transcends borders, as it is "a state of being, more than just the name of suburb or a home."[28]

One of the many pivotal moments recounted in the memoir is the beginning of Cepeda's story in the Dominican Republic in 1971, when her father "dropped into town from Nueva York and into her [mother's] life like Changó himself, with a drum in one hand and his dick in the other."[29] The journey continues with her mother's arrival in Harlem in 1972, Cepeda's birth in the spring of the following year, and her constant vaivenes across transnational boundaries between the US and the Dominican Republic. Cepeda's constant travels—which later take her to Africa and Europe—expand and frame her identity in a transnational and global Afro-Latinx configuration. The experiences she narrates and the tools she employs to emphasize Afro-diasporic aspects of her cultural identity, especially hip-hop culture, as well as the emphasis on Dominican/Latinxs racial formation foreground Black identity in Dominican and Latinx cultures and literatures in the US. Cepeda's *Bird of Paradise* continues the genealogical branching of New York City Latinx narratives by Afro-Latinx writers of Spanish-speaking Caribbean descent, such as Piri Thomas, Nicholasa Mohr, and Marta Moreno Vega. Like her predecessors, in *Bird of Paradise*, Cepeda portrays her strong connections to Black Caribbean and African American cultures, foregrounding her Afro-diasporic heritage and the social and cultural alliances formed with African Americans and Black Caribbean communities in New York City, given their geographic proximity and shared socioeconomic struggles.[30]

From an early age, Cepeda's life was marked by instability, violence, and a constant negation of her identity by others. Shortly after her arrival in New York City in 1981—the year she moves in with her father and his wife, Alice—her father decides to start calling her Rachel to erase any trace of her Dominican identity and impose on her the same "white" behaviors that he adopts in his own performance of latinidad. Although on one occasion she decides to succumb to others' insistence on calling her Rachel, it is evident throughout the text that just as the Dominican Republic will always be an essential part of who she is, she will always be Raquel or Raquelita.[31] She writes, "I always loved my name, especially when I was referred to as Raquelita, *un nombre de cariño*, by people like Mama and Paloma, who knew me before now."[32] Perhaps the most pivotal assertion of her connection to her dominicanidad, which her father and her "new masters" so wanted to eradicate, comes with her self-awareness of the multiple layers of her identity:

> The Dominican Republic is my holy land, my Mecca. It's equal parts archeological site and ancestral shrine, a place where I can go to get centered when I start feeling off-kilter. While America will always, I think, feel foreign to me, New York City is my home. This is where I construct my own identity freely and reject labels imposed on me. My foundation may be *por allá*, but myself is firmly rooted here.[33]

Cepeda's acknowledgment of the Dominican Republic as her foundation is by no means romantic. Instead, there are key moments during the narration that reveal the complexities of Dominican national, cultural, and racial discourses as they relate to the long-standing tensions between the Dominican Republic and Haiti, to provide an example that shaped her political consciousness. In her accounts, we find oscillating viewpoints: one that reproduces anti-Haitian sentiments embedded in the collective consciousness of the Dominican people and the state and another that challenges Cepeda's own internalization of said sentiments and offers alternative narratives to a one-dimensional perspective on Haitians. As the memoir unfolds, the awakening of her new consciousness becomes clearer, opening new possibilities and narratives of Haitian-Dominican relations in the diasporic space.

Chapter 3, "Journey into the Heart of Darkness," an overt reference to Joseph Conrad's *Heart of Darkness*, presents a series of stereotypes about Haitians that indirectly speak to the impact of European and US imperialism on Dominicans' anti-Haitian sentiments. When Cepeda is five years old, she moves to San Francisco with Rocío and her boyfriend, Pascal, also known as Papito, a Haitian man who becomes abusive to both Cepeda and her mother. Her description of Pascal and his brothers, Gerard and Jean, reveals how discourses of colorism and anti-Haitian sentiments travel with and reproduce within the Dominican diaspora. In other words, she is colorist in her descriptions of the Haitian men that she comes in contact with while in San Francisco. Gerard, Papito's youngest brother, is the lightest-skinned of the three brothers. He is described as having "a pretty face the color of brown sugar," and when he is around, "there [is] peace." In contrast, Jean is "a darker skinned version of Papito and way more sinister," which leads Raquel to ponder "that what Dominicans said about *haitianos* was true: Their darker skin did make them more evil."[34]

Then, in what can be read as an attempt to break away from the reproduction of *anti-haitianismo*, Cepeda begins a reflective process whereby she questions how her personal experiences with Papito and his family, as well as the anti-Haitian ideology embedded in the stories that she grew up hearing on the island, shaped her perceptions and notions of Haitians. Through her writing, she confronts and exorcises her prejudices and builds bridges between diasporic subjects from Hispaniola in New York City.

Cepeda describes how her contact with the Haitian diasporic community, as she makes her way back to New York City and engages more with Afro-diasporic and US Black communities, reframes her perspectives and awakens her to a new consciousness in which being Dominican is no longer equated with being anti-Haitian. In chapter 6, "Jesus Christ and the Freakazoid," she confesses, "All the bullshit Dominicans talk about Haitians rushes into the foreground of my mind. I am embarrassed by it." She acknowledges that "it's part of the baggage our parents and grandparents lug over from the *madre patria*."[35] Throughout this and the previous chapter, "An Awakening," it is clear Raquel soon learns that, as Sophie Maríñez notes, Haitians and Dominicans "are equalized and lumped together with 'Blacks,' a category that erases the specificity of their national historical past and ethnicities. And leads them to learn from, adopt, or join forces with others in a heterogeneous African diaspora."[36]

This sense of solidarity becomes evident in the support Cepeda receives from her friend Claudine Jean-Baptiste, the daughter of a Haitian nurse from Port-au-Prince, when everyone at school makes fun of Raquel's unfashionable winter outfit. "The first time I'm forced to wear the polar bear to school," she says, "everyone does poke fun of me except my best friend, Claudine Jean-Baptiste."[37] Her friendship with Claudine opens the door to forge other connections with Haitian youth in New York City, such as Marie Christophe and David Jude Jolicoeur, a.k.a. Truoy, one of the founding members of the Long Island hip-hop trio De La Soul. Reflecting on her friendship with Marie, Raquel wonders if they would have been able to be friends in the Caribbean and raises questions about the impossibility of unity in such a fragmented and bordered space: "I glance over at Marie, noticing her red lipstick perfectly framing a set of full pouty lips. I wondered if we would have been friends had we been living in DR or Haiti. I imagined thousands of friendships disintegrating into the arid Caribbean air—POOF—before they could even begin. Teenagers, separated by an imaginary line, who will never laugh together or share fresh clothes. I can't imagine it."[38] New York thus bridges the cultural and national divides between Haiti and the Dominican Republic. Raquel goes on to marry Sacha Jenkins, who is half Haitian and shares a "love for and roots on the island of Hispaniola, Sacha in Haiti by way of Queens."[39]

We can thus situate Cepeda's memoir in a Dominican diasporic literary tradition that, as Maríñez points out, "has been crucial in developing an empathy toward Haitian immigrants that the normalization of anti-Haitian sentiments prevailing in the Dominican Republic would seldom promote" by first confronting us with the story of Papito and then showing us that there are other possibilities of relationships between Dominicans and Haitians.[40] The emphasis on these alternative narratives and dynamics of Haitian-Dominican relations in the diaspora creates a potential space to debunk one-sided scripts of Haitian-Dominican relations carried from the island nations. It is also relevant to reframe—as the case of Cepeda illustrates—notions of racial identifications for second-generation Dominicans in the United States.

ON BEING BLACK AND LATINA

Cepeda grew up in a world where, to borrow from Torres-Saillant, "race has implications that impinge on one's survival."[41] Not only did she learn that race matters through the transference of her parents' experiences before and upon their arrival in the United States, but she also developed a racial consciousness through her own experiences growing up in simmering racial tensions within New York City. Raquel's constant assertions of her ethnicities (dominicana, dominiyorkian, and Latina) and her race (Black) are central to her reconciliation of the many layers of her identity. They are also a strategy for coping with and dismantling racialized geopolitics of US-Hispaniola relations and for understanding her "grounding in the history of African peoples in the Caribbean as well as in the history of women of color in the United States."[42] As such, Raquel's memoir traverses the rigid borders between Latinidad, Dominicanidad, and Blackness.

In *Embodied Economies: Diaspora and Transcultural Capital in Latinx Caribbean Fiction and Theater*, Israel Reyes coins the term "embodied economies" to describe contradictory patterns of values and practices among Latinx Caribbean migrants/immigrants. In his comparative analysis, he looks at how Latinx Caribbeans embody cultural practices, social and cultural values, and forms of empowerment that either "align or come into conflict with state power, hegemonic discourses and institutions, and global markets."[43] *Bird of Paradise* shows these counterpoints through the intrafamilial tension between two attitudes toward the performance of latinidad, one more assimilative and the other more dissimilative to mainstream US society. This polarity is captured in Cepeda's portrayal of her ethnoracial affirmation and that of her father, as expressed in the preface to the book: "Race and identity have been a source of bitterness between my father and me since before I can remember."[44] Raquel's father, Eduardo, adopts "white middle-class forms of embodiment in order to mitigate any ethnic and racial identity markers that might hinder [his] trajectory of upward mobility."[45] At the same time, his daughter identifies with minoritized racial groups. In other words, Raquel is inclined toward what Wendy Roth calls a "Black-centric" schema and asserts her ethnic identity as Dominican, while Eduardo favors a "White-centric" schema and rejects his national origins, Dominican heritage, and Black racial identification.[46]

In *Introduction to Dominican Blackness*, Torres-Saillant makes the argument that "Dominican youngsters who are brought up in this country [the United States], where bipolar racial categories reign supreme, are likely to adopt the racial classifications administered by their environment."[47] He then proceeds to quote Tanya Katerí Hernández's study of the 1990 census in which she finds that "the longer Dominican youngsters have lived in the US, the higher the chances they [racially and ethnically] identify as blacks."[48] Along these lines, Alejandro Portes suggests that there are various trends for how second-generation immigrants claim their ethnic identity. For some, it becomes optional, while for others, their "ethnicity and the social networks linked to it will become a key resource and a strong basis for self-identity and pride." Portes also identifies a third trend among youth, for whom ethnicity becomes synonymous with subordination and prejudice.[49] For Raquel, her Black racial identity and her dominiyorkian and Latina ethnic identities are equally important—a challenge to the notion that Blackness, Latinidad, and Dominicanidad are mutually exclusive.

The role of race in Cepeda's identity construction compels her to look at official US American and Dominican racialization practices. She recognizes that Latinxs tracing their roots beyond their parents and grandparents often "hit major roadblocks because the definitions of race throughout Latin America are often radically different from those in the United States."[50] Yet she also considers the similarities between racialization practices in the US and the Dominican Republic. Throughout the second part of the book, she challenges the accuracy of racial classification systems both on the island and in the US by pinpointing the discriminatory practices embedded in the ways Black Latinxs and Black Dominicans are undercounted. Her considerations, especially when she speaks about the US, are timely given the changes by the Office of Management and Budget to conflate Latino/Hispanic ethnic identity with the list of racial categories, which will continue to exacerbate the general hegemonic notions of Blackness as exclusive to African Americans.[51] In the following passage, Cepeda underlines the impact of the arbitrary recording of race on the erasure of Black Latinxs in the US census. She then considers the difficulties similar official classifications in the DR pose to her and her family when tracing their racial lineage:

> There's something else we need to consider: how people classify us in the United States. Looking at the race section on birth and death records is about as reliable as looking at the race section on census records and even, say, New York's sex-offender database, where phenotypically Black and mixed-race child molesters who have Spanish surnames are often listed as Hispanic and white. In death, the race and other particulars of two of my grandparents were wrongly recorded. Let's say Dad's mother wasn't adopted. By all accounts, the woman and man who raised her have been described as both Black and white and *indio* and Black. In death, her race was listed as white, entombing her true identity for evermore. Ercilia's case is hardly anomalous, making the search for our ancestral origins all the more challenging.[52]

Cepeda's consideration of the impact of racial classification systems on US Latinx and Dominicans on the island illuminates how official unrecording of Blacks exacerbates the rejection of Blackness by Dominicans in the diaspora, such as in the case of Cepeda's father, Eduardo. Like many of his Latin American and Caribbean counterparts, Eduardo comes from contexts in his homeland and hostlands that, similarly to Frank Bonilla's observations of the Puerto Rican diaspora, "taught him to assume blackness as a misfortune."[53] This explains his obsession with delinking himself and Cepeda from Blacks and Afro-diasporic cultural expressions.

In an interview with Dr. Brenda Greene on the program *Writers on Writing*, Cepeda spoke about her father's negative feelings regarding his origins and his assimilative behavior to US dominant white culture.[54] Throughout the memoir, Eduardo, a first-generation Dominican, is aware of the socioracial implications of categorizing himself as Dominican, Latino, or Black. Therefore, he assumes an assimilative stance toward mainstream society and performs white Americanness while dissociating himself from stereotyped and discriminated-against ethnic and racialized clusters. Eduardo exemplifies "passing" by adopting "white" behaviors, such as forcing Raquel to play tennis and play the piano, marrying a Finnish woman, and moving from Harlem to the "whiter" neighborhood of Inwood, to "a block where white people still live."[55] His performance affirms the complexities of Latinx identity formation as it is mediated by gender, class, and race.[56] Indeed, Eduardo's behavior perfectly embodies Roth's persuasive arguments on the relationship between class and race among Latinx migrants who often enact, and embody, whiteness as a means "to convey a higher-class status":

> Because Latinos are stereotyped as being poor, less professional, more likely to be "up to something" than Whites, the styles and mannerisms that people associate with acting American are often those intended to convey a higher-class status. The associations between race and class are deeply ingrained, such that "performing class" is often interpreted as "performing race" as well.[57]

As the story develops, we discover that although Eduardo's physical traits are more closely aligned with a racial schema of Blackness than whiteness, he insists on negating his Blackness. This phenomenon of negation can be attributed to a superposition of racial and ethnic categorizations from his home and host nations. In other words, Eduardo's denunciation of Blackness responds to the stigmatization of the category "Black" in the United States and the Dominican Republic, where Blackness is associated mainly with African Americans and Haitians, respectively.[58] Cepeda questions such stigmatization:

> All the bullshit Dominicans talk about Haitians rushes into the foreground of my mind. I am embarrassed by it. Marie finds it confusing that the *plátanos* over here spewing the worst venom about the *prietos* on the island often look just like them. It's part

of the baggage our parents and grandparents lug over from the *madre patria.*[59]

Eduardo's latinidad is also marked by his deprecation of Dominicans, including Raquel's mother, Rocío, such as "They chu'd *take* all of dose Dominicans and *kill* 'em" or "You going to be like *dose* ga'bage Dominicans on welfare—like your moth'a."[60] His refusal to identify himself as Dominican and his insistence on separating himself from anything related to Dominicans results from his awareness of the prejudice and stereotyping of Dominicans and other Latinx groups in New York. Cepeda reflects on this upon her arrival at her Seaman Avenue apartment in 1981:

> I hear people walking their dogs outside complaining about there being too many Dominicans and other Spanish-speaking people flooding this side of the block. They already made a mess of the building directly across the street from Mami's old place by playing dominoes and music through the night, and talking too loudly for the sensitive ears of the block's white settlers. These new people are invading the area like they do the trains, walls, and parks when night falls. Every morning they leave evidence in the form of elaborate murals that stretch ten feet high and more across, painted on the concrete barricade wrapped around large sections of the park's baseball fields.[61]

The juxtaposition of Eduardo's and Raquel Cepeda's journeys elucidates the nuanced process of intergenerational ethnoracial self-identification of Dominicans in the United States and their process of identity formation in the host city. In her analysis of *Getting Home Alive, Loving in the War Years*, and *Borderlands / La Frontera*, Torres elucidates how the Latina author of each one of these three texts claims her identity precisely in that which she has been taught to repudiate: "all the cultural and gender socialization and misinformation which has left them in a maze of contradictions." Thus, according to Torres, "their works show fragmentation of identity, and the inability to speak from a unified, noncontradictory subject position."[62]

A similar argument could be made for Cepeda's memoir. In it, we find a contradictory subject position that, following the steps of Afro-Latinx memoirists Piri Thomas and Marta Moreno Vega, finds in autobiography a medium to "demand inclusion as legitimate members of the national community while asserting their right to proudly display the trappings of their difference."[63] As readers, we witness and sometimes relate to Cepeda's pressures to choose between cultures, ethnicities, and races. She is constantly being pushed by her father to question and deny her ethnic and racial identities. However, unlike her father, Cepeda's search for her identity leads her to defy all prescriptions imposed on her, both in her parents' home nation and in the United States. On various occasions, Cepeda explains that although she grew up in an environment where she was "discouraged from celebrating, much less expressing, the Dominican half of [her] hyphenated identity," the book is an account of her resistance to "the pressure to bend and how [she] constructed [her] own identity."[64]

If anything, the book is a testament to her refusal to acquiesce to the demands of her father and other members of her family and community to deny her Dominican heritage, her Blackness, and Afro-diasporic cultural practices. Ultimately, she integrates the multiple layers that make up the tapestry of her identity, leading her to self-identify as a Latina dominiyorkian who is knee-deep in New York City's cultural movements, especially in hip-hop culture, as I explain in the following pages.

We can see a double movement: one of opposition to the demands on her identity by her family and another toward affiliations with Afro-diasporic heritage and cultural practices. Concerning race and racialization practices in the United States, Cepeda consistently challenges the US Black-white racial binary by positioning herself as an Afro-diasporic Latina who has strong affiliations and commonalities with Blacks in the United States. Tanya Saunders and Raquel Rivera argue that although in the US, latinidad is not often associated with African Americanness, it is a fact that the majority of Latinas/os are of African descent and that the two groups share similar socioeconomic experiences.[65]

Further, Masiki situates *Bird of Paradise* in a Latinx memoirist tradition that is mediated and influenced by US Black nationalism and African American culture and literature. He contends that *Bird of Paradise* is a "post-soul" memoir and that its engagement with a modality of Black nationalism "complicate[s] and expand[s] what it means to be and become Latina, underscoring the copiousness of Latinidad and the commensurability between Latino and African American Studies."[66] In this sense, Cepeda's self-ascription of Blackness acknowledges the shared legacy of oppression and marginalization that dates back through colonial history and persists in the Black American, Caribbean, and Latin American migrant/immigrant communities of inner-city New York. The memoir bridges the often-wide divide between US, Caribbean, and Latinx Blackness. Read through the lens of García-Peña's nuanced historicization of Black Latinidad, the memoir also shows the erasure of Black Latinxs in US Black cultural archives, especially with the absence of Latinxs of the

Spanish-speaking Caribbean in the historicization of the incipient years of hip-hop culture. This could be a result of "naming all Black experiences through hegemonic blackness."[67] In *Translating Blackness: Latinx Colonialities in Global Perspectives*, García-Peña challenges dominant hegemonic narratives of Blackness that represent Black people and their histories as a monolith and explains the effects of said rigid representations on Black Latinxs:

> For Black Latinx immigrants living in the Global North, translated half truths often separate them from Black nationals, further marking their unbelonging to the nation. The impossibility of full recognition leaves them, as in the case of Black Latinxs in the United States, outside of even minoritarian discourses of contestation (Latinidad and hegemonic blackness), their blackness called into question because of their linguistic and cultural differences.[68]

In Cepeda's case, her upbringing in an urban-centered community among Spanish-, French-, and Anglo-speaking Caribbean and Black American youth was pivotal to her identification with hip-hop culture. Hip-hop becomes a common thread connecting her with other Afro-diasporic groups, functioning as a mechanism of survival to resist a discriminatory environment, and serving as a "weapon" with which to confront her father's adherence to strictly "white" behavior at home. Moreover, it confirms the presence of Afro-diasporic Caribbeans from Spanish-speaking countries in the unfolding and development of hip-hop culture in New York City and centers stories of Black Latinxs such as herself who remained sidelined, expunged, and silenced in hegemonic narratives of Black cultural expressions in the US.

HIP-HOP IN NEW YORK: A DOMINICAN AMERICAN IN THE MIX

The popularity of hip-hop surged amid New York City's dire economic depression in the mid–1970s in the South Bronx.[69] In this context, marginalized African Americans, as well as Afro-diasporic communities from the Caribbean and Latin American, sought out a cultural expression that could articulate their struggles, raise social critiques, and ultimately help them survive their immediate surroundings. Tricia Rose notes that "hip hop gives voice to the tensions and contradictions in the public urban landscape during a period of substantial transformation in New York and attempts to seize the shifting urban terrain, to make it work on behalf of the dispossessed."[70] In a similar vein, Saunders highlights that "hip-hop has been recognized as a transnational/transcultural art form that is linked to social critiques of modernity."[71] Thus hip-hop became the utterance of a youth culture in New York City, a means of expression that sought to shed light on what was happening in the inner city, which mainstream media could not project or understand. Raquel inserts herself in the wider hip-hop culture by tapping into a cultural and sonic archive that encompasses cultural references and icons mostly associated with hip-hop culture: fashion, graffiti art, film, dance, and rap. There she finds the lyrics, voices, movement, and images that speak to her personal struggles and those of her community.

In a 2014 conversation between Joan Morgan and Brittney Cooper at the HipHop Literacies Conference, Cooper read from "Hip Hop Generation Feminism: A Manifesto" and historicized her affiliations and that of the Crunk Feminist Collective with hip-hop culture. In her manifesto, she explains why as feminists they identify with hip-hop culture:

> We are members of the Hip Hop Generation because we came of age in one of the decades, the 1990s, that can be considered post-Soul and post-Civil Rights. . . .
>
> We identify with Hip Hop because the music, the culture, the fashion, and the figures provide the soundtrack to our girlhood and our young womanhood. Our coming-of-age happened in the linguistically and rhetorically rich cultural milieu and transformation that was the 1990s, the decade of the woman, but also the decade of the female emcee: Queen Latifah, MC Lyte, Da Brat, Left Eye (and TLC), Foxy Brown, Lil' Kim, and Lauryn Hill. . . .
>
> We grooved to sounds of the G-Funk era and wept at the murders of Tupac Shakur and the Notorious B.I.G. We are Hip Hop's middle children, folks who fell in love with Hip Hop at the tale [sic] end of the "Golden Age," came of age during the "Modern Era" and find ourselves increasingly concerned with the gender and race politics of Hip Hop in the "Industrial Era."[72]

Although Cepeda is seven years older than Cooper, and some of the cultural and iconic references they cite may differ, hip-hop was also the soundtrack of Raquel's generation. She grew up during the years when hip-hop culture was crystallizing and had not yet shifted to the dominant culture. Hip-hop was the language and sound of a peer group that lived on the margins of postindustrial America.[73] Moreover, Cepeda is the dominiyorkian middle forgotten child who "fell in love with Hip Hop" at the beginnings of its golden age and remained in love with it at the end. Gender and race politics, as well as social injustice, are foremost in her concerns. At the core of her identity is hip-hop, a regenerative source that bridges and connects urban youth of her generation across the US. Cepeda situates Public Enemy's classic album *It Takes a Nation of Millions to Hold Us Back* (1988) at the center of her identity formation. Reflecting on the power of hip-hop as a tool to negotiate the personal and urban crises she and her US Black, Latino, and Afro-diasporic counterparts faced, Raquel notes:

> When Public Enemy releases *It Takes a Nation of Millions to Hold Us Back*, it ignites me, gives me life. I feel free to express myself, using their seething vocabulary and attitude to articulate what I'm feeling. Something about the music and lyrics speak to my anxiety. It compels me to question everything I'm being taught at the Catholic high school I'm attending in Yonkers.[74]

She cites one of the verses from "Don't Believe the Hype," the third song on the album: "The enemy could be their friend, guardian." She feels that "Chuck D is speaking to me."[75] Raquel is referring to a different "enemy"— her father Eduardo, with his attempts to force his ideas of ethnic and racial identifications on her through cultural impositions and physical violence. But the act of identifying with the struggles in an album that claims "the right to be hostile" and functions as a cultural and political response to oppression and a counternarrative to official truths is quite significant in Raquel's journey toward becoming Latina and Black.[76] In doing so, she challenges the historical elisions that did not account for second-generation Latinxs' "personal, historical, and geographical discontinuities."[77]

Cepeda's personal story as it links to her participation in hip-hop culture becomes a site of contestation of ethnoracial identifications anchored mainly in the Hispanocentric foundations of hegemonic Dominicanidad and Latinidad and in the anti-Black sentiments cemented in the collective psyche of first-generation immigrant parents. By claiming hip-hop as central to the construction of her identity, Cepeda negotiates with hegemonic notions of Dominicanidad and Latinidad as they relate to the historical elisions of Blackness and Afro-diasporic cultural expressions in US public spheres and official scripts. Thus it makes sense that Public Enemy resonates so strongly with Raquel, especially when the group reminds her (and us) that "Left or right, Black or White / They tell lies in the book / That you're readin' / It's knowledge of yourself / That you're needin'."[78] Cepeda takes on the role of historian, chronicler, and participant in a culture that was fundamental to her identity formation and that of her generation coast to coast. The bridge established between East and West Coast hip-hop culture indexes Raquel's conceptualization of hip-hop as a language of unity. Through the language of hip-hop deployed in the memoir, we can see that the same coalitions and strategies created to endure the racial backlash of working-class neighborhoods in postindustrial New York City are linked to similar experiences in the urban space of Los Angeles.

In many of her works, sociologist Raquel Rivera focuses on the exceptionality of Puerto Rican latinidad compared with other Latinx groups since, according to her, their historical presence in the United States situates them closer to the African American experience.[79] Cepeda's *Bird of Paradise* underscores the sociocultural identifications of second-generation Dominicans with African Americans and other Afro-diasporic groups in New York City, applying Rivera's arguments to the experiences of other Latin American and Spanish-speaking Caribbean migrant/immigrant communities, such as Dominicans. Although in many instances, *Bird of Paradise* lays out interethnic racial tensions,[80] the author also often highlights moments of unity and intrasolidarity that emerge from shared social struggles and discrimination, as well as the presence of elements of hip-hop culture in Brown and Black communities in urban New York. In this sense, the memoir portrays Johnson's descriptions of Black and Brown expressive cultures as "concrete social sites where new forms of social relations are envisioned, constructed, and enacted."[81]

The centrality of hip-hop in this memoir underscores its concrete social value as an alternative archive containing the memory and history of minoritized urban ethnic youth and as a mosaic composed of the multiple experiences, mutual influences, and shared struggles of African American and Latinx communities from which new epistemologies can emerge. Cepeda writes of the solidarity that emerged in the midst of social crisis, such as during a period of high racial tension in New York when a "subway vigilante" claimed he acted in self-defense in the infamous shooting of four Black teenagers: "Bernard Goetz has convinced me that everybody in the city, not just Papi, feels that Black and Latino kids are no better than subway tunnel rats. Around our way, the resentment we feel encourages kids who may not otherwise fuck with each other to form alliances." Hip-hop was, then, a connection, a language of unity that functioned as a tool of survival: "[It's] this thing we love that loves us back, . . . our lingua franca."[82] Thus Cepeda's emphasis on the interconnections between Afro-Caribbean and African American experiences as well as their insertion in hip-hop culture is crucial to create coalitions and strategies to survive amid the racial backlash of working-class neighborhoods in the period of urban renewal in New York City.

In *From Bomba to Hip-Hop*, Juan Flores asserts that "popular culture is energized in 'moments of freedom,' specific local plays of power and flashes of collective imagination."[83] Hip-hop is at the center of Cepeda's reflections on the struggles of urban Blacks and Latinxs in the late 1970s, 1980s, and early 1990s. It served as a tool of resistance, a cultural and political expression from the margins where the fight—la lucha—was recorded in an alternative historical archive:

> At the dusk of the 1980s, and now, the onset of the '90s, social awareness is at the forefront of rap vérité. Hip-hop storytelling, illustrated most vividly by N.W.A. on the West Coast and Public Enemy on the East, is starting to eclipse its other expressions by assaulting all those who'll listen with the fucked-up truths about society's mores and politics. A spirit of resistance is being captured in the zeitgeist. The aftershock of the crack era shredded our families and, in turn, sent us into our communities looking for role models in all the wrong places. Police brutality, while hardly a new phenomenon, was finally caught on video in the savage beating of Rodney King in Los Angeles. Shit is tense, and there's been no time in hip-hop like the present for a revival of Clarence 13X's Five Percent ideology.[84]

As Rivera points out in *New York Ricans from the Hip Hop Zone*, during the 1980s and 1990s, hip-hop "frequently was described by African American participants as 'a Black thing, you wouldn't understand.'" She also notes that "starting in the mid-1990s it became increasingly common to hear hip hop explained in everyday conversation, as well as in mass media and academic forums, as a 'Black and Latino' phenomenon."[85] By situating hip-hop at "the core" of her Latina identity in New York City, Cepeda breaks away from the notion that latinidad and Blackness are mutually exclusive. In a conversation with Raquel, her friend Susana tells her, "I can't understand why you like all that Black shit," to which Cepeda answers, "What do you mean 'Black shit'? Hip-hop is *our* shit, too."[86]

Cepeda's participation in hip-hop culture, her Afro-diasporic ethnocentricity, and the telling of her marginal story are fundamental to her performance of ethnoracial Dominican/Latinx identities. By talking about what hip-hop has done for her generation, Cepeda asserts her participation in hip-hop culture, which has led Masiki to assert that the memoir underscores "the fact that New York Caribbean Latinos were essential to the genesis and evolution of hip hop culture" as creators or active participants.[87] Further, throughout the text, Cepeda refers to the importance of the musical genre and some of its more prominent figures from the 1970s through the 1990s in the formation of her identity.[88] "In New York City," she writes, "I'm creating my own identity, one in which hip-hop culture, now in full effect, is at the core." As she puts it, "Hip-hop—my participation in the culture as a magazine editor, critic, and documentary filmmaker—has been the proverbial key that's opened the door for me to roam this breathtaking planet. And traveling, when my racial origins almost always come up, has reinforced my desire to know where my ancestors came from, beyond my parents' homeland."[89] Hip-hop is seminal to Cepeda's exploration, consolidation, and performance of an Afro-centric Dominican latinidad in opposition to that of her parents, especially her father.

Cepeda's memoir is fundamental to the (re)construction and continuous redefinition of dominicanidad/latinidad as experienced by an Afro-Latina in New York City, a product of the cultural interchanges between African Americans and other Afro-diasporic communities. She challenges the historical opposition to Blackness in constructing Dominican identity both on the island and in its diaspora in the United States. Moreover, the diverse experiences of being Latina, Dominican, and Black in her memoir make discernible the fact that the intersections between gender, ethnicity, class, cultural affiliations and expressions, and race are central to understanding the enactment of latinidad in the United States.

BECOMING WRITABLE, AUDIBLE, AND READABLE: ELIZABETH ACEVEDO'S *THE POET X*

The Poet X is an ode to young Black Latinas growing up in the borderlands between the Dominican Republic and New York City. In this debut novel, multi-award winner and renowned Afro-Dominican American poet laureate and writer Elizabeth Acevedo foregrounds relevant issues affecting the coming of age of dominicana, Latina, and Black girls in Harlem. The novel also highlights sexuality, intergenerational clashes with family members, the discovery of self, and the influence of hip-hop culture and spoken-word poetry in protagonist Xiomara's process of ideological emancipation from her parents and immediate communities, as well as her growth and development as a slam poet. Xiomara's fictional path toward finding her identity through hip-hop and spoken-word poetry is much like Cepeda's personal account. Writing and hip-hop are central to finding their voices and becoming audible and visible. As Raquel says,

"Writing keeps my soaring temper in check and my fists from pounding some girl harder than Papi does me."[90] Similarly, in the poem "Final Draft of Assignment 1 (What I Actually Turn In)," Xiomara confesses, "Sometimes it seems like writing is the only way I keep from hurting."[91]

In my analysis of *The Poet X*, I focus on how Xiomara shows how she, a Black Latina girl, writes her way into her present and future while dealing with her past. Further, the connections between two generations of Afro-Dominican American writers—Cepeda and Acevedo—coming of age in New York City attest to how their immersion in hip-hop culture within their respective historical, cultural, and social contexts is crucial not only to writing their way into the future but also to reflecting on and healing las heridas abiertas of the past, as well as resisting the challenges Afro-diasporic girls and women face in the present as they cross the literal and metaphorical borderlands between New York City and Hispaniola. I see these two books as joint literary efforts toward the liberation of Black Latinas who articulate their identities by focusing on some of "the questions and issues that grow out of the aesthetic and political prerogatives of hip-hop."[92]

Acevedo belongs to a generation that establishes close kinships between rap and poetry as means to bridge the gap between both genres. Despite having been written in a different era and being a different literary genre, Acevedo's *The Poet X*—like Cepeda's *Bird of Paradise*—amplifies the voices of Black and Brown urban disenfranchised youth, particularly Afro-Latina girls and women. Throughout the novel, Acevedo's poetic language, the cadence of rap, and some of the iconic figures of hip-hop culture in the last two decades weave together to create a narrative that amplifies Xiomara's voice. Thus hip-hop culture empowers Xiomara to confront cultural and religious, familial, and social expectations in the quest to find her own voice as a Black Latina girl entering womanhood in a world where Black women are constantly fighting for self-representation rather than being the objects of dominant stereotypes imposed on their bodies.[93]

Although to date there has been little scholarship on *The Poet X*, scholar Macarena Martín Martínez has centered the agency of Black Latina girls through the (re)conceptualization of Xiomara's body as a site of activism and the source of new epistemologies.[94] Moreover, Zamora has focused on the sexualized violence that the church wields and how that affects the bodies of Black Latina girls and their embodied experiences as a source of creativity.[95] In both approaches, the bodies of Black Latinas are enlivened through spoken-word poetry and performance. Adding to this existing research, my approach to *The Poet X* considers how the presence of hip-hop and spoken-word poetry in the novel is crucial for Xiomara's contestation of and resistance to Euro-American epistemologies. In the novel, rap is the most prevalent element of hip-hop culture that Acevedo deploys to tell Xiomara's story. In the words of Mark Dery:

> Rappers invert the natural "European" order of things by stripping music of its harmonic content and supplanting it with rhythm, timbre, boasting, bullying, wisecracking lyrics delivered in a voice that hovers between speech and song. Rap's plaster-cracking volume functions simultaneously as a metaphor of empowerment ("Today the button on my boombox, tomorrow the world") and as an artistic parallel to fingernails on a blackboard, setting establishment teeth on edge.[96]

Dery's definition is helpful in considering how rap in *The Poet X* is yet another tool to dismantle Eurocentric thought and the "'European' order of things." Similarly, as Esther Álvarez López reminds us, Latina artists use spoken-word poetry "to articulate their identities from the perspective of racial, gender, and colonial (sub)alter(n)ity."[97] Thus Acevedo's deployment of spoken-word poetry in the novel dismantles and decolonizes Eurocentric epistemologies while actively affirming body-positive attitudes and resisting the colonial and patriarchal assumptions imposed on the bodies, experiences, and (self-)perceptions of Afro-Latinas. As the plot advances, Xiomara becomes "the poet X." This transformation illustrates the potential of Afro-Latina spoken-word poetry "to be transformative, enact alternative ways of thinking and being, and imagine new, more equitable forms of social [and intrafamilial] relationships."[98]

Acevedo's *The Poet X* articulates a hip-hop feminist consciousness and epistemology anchored in undoing the often-contradictory hypersexual imaginings and censuring of Black women. Xiomara's journey could be read through the lens of hip-hop feminists Durham, Cooper, and Morris, as it reframes "the narrative of excess and pathology [that] has seriously limited how black and brown sexualities can be made intelligible in popular culture and academic discourse, both of which tend to represent women of color either as ladies and queens or as bitches and whores."[99] In the poem "Church Mass," Xiomara speaks of her experiences listening to Father Sean, the priest at her church, reflect on the scriptures. As Xiomara grows older and more conscious of her body and all the moral impositions on women's and girls' behavior, she starts to enjoy church less and grows to resent the dichotomous representation of women as either good or bad, depending on the expression of their sexuality. In addition to challenging, criticizing, and rejecting Catholic patriarchal discourse, Xiomara also calls attention to the place Black girls and women hold in a faith community that does not represent them or their experiences.[100]

> When I'm told girls
> Shouldn't. Shouldn't. Shouldn't.
> When I'm told
> To wait. To stop. To obey.
> When I'm told not to be like
> Delilah. Lot's wife. Eve.
>
> When the only girl I'm supposed to be
> was an impregnated virgin
> who was probably scared shitless.
> When I'm told fear and fire
> are all this life will hold for me.
>
> When I look around the church
> And none of the depictions of angels
> Or Jesus or Mary, not one of the disciples
> look like me: brown and big and angry.
>
> When I'm told to have faith
> in the father the son
> in men   and men are the first ones
>
> to make me feel so small.
>
> That's when I feel like a fake.
> Because I nod, and clap, and "Amén" and "Aleluya,"
> all the while feeling like this house   his house
> is no longer one I want to rent.[101]

This poem is about the realization of not belonging, which implies a loss of community and a feeling of homelessness, but also liberation. There is an estrangement between the prayers Xiomara utters and herself. I connect this passage in the novel with the moment when Xiomara finds a new home in a community marked by the sounds and experiences of hip-hop.

Through Aman, her romantic interest, and Ms. Galiano, the teacher who motivates her to find her voice as a poet, she becomes immersed in hip-hop and poetry. She joins a poetry club and begins to write, inspired by the hip-hop songs she listens to. Her poetry dialogues with similar preoccupations and experiences expressed in the sonic archive of these artists: frustrations, fears, rage, disappointment, sexual desires, social injustices, issues of belonging, and the struggles and strategies of empowerment of Black women and men. Rap music plays a pivotal role in Xiomara's life, providing her with a creative outlet to express her inner struggles, intergenerational clashes with her mother, and her overall place within a social milieu that does not fully embrace her as a legitimate member of the communities surrounding her. Thus she finds solace and a space of belonging in the music she listens to with Aman, as illustrated in the poem "Smoke Parks," where Xiomara says, "I close my eyes and let myself / find in music what I've always searched for: / a way away."[102] Music becomes her escape, the only refuge to find the empowerment she does not have at home or at church.

The novel is divided into three parts that show a progression toward the solidification of Xiomara's voice, words, and self-representation. Each is named after a passage from the Bible, which is transfigured as the story develops in the poems included in that part of the book. Part 1 is titled "In the Beginning Was the Word"; part 2, "And the Word Was Made Flesh"; and part 3, "The Voice of One Crying in the Wilderness."

In part 1, Xiomara is introduced to hip-hop, a soundscape where she finds a new language to question and combat the silencing, hypersexualization, and dehumanization of Black girls ingrained in her Catholic upbringing. Xiomara's poetry is inspired by the ethos of songs by some of the most widely recognized hip-hop icons of her generation. In the novel, artists such as Beyoncé, Nicki Minaj, Cardi B, J. Cole, Drake, and Kendrick Lamar are referenced, and in some cases, their lyrics appear as intertexts in the novel. These well-known rap figures of Xiomara's generation populate the verses of *The Poet X*, and "with old-school rappers like / Jay Z, Nas, and Eve," they become the motor that moves Xiomara's body to "want to rebel. To speak up." The closing verses of the poem "Asylum" reveal the centrality of music in Xiomara's journey toward finding herself, her voice, and agency through the music she listens to: "And even that young I learned, music can become a bridge / between you and a total stranger."[103] To paraphrase Lorena Alvarado, the engagement with the sonic archive of these musical icons—or in Xiomara's words, "total stranger[s]"—has a direct impact on their listeners' lives. These rappers and their creations become seminal to the critical stance she takes against the role of women in Latinx households that are still very much influenced by Catholic patriarchal discourses.[104]

In parts 2 and 3, Xiomara becomes more aware of the power of her voice through writing poetry and performing it in public. She is no longer ashamed of her body but claims it as the source of her creativity. In

"Catching Feelings," she compares her body to a Country Club soda bottle that after being "shaken and dropped" will "pop open / and surprise the whole damn world." Toward the end of the novel, writing about her embodied experiences becomes an act of spiritual healing: "It almost feels like / the more I bruise the page / the quicker something inside me heals." A similar sentiment is echoed in the closing poem, "Assignment—First and Final Draft," in which Xiomara asserts, "Learning to believe in the power of my own words has been the most freeing experience of my life. It has brought me the most light."[105]

Xiomara's awareness of the power of her words and their ability to heal her and help her accept and assert herself illustrates Audre Lorde's claim that poetry is not a luxury for Black women. Rather, "it is a vital necessity of our existence. It forms the quality of the light within which we predicate our hopes and dreams toward survival and change made into language, then into idea, then to more tangible change. . . . It lays the foundations for a future of change."[106] For Xiomara, poems such as "At the New York Citywide Slam," "Celebrate with Me," and "Assignment—First and Final Draft" become "a bridge across our fears of what has never been before."[107] In "Celebrate with Me," Mami and Papi celebrate her success in the New York Citywide Slam, hinting at the possibility of change, (self-) acceptance, and the tangible action and power of poetry:

> I catch Mami's eyes in the doorway
> of the living room; she smiles at me and says:
> "Pa'lante, Xiomara.
> Que para atrás ni para coger impulso."
> And she's absolutely right,
> there will be no more backward steps.
> And so I smile at them both
> and step forward.[108]

The silence imposed at home, in her church, and in her community is mitigated by the creative power granted through a sonic archive deemed profane and morally corrupt by her mother and the church.

In *Listening to Salsa*, Aparicio highlights the importance of establishing distinctions between women as passive listeners, the "listening woman," and women as meaning makers and active listeners, "listening (as) woman." Aparicio examines how Latinas become active subjects of their own identities through the act of listening to music. Listening is not conceived as "merely a passive behavior, an ideological consent but rather constitutes a potential instance of rewriting culture."[109] Read through this lens, listening to rap and subsequently writing poetry in response to that sonic archive are vital to conceptualizing Xiomara's identity as a Black Latina girl of Dominican heritage coming of age in New York City. She records and articulates her experiences through listening to other Black women and men who, despite coming from different origins, have experienced similar silencing and have been subjugated to violence by social structures that constantly discriminate against them. She begins to feel understood, heard, and seen through listening and becomes an interlocutor through her writing. As Martín Martínez points out, slam poetry is yet another tool for reclaiming the body and performing the written word through Xiomara's own body, opening new avenues of agency and knowledge production for Afro-Latinas in which "embodied practices such as sexual desire and self-representation through performative and embodied poetry are mechanisms to combat the cultural constructions against Black female bodies."[110]

The novel's references to female rappers such as Beyoncé, Cardi B, and Nicki Minaj significantly amplify the voices of Black women, emphasizing the historical violence of the silences imposed on them in private and public spaces. By listening to these women and considering some of them to be her role models, Xiomara not only defies the rules imposed on her within her household and church community but also questions, in the words of Brittney Cooper, century-long politics of respectability anchored in "elitist, heteronormative, and sexually repressive ideas about proper Black womanhood."[111]

Out of the three female rappers mentioned in the novel, US Afro-Trinidadian singer and performer Nicki Minaj is the one Xiomara "fell in love with."[112] This is of particular importance, given the attention Minaj has garnered among critics and scholars because of her hypersexualized self-representation, blatant sexual expression, and explicit language and imagery. Most of the criticism of Minaj surged after the release of her video "Anaconda" in 2014.[113] Journalist and anthropologist Sophie Kleeman asserts that the video is frustrating because, "instead of using her position to bring something new to the table and expand the conversation, Minaj simply reverts to the hypersexualization of women and their bodies—in other words, she gives us more of the same."[114] Xiomara, however, makes an insightful distinction between the persona that is projected in the highly criticized video and who the woman Minaj really is. Further, she raises questions about society's swift condemnation of Minaj's lyrics, bodily representation, and use of profanity, presenting a humanized image of the rapper. She writes in "Final Draft Assignment 3":

I've always found Nicki Minaj compelling. Although she gets a bad reputation for being "overly sexual" and making songs like "Anaconda," I think the persona she portrays in her videos is really different from who she is in real life. So, the question should be, "Does society distinguish between who someone actually is and the alter ego they present to the public?" For example, Ms. Minaj may have lyrics that some people feel are a bad influence, but then she's always tweeting people to stay in school.

I also think society puts a negative spin on her music by saying she's allowing men to dictate how she raps, but a lot of her music shows a positive outlook on physical beauty. She is well developed and people always have a lot of negative things to say about her because of her body and how she talks about it and sex, but instead of being ashamed or writing something different, she celebrates her curves and what she wants.[115]

Toward the end of "Final Draft of Assignment 3," Xiomara explains the positive influence Minaj has had on young women like her—"those who can relate."[116] In spite of the contradictory nature of a video like "Anaconda" and Minaj's controversial public persona and sonic archive, she plays a vital role in helping Black girls and women "reclaim agency of their own bodies and sexualities."[117] Minaj is instrumental in reconceptualizing the gender roles and politics of respectability imposed on Xiomara, as well as confronting hegemonic narratives of Black girlhood and womanhood. After listening to Minaj, Xiomara discovers that "profanity can play such an important role in the output of both rappers and the poets they inspire."[118]

In the poem "Cuero" ("the Dominican word for *ho*"[119]), we see how Xiomara rewrites the script of her own identity as a *cuero* and makes use of profane language to define who she is and assert that all the stereotypes associated with this term are layers of her identity: "[a] spectacular girl. With too much ass. Too much lip. Too much sass." She also points out that cuero can be "[a] plain girl. / With nothing llamativo—nothing / that calls attention. A forgotten girl." In the last verses of the poem, she affirms that she embodies the contradictions embedded in the definition of what a cuero is, and therefore she is a self-proclaimed cuero. "I am a cuero, and they're right. / I hope they're right. I am. I am. I AM."[120]

A similar argument could be made about the role of the references to Beyoncé in the novel. Beyoncé's "Ring the Alarm" and Nicki Minaj's "Feeling Myself," featuring Beyoncé, inspire Xiomara to write two poems that borrow the titles of these songs. The poem "Ring the Alarm" emphasizes Beyoncé's call to reflect on the historical oppression, repression, and policing of, and violence against, Black women, as shown in the 2006 video of the song in which Beyoncé is restrained and handled by law enforcement in what appears to be an interrogation room.[121] Daphne Brooks notes that Beyoncé's urgent call for someone to "ring the alarm" is a reminder "of not only powerful black women who have been chastised and punished for 'misbehaving' in recent years, but also of the growing number of black women who are or have been in lock-down with little opportunity for recourse or rehabilitation."[122]

In Xiomara's "Ring the Alarm," the young protagonist is empowered and makes decisions that will change how she relates to her sexuality. When a fire alarm goes off at school, she tells Aman that they should go to the park and skip school, not to listen to Drake, but to be alone. In the last verses of the poem, Xiomara expresses her sexual desires toward Aman and acts on them: "I lean back against him, / feel his body pressed against mine. / 'Drake isn't the one that I like.'"[123] Xiomara's poem is yet another step toward her sexual empowerment. The same can be appreciated in the poem "The Day," where she feels confident to describe some details of her intimate encounters with Aman:

So I press my lips to his
His mouth is soft against mine
Gently, he bites my bottom lip

And then his tongue slides in my mouth.
It's messier than I thought it'd be.

He must notice, because
his tongue slows down.

And my heart is one of Darwin's finches trying to fly.[124]

Despite the contradictions that the works of Nicki Minaj and Beyoncé may evoke concerning gender politics and feminism, as Durham, Cooper, and Morris write, their sonic archive is "creative, intellectual work of hip-hop feminism [that] invites new questions about representation, provides additional insights about embodied experience, and offers alternative modes of critical engagement."[125] In this sense, Acevedo's *The Poet X* shows the impact of women rappers in the articulation of Black women writers' storytelling through hybrid mediums such as a novel in verse. In keeping with Aparicio's argument, *The Poet X* "destabilizes the modern(ist) notion of art as a space exempt from the 'vulgar' reality of the masses."[126] The central role these artists have in Xiomara's awakening to new knowledge of self and community indicates the value Acevedo gives to the cultural production of women in hip-hop as "knowledge makers and culture creators" in the novel.[127]

The Poet X not only bridges artistic genres to loosen the borders of creativity and knowledge making but also attempts to bridge traditional gender divisions in hip-hop culture. Acevedo could have avoided including male rappers in the novel as influences on Xiomara's becoming. The choice to integrate them into her story and find selective affinities with them goes hand in hand with bell hooks's observations that "men are in our [women's] lives whether we want them to be or not, that we need men to challenge patriarchy, that we need men to change."[128] The references to J. Cole, Kendrick Lamar, Kanye (a.k.a. Ye), and Drake in addition to the female rappers resonates with Gloria Anzaldúa's notions of bridging differences "to attempt community" and knowing when "to keep the gates open" to those outside our groups.[129] The poems "Can't Tell Me Nothing" and "Poetic Justice" take their titles from rap songs by Kanye West and by Kendrick Lamar, featuring Drake, respectively. Despite the many controversies surrounding these rappers, they are today's hip-hop royalty, and they are some of the most influential hip-hop artists across the globe.

By listening to Lamar's song, Xiomara moves closer to other kinds of knowledge and experiences where Black men in hip-hop are redirecting the masculinist, exploitative, and violent discourse toward women that is deeply rooted in hip-hop culture. Lamar's presence in the text and the shared title of one of his songs with one of Xiomara's poems is yet another bridge that connects the East and West Coasts, genres, and genders to celebrate Black women's beauty and sexuality through writing and raises the possibility of steering away from hip-hop's historical masculinist, exploitative, and violent discourse. This is illustrated in the following verses of Lamar's song "Poetic Justice":

> I mean I write poems in these songs dedicated to the fun sex
> Your natural hair and your soft skin and your big ass in that sundress, ooh
> Good God, what you doing that walk for?
> When I see that thing move, I just wish we would fight less and we would talk more
> And they say communication save relations, I can tell
> But I can never right my wrongs unless I write them down for real, P.S.[130]

FIGURE 1.1. *Cover of Los Virtuosos album* ¡No me empuje! *(1975).*

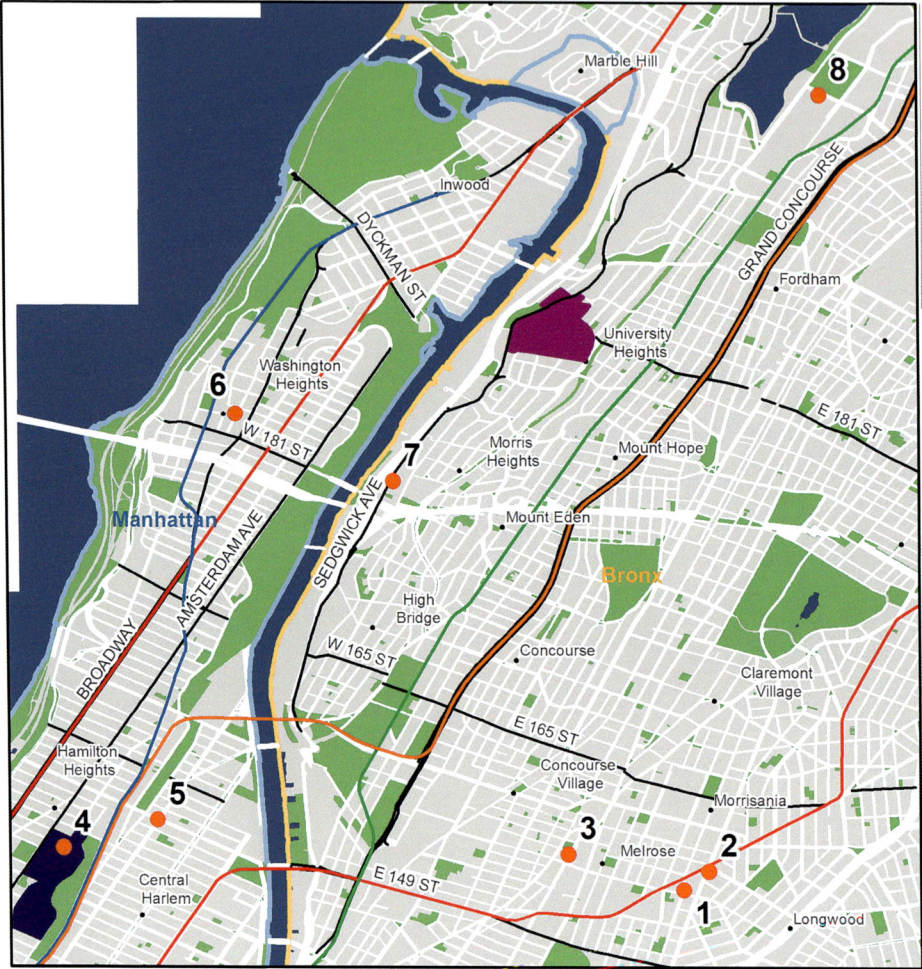

1. 750 Union Avenue, Bronx, NY 10459
2. Casa Amadeo, 786 Prospect Avenue, Bronx, NY 10455
3. La Casita de Chema, 749 Brook Avenue, Bronx, NY 10451
4. CUNY Dominican Studies Institute,
   The City University of New York,
   1860 Convent Avenue New York, NY 10031
5. 300 West 145th Street, New York, NY 10039
6. 44 Bennett Avenue, New York, NY 10033
7. 1520 Sedgwick Avenue, Bronx, NY 10453
8. Lehman College of the City University of New York,
   250 Bedford Park Boulevard, Bronx, NY 10468

FIGURE 3.1. *Digital map of Upper Manhattan and the Bronx by Meagan Duever.*

Legend

Rail Lines

 ——— 1-2
 ——— 4
 ——— A-C
 ——— D
 Bronx Community College
 City University of New York

FIGURE 4.1. *Image with texts from* Levente no. Yolayorkdominicanyork *by Adriana Vásquez-Ornelas.*

FIGURE 4.2. *Josefina Báez and musician Carlos Snaider standing on a cloth labyrinth during the first public reading of* Comrade, Bliss Ain't Playing *in New York City.*

FIGURE 4.3. *Staging of* Comrade, Bliss Ain't Playing, *with a second labyrinth in the center of the room and a third labyrinth on the altar decorated with food.*

FIGURE 4.4. *Image of Josefina Báez by Giovanni Savino.*

Aside from their impact on hip-hop culture, US rappers Kanye West and Kendrick Lamar are known for being outspoken about politics, employing music to ventilate struggles with their religious beliefs, and using their writing to articulate what affects people. Given the affinities between Lamar and Xiomara, I speculate that Acevedo's choice to include him and title a poem in the novel after the widely known song "Poetic Justice" is intentional, as it shows the possible bridges that can be built between genres to shift the violent and hypersexualized narratives of Black women in hip-hop culture. Although at first glance, Lamar's song may be construed as a reproduction of stereotypes about Black women, a close reading of some of its verses unfolds a different narrative: the song is a tribute to Black women's empowerment, beauty, and expression of their sexuality. Further, the song underlines the need for men to write about women, to be more empathic toward them and understand the complexity of the road Black women must take to break the historical silences that have delineated their existence:

> If I told you that a flower bloomed in a dark room, would you trust it?
> I mean I write poems in these songs dedicated to you when
> You're in the mood for empathy, there's blood in my pen
> Better yet, where your friends and 'em? I really wanna know you all.[131]

Aside from sharing similar sentiments toward religion and faith, Lamar and Xiomara resort to rap and poetry, respectively, to express their urgent need to write as a means to capture and reflect on "the complexity of black life and the struggle for the fullness of black humanity."[132] Both Lamar's song and Xiomara's poem amplify how the 1993 film *Poetic Justice*, directed by hip-hop filmmaker John Singleton and starring Janet Jackson, Tupac Shakur, and Regina King, centers the experiences of Black urban women and men surrounded by violence and coping with trauma. The film depicts Justice's urge to "write about whatever is in my heart" and to cope with the traumas of her life and community. Justice finds the answers to her pain in a binder containing the poems she writes to heal and to celebrate Black female beauty in all forms. The widely known poems "Alone" and "Phenomenal Woman" by Maya Angelou are two of the pieces attributed to the fictional character Justice. As Justice, played by Janet Jackson, reads Angelou's poems, the viewer recognizes the ambiguities of authorship and the shared experiences and struggles in the reenactment of the voice/s of Black women's writings. The latter evinces how poetry can achieve solidarity between Black women.

The links between Angelou's poems (filtered through Justice) are also central to Lamar's song and Xiomara's poem. Xiomara writes Justice into her poetry and, by extension, amplifies the ethos of Angelou's poetry: to center the bodies and experiences of Black women. Toward the end of the novel, Xiomara describes how she is practicing in the living room of her house in front of her family and finds that even though she opens her mouth, she is unable to speak: "I open my mouth / and silence. I can't do this. I can't perform / in front of them." In the last verses of the poem, after closing her eyes, the words begin to "unwrinkle themselves," and she "let[s] them loose / and the other words follow."[133] As is true of Justice in the film, once she becomes one with her words, they let loose and break the silences that have consumed her.

The Poet X is a tribute to the strength and transformative power of words and how hip-hop, as an artistic expression, can liberate and empower Afro-Latina women. It is a masterful amalgamation of poetry, hip-hop, and narrative, a poignant and vibrant novel in verse that resonates particularly with Afro-Latinas whose identities have been influenced by hip-hop culture and who find themselves in its sonic archive and historical development. Through the mixture of rap and poetry, *The Poet X* continues to amplify the voices of generations of youth who have gone unheard.

By bringing Acevedo and Cepeda together in this chapter, my hope was to create a common groove through two sonic literary texts that raise the voices of Afro-Dominican women from New York over the course of approximately five decades. In chapter 4, I delve into the works of Josefina Báez, someone who is no stranger to creating from the margins and making audible the voices of disenfranchised Afro-dominicanyork migrant communities in New York City and beyond.

CHAPTER 4

Storytelling from the Borderlands:
The Journeys of a Dominicanyork Writer
and Performer

Why am I compelled to write? . . . Because the world I create in the writing compensates for what the real world does not give me. By writing I put order in the world, give it a handle so I could grasp it. I write because life does not appease my appetites and hunger. I write to record what others erase when I speak, to rewrite the stories others have miswritten about me, about you. To become more intimate with myself and you. To discover myself, to preserve myself, to make myself, to achieve self-autonomy.

GLORIA ANZALDÚA, "Speaking in Tongues: A Letter to 3rd World Women Writers"

Circles of women surround me.
They brush sorrows
off my shoulders
like dust
and sprinkle moon water
on my face
so that I may wake to dreams
of my own designs.

NAOMI H. QUIÑONEZ, "Circles of Women"

When I attended the one-man show *Latin History for Morons* at Studio 54 on December 22, 2017, Colombian American stand-up comedian, performer, screenwriter, and actor John Leguizamo spoke about the absence of Latinx heroes in the historical archive of the United States. As a Latina woman and scholar to whom representation matters, I could not help but notice that most of the figures underscored in Leguizamo's "lesson" on Latinx history happened to be men.

During the performance, I compiled a list of the Latina sheroes who have been central to my personal and professional development. First on my list were the women of my family: my *tatarabuela* Amanda, my *bisabuela* Chicha, my *bistía* Cela, my *tíabuela* Luz, and my core, my *abuela*, my *mami*, María Altagracia Marte Uribe. In many ways, they have been enmeshed in the transnational history between the Dominican Republic and the United States; most of them are no longer with us, and those remaining were and are unaware of their significant contributions to US American and Dominican societies. The next part of the list included María Amparo Ruiz de Burton, Gloria Anzaldúa, Cherríe Moraga, Julia de Burgos, Julia Álvarez, Marta Moreno Vega, Dahlma Llanos-Figueroa, Esmeralda Santiago, Judith Ortiz Cofer, Sandra Cisneros, Rita Moreno, Magda López, Migdalia Cruz, Alina Troyano, Nelly Rosario, Angie Cruz, Camila Henríquez Ureña, Josefina Báez—but my thoughts were interrupted by the sounds of a famous merengue, "La Vaca," in Leguizamo's performance. This abrupt intervention by a song that refers to women as *vacas* (cows) led me to think yet again of the importance of revisiting sonic archives to highlight how even the work of progressive Latino men, such as Leguizamo, continues to reproduce patriarchal and hegemonic discourses that objectify women and keep them in the shadows.

Rather than getting angry or writing a piece to denounce Leguizamo's *Latin History for Morons* for this unfortunate flaw, I left the performance motivated to continue my unfinished list, to write about Latina women. More specifically, I left Studio 54 thinking of the threads that connect the works of the women in my previous chapter with three texts of one of their predecessors, a writer and performer who deploys sonic archives in her writings and performances to delve deeper into the diasporic experiences of Dominican women in New York City. I found another reason to continue creating spaces for the works of Afro-diasporic dominicanyork women who have yet to be read, heard, and legitimized in the Latinx cultural and literary canon.

In her introduction to "Las tertulias de las escritoras dominicanas en Estados Unidos: Una historia," Daisy Cocco De Filippis notes, "Historically, scholarship on Latinos in the US has not included the literary work of Dominicans."[1] The CUNY Dominican Studies Institute and Dominican studies scholars from various generations, starting with Cocco De Filippis, Silvio Torres-Saillant, and Ramona Hernández, noticed this absence. As a result, they have focused their efforts on the crystallization of a field of study geared to fill this void. In 1997, Cocco De Filippis—to name one example—decided, along with writer Marianela Medrano, to create "a space for production, reflection, and support for a collective of women producing at the margins of the US literary establishment and even of the Latino academic and literary community."[2] After rereading Josefina Báez's texts in 2020 in tandem with Elizabeth Acevedo's and Raquel Cepeda's work, the words burned through my skin and purified me, taking me to a place where the collision of my memories, the many worlds I inhabit, the many traumatic yet strengthening experiences opened new possibilities to think about who I am to myself and my community. So during a pandemic that changed the way we feel, read, write, and engage with our many worlds, I was even more committed than ever to continue the work of Cocco De Filippis and Medrano by establishing connections between the literary productions of dominicanyork/dominiyorkian/Afro-Dominican women who articulate their experiences from New York City and through the intersections between popular music and literature.

Over the last two decades, there has been a steady increase in the cultural production by women documenting the experiences of Dominican Americans in New York City through literature, performance, and slam poetry. Notable examples include the works of Rhina Espaillat, Josefina Báez, Julia Álvarez, Annecy Báez, Angie Cruz, Nelly Rosario, Loida Maritza Pérez, Ana-Maurine Lara, Miriam Ventura, Dinorah Coronado, Raquel Cepeda, Elizabeth Acevedo, Naima Coster, Amanda Alcántara, Lorraine Ávila, Melania Luisa Marte, and Cleyvis Natera. In this growing body of literature, these Latina writers "theorize in the flesh" to bring forth the complexities of being Dominican American/dominicanyork and Latinas in a transnational context.[3] They engage with the current reality of the Dominican subjects in New York and Hispaniola while also engaging with the intergenerational nuances of Latinx identity formations from the mid-1960s to the present. Their works are seminal to understanding the transnational dynamics that shape Dominican identity formation in the borderlands, the symbolic and material location of marginal subjectivities, between the United States—especially New York—and Hispaniola. They also become archives of contra*diction*—to borrow Lorgia García-Peña's terminology—countering the historical invisibility of the Dominican American experience in the US Latinx literary canon, especially as narrated and embodied by Black Dominican women writers and artists.[4]

This final chapter pays homage to the life and the trajectory of Josefina Báez. Here I part ways with the comparatist approach I used in the previous three chapters. Báez's extraordinary legacy, larger-than-life figure, and daring works stand alone. Despite this shift in methodology, the general scope of the chapter remains the same: highlighting how the bridge between sound and literature produces alternative forms of knowledge that challenge essentialist definitions of Dominicanidad, Latinidad, and US Americanness. I must point out that the biggest lesson I have learned from Báez has been to embrace change. Thus my decision to keep the threads that connect this book while altering how I do it responds to my deployment of change as "Lo constante. Esencia de la existencia."[5] (The constant. The essence of existence.) In the following pages, I read and analyze Báez's life and works following Anzaldúa's reflections on women of color's relationship to writing and creating alluded to in the epigraph at the beginning of this chapter. Báez's texts, lectures, and performances respond to her urge to write, create, and perform as a way to record what others erase about her and those like her—to become more intimate with herself and others. Therefore, her texts, both verbal and corporeal, are survival strategies for life in the borderlands; they challenge homogeneous notions of the migratory experience through the insertion of silenced (her)stories in ontological and epistemological discourses of dominicanidad, latinidad, and US Americanness.

JOSEFINA BÁEZ: A DOMINICANYORK IN THE MIX

Josefina Báez, a self-identified dominicanyork storyteller, writer, dancer, and performer, was born in La Romana, Dominican Republic, to a working-class family. Báez is a key figure in the representation of the experiences of Dominican immigrants in New York City and a salient example of women narrating from the margins and against the current. She arrived in New York City in 1972 at age twelve and, similarly to other Latina writers, has straddled multiple cultures, languages, social classes, nationalities, and race constructions. As García-Peña has noted, Báez's arrival in the United States coincided with the aftermath of a "strong anti-immigrant sentiment" after the Great Depression, culminating in the Bracero Program, beginning in 1942, and the Zoot Suit Riots and Operation Wetback of the 1950s.[6] This period also saw the criminalization of Latinxs (mostly of Puerto Rican and Dominican descent) and other Afro-diasporic communities during the "crack years" in New York City. These elements alongside the traditions learned during her childhood and frequent trips to her hometown of La Romana, as well as the diverse sounds and the cultural transformations she undergoes as a migrant body in constant movement, are consubstantial to her work. Torres-Saillant and Hernández write of Báez and her artistic production:

A black woman whose ancestral line links her directly to the African descended sugarcane workers of the *bateyes* of La Romana, Báez draws in the mental transformations set in motion by migration to peruse many of the social, political, and cultural myths of the Dominican Republic. The linguistic, religious, and ethnic diversity of New York fuels the discourse of the performance texts, which ingeniously indict the negrophobia, conservatism, misogyny, homophobia, Eurocentrism, and upper-class bias that characterize official Dominican discourse as reflected in the pronouncement of Catholic Church leaders, mainstream politicians, and state-funded intellectuals in the sending society. At the same time, she celebrates the cultural hybridity that diaspora Dominicans normally develop while poking fun at the xenophobic prejudice that often causes others in the larger American society to raise a disapproving eyebrow in the face of Dominican difference.[7]

Such experiences have been fundamental to Báez's ability to negotiate and resist monocultural and monolingual conceptualizations of identity as she portrays it in both the written and performance versions of *Dominicanish*.[8] In the words of Emilia Durán Almarza, Báez's works have challenged "the illusion of homogeneity in the definition of Americanness for decades, creating transnational social networks that transcend traditional national and ethnographic boundaries."[9] As Torres-Saillant and Hernández put it, "The creed informing Báez's work invariably gives priority to artistic experimentation, audience development, and authentic representation. When approaching the human experience, she focuses especially on the life of her people as cultural, political, and linguistic minority in the United States."[10] Her corpus of works becomes what Diana Taylor calls "vital acts of transfer," in which social knowledge, cultural memory, and identities are transmitted to readers, spectators, and cocreators across metaphorical and literal borders.[11]

Since the early 1980s, Báez has been a participant in several initiatives aimed at encouraging and making visible the artistic and literary activities of women in New York. She frequently participated in the writers' gatherings organized by Cocco De Filippis in the 1990s, in which "autoras interesadas en compartir inquietudes comunes como escritoras y como mujeres que están aprendiendo a sobrellevar la vida en una nueva cultura y en un país ajeno" (authors interested in sharing common concerns as writers and as women who are learning to cope with life in a new culture and a foreign country) would meet on a monthly basis "para celebrar su existencia como mujeres que piensan y escriben"[12] (to celebrate their existence as women who think and write).

Báez's multifaceted means of expression have situated her as one of the most versatile dominicanyork women writers and artists.[13] Narrative fiction, theater, poetry, performance, and texts for performance are some of the forms through which she explores and reflects on the experiences of women who inhabit the borderlands between homeland and hostlands. To invoke Anzaldúa, Báez's works are influenced by her constant straddling of two or more cultures. Her consciousness emerges with "a plural personality. She operates in a pluralistic mode—nothing is thrust out, the good, the bad, and the ugly. Nothing rejected. Nothing abandoned."[14] Báez's works are not attempts to create a romanticized and simplistic portrayal of Dominican migratory experiences. Rather, she integrates elements that at times are dissonant, in conflict, and in contradiction with each other.

Báez's artistic production is rooted in the intersection of five fundamental identities, which she calls a "penta-thematic circumference": her spirit/consciousness, gender, skin color and physical features, working-class origins, and immigrant condition.[15] The permanence of these elements allows Báez to remain in active dialogue with history, her present reality, and her communities. Thus her engagement with the sounds and orality of everyday life suggests that her works "transcend the social spaces of the masses."[16] Her works exemplify Lorena Alvarado's observations of how Tato Laviera's "attention to music and nonmusical sounds, voices, and vernacular auralities produces a radical archive of the unheard and overheard."[17] Báez's artistic production is situated within a Latinx literary tradition that, as Cocco De Filippis writes, "florece al margen, la voz de los que no tienen voz, por definición la clase obrera, los pobres, los autores cuyo discurso literario no imita el lenguaje, los temas y estilos de la corriente principal"[18] (flourishes on the margins, the voice of those who do not have a voice, by definition the working class, the poor, the authors whose literary discourse does not imitate mainstream language, themes, and style).

In 1986, Báez founded Latinarte/Ay Ombe Theatre, which promotes Latinx and Dominican arts, artists, and culture in a space where the creative process emerges from the artists' autobiographies. Torres-Saillant and Hernández describe Báez's theater as a space that "showed the possibility of producing work that is creative in form and content even in an immigrant community that has not yet reached the maturity and social sophistication required for the establishment of expensive and permanent theatrical ventures with large, conscientious audiences to support them."[19] Her theater practice integrates her own life experiences and the immigrant experience of the Dominican diasporic community in New York City with her wide knowledge of dance, theater, and Eastern spiritual practices acquired during her many travels to Russia and India. Báez's approach to theater, for which she has coined the term "performance autology," aims to heal the spirit through creative work. She uses theater, performance, and literary texts to explore and comment on life in the borderlands and to heal las heridas abiertas of border crossers such as herself, who are constantly confronted with rejection in both the Dominican Republic and New York City.

Her works represent the journeys of a writer, a migrant artist, and a woman performer for whom "home is where theater is."[20] Thus home to her is a stage at a given moment, a border, a neither-nor location. Báez, much like Anzaldúa, is a turtle: wherever she goes, she carries her home on her back.[21] I read, hear, and see *Dominicanish* (2000), *Comrade, Bliss Ain't Playing* (2008), and *Levente no. Yolayorkdominicanyork* (2011) as concomitants with the life processes of a migrant author, a dominicanyork in a constant journey between el aquí and el allá. Báez herself describes these three books in the following terms:

My life's film had been scheduled
To be seen three times.
When I was an infant, I pretended that I was sleeping most of the time.
In that first showing, intermissions
were programmed just for the usual biological needs.
. . . .
Recently, I have attended the 2nd viewing
Midlife.
Menopause.
Light not at the end, but while in the path in the tunnel.
. . . .
I know. I know
She is scheduling the 3rd showing.
For me to continue in the tunnel.
In the present.
In this bus.
With no beginning.
With no end.
In the light.
To the light.
Now looking to the right,
I see myself
in many life's stops.[22]

Each one of the texts represents the multiple experiences of dominica-nidad as lived and experienced by immigrant women in New York City. Báez's works, then, become an invitation to create a new Archive of Dominicanidad—multiple Ni és where New York is an essential place for understanding Dominican identity "en sus bordes más intensos"[23] (from its most intense borders). By understanding dominicanidad in this way, we can conceptualize the borderland between the Dominican Republic and New York City as a condition, a space that embraces heterogeneity and allows us to reflect on, challenge, and reframe official discourses of dominicanidad in the homeland and hostlands. Following García-Peña's invitation to think of the border space, the in-between, the Nié, as bor-der embodiment—the bodies that carry the borders that have silenced, excluded, and marginalized them and have denied them access to "full just citizenship, and from public, cultural, historical, and political repre-sentations" in the homeland and hostlands—I consider the relevance of this third space as both a site for identity negotiation and an embodiment of the many borders (material and symbolic) that have rendered Domini-can/dominicanyork women's subjectivities invisible.[24]

In an interview with Báez in 2016, I asked why popular music is so present in her texts. She responded, "Popular music is part of me, that [which] feeds me. . . . Popular music specifically informs and forms me. *Me forma y me informa*. I am part of that history. . . . They are talking about me. The people I am listening to, they are contemporary artists. . . . We lived the same, and we took it in a very specific way."[25] Although some scholars have been attentive to the intertextual dialogue between popular music and Báez's works, especially in *Dominicanish*,[26] there has not been an in-depth analysis of her deployment of the sonic (popular music, the orality of everyday, silence) in her overall oeuvre.

Borrowing from Frances Aparicio, in this chapter I pay close atten-tion to Báez's engagement with popular music, the orality of *lo cotidiano* (the quotidian), and silence as a "gesture of resistance" and "references [by which] to examine differentials of race, class, gender, and sexuality." In her analysis of Laviera's poetry, Aparicio underlines how the binary separation between the oral and the printed word "subordinate them within the colo-nizing ideologies of dominant institutions such as schools and the govern-ment." She goes further, asserting that this "legacy of the Western world led to the marginalization of racial, cultural and academic capital."[27] After teaching Báez's texts for over thirteen years, I have heard many times from students how hearing the author read verses aloud or our oral readings of the texts provide new meanings and understandings that reading alone did not convey. Thus, similarly to Tato Laviera and other prominent poets of the Nuyorican poetry movement, Báez's integration of the sonic and quotidian in her texts are "attempts to reclaim, validate, and celebrate these oral traditions, thus giving them a public 'voice.'"[28] The fact that Báez's texts are written to be read out loud, read in public, or performed evinces the importance of orality in her theory and practice of artistic creation.

STORYTELLING TRANSITIONS: THE CASE OF *DOMINICANISH*

Dominicanish, first performed in 1999 and published as a text for performance in 2000, is the first work of Báez's foundational trilogy, along with *Levente no. Yolayorkdominicanyork* and *Comrade, Bliss Ain't Playing*, which I analyze in this chapter. In them, she digs into the open wounds of migration and explores the fluid nature of identity. *Dominicanish* focuses on issues related to language, cultural transformation, and sociopolitical situations that have an impact on the process of adaptation for a young Dominican migrant in a new geographic context. It is a piece spanning adolescence and young adulthood. It embodies a young woman's encounter with a new world and her various attempts to learn, master, and transform the governing codes of her surroundings as she comes of age in New York City. In *Performeras del Dominicanyork: Josefina Báez y Chiqui Vicioso*, Durán Almarza describes *Dominicanish* as the metamorphosis of a little migrant into an adult woman who is faced with a process of redefinition and acceptance of her ethnic and linguistic identity as a dominicanyork.[29] In it, both Spanish and English undergo a process of continuous reformulation to account for the transformation of the young woman. Reflecting on learning English, the narrator states:

> I thought that I will never learn English
> No way I will not put my mouth like that
> No way jamás ni never no way
> *Gosh* to pronounce one little phrase one must
> become another person with the mouth all
> twisted   Yo no voy a poner la boca así como
> un guante.[30]

Much has been said about this particular passage of the written text and the embodiment of the painful and abrupt introduction to a new language in the 1999 staged performance of *Dominicanish*. García-Peña deems this encounter a "linguistic trauma" that "embodies the dislocation of experience."[31] Danny Méndez highlights how the quoted verses "emphasize[s] the pure corporality of language" and notes that "to learn English is to learn a bodily movement."[32] Ramón Antonio (Arturo) Victoriano-Martínez notes that "al cambiar de lengua, el inmigrante debe transformarse en otra persona, usar otra máscara"[33] (when changing languages, the immigrant must transform into another person, wear another mask). In my analysis of the following verses, I emphasize how the contradictions embedded in Báez's works, as well as the pain, struggle, and feelings of not belonging, are transformed into verbal creativity in *Dominicanish*. This text attests a process of becoming and coming to terms with the bodily suffering that results from being forced to learn and speak in a foreign language. This process starts with the first verses, in which the reader can find a multiplicity of meanings resulting from the "mispronunciation" of English with a Dominican Spanish accent:

> every sin' is vegetable.
> Vegetable vegetable
> Refigirator refrigirator fridge
> Comfortable comfortable comfortable
> Wednesday sursdeis zerdeis
>
> Once in a while every sin'
> Son sin' something sin.[34]

The newly embodied painful movements the narrator undergoes as she learns this foreign language generates new linguistic possibilities in which an English morpheme is transformed when pronounced in Dominican Spanish. These new alternatives can be read as a metaphor of how a cultural border crosser deals with linguistic limitations by extending the rigid meanings of one word. One such instance is the shifting understanding of the word "comfortable" in the verse "Comfortable comfortable comfortable." The phonetics of the first word are the standard US English pronunciation of "comfortable." The second is a mix between the Spanish pronunciation of "confort" (with a Dominican accent) and the US English standard pronunciation of "able" (I interpret the latter as "hable," where the word could become "hable con confort" or "speak comfortably.") The third iteration of the word is a combination of "confor" and "table," where the latter word is pronounced in Dominican Spanish with a syllable break: "ta-ble." Although such subtleties can be appreciated only by listening to the author perform it, the repetition alone suggests that in her multiple attempts to learn the "proper" US English pronunciation of this morpheme, the young migrant is never repeating the same sound or doing the same corporeal gesture. Hence every iteration has a different meaning, and one word can give us multiple possibilities.

Further, although it is evident that the collision between the two languages may seem limiting, painful, uncomfortable, and even disempowering for the young narrator, it generates new linguistic avenues through which English words pronounced in Dominican Spanish give way to the creation of new text and meaning—new possibilities of communication in which the narrator, a linguistic border crosser, is constantly "chewing English" and "spitting Spanish."[35] Méndez asserts that authors like Báez and her counterpart, Loida Maritza Pérez, "reconfigure very particular understandings of *dominicanidad* as women in the context of the Dominican diaspora in New York City by explicitly proposing new language . . . that is simultaneously engaged in the process of undoing and doing the coordinates that make up the individual and collective notions of home they each experience in gendered and racial terms in the United States."[36] In this sense, *Dominicanish* is fertile ground for understanding how language becomes one of the mechanisms employed by dominicanyork women to reframe understandings of dominicanidad in the diaspora.

Dominicanish can also be understood as an indictment of linguistic discrimination, what Anzaldúa calls "linguistic terrorism," a form of hostility, delegitimization, and discrimination toward speakers of Spanish, English, and other linguistic varieties that derive from the contact of these two languages.[37] Camilla Stevens and Victoriano-Martínez note that one such instance is Báez's allusion to *Saturday Night Live*'s fictional baseball player Chico Escuela, who became infamous for his constant utterance of the phrase "Baseball has been berry berry berry good to me" with a heavy Spanish Caribbean accent.[38] In his analysis of the verse where this phrase appears in *Dominicanish*, Victoriano-Martínez argues that it "podría interpretarse como una alusión a Sammy Sosa bromeando en el 1998, año en el cual el famoso jugador dominicano disparó 66 cuadrangulares en su "carrera" contra Mark McGwire por quebrar la marca de más 'jonrones' en una temporada del beisbol de Grandes Ligas"[39] (could be interpreted as an allusion to Sammy Sosa joking in 1998, the year in which the famous Dominican player hit sixty-six home runs in his "career" against Mark McGwire for breaking the record for the most home runs in a Major League Baseball season). Although this is a plausible interpretation, given the exaggeration in the Dominican accent pronunciation with which Sammy Sosa uttered how baseball had been good to him, it is important to highlight that the phrase "baseball has been very very / very good to me" in *Dominicanish* is a more direct reference to Afro-Cuban outfielder and third baseman Saturnino Orestes Armas Miñoso Arrieta, better known as Minnie Miñoso.[40]

Miñoso was the first Black Latino ballplayer to be drafted by a white Major League Baseball team in 1951, and on many occasions he repeated this phrase, which is embedded in the collective consciousness of Chicago White Sox fans. The emphasis on Miñoso's accent, the racial slurs hurled at him during games, and his very late induction to the National Baseball Hall of Fame in 2022—despite his undeniable talent and contributions to baseball, multiple accolades, and the admiration of his colleagues and fans—is evidence of the long-standing discrimination against Black Latinx migrants/immigrants in the United States.[41] The case of Miñoso thus illustrates the multiple forms of discrimination endured by Black Latinxs in the US for being Black and immigrants who barely spoke English or spoke it with an accent. Further, Miñoso's contradictory invisibility, despite his triumphant journey in the MLB, is indicative of the negative effects of approaching Blackness from a US-centered vantage point that deems Spanish-speaking Blacks from the Caribbean foreigners, especially during the periods of early mass migration of Puerto Ricans (1940s–1950s), Cubans (1960s–1980s), and Dominicans (1970s–1990s) to the US. At the same time, it could be interpreted, in keeping with Wendy Roth's argument in *Race Migrations: Latinos and the Cultural Transformation of Race*, as a conscious attempt by US Latinxs to distance themselves from Blackness.[42]

As a careful observer, young Báez picked up on the exclusionary dynamics toward Afro-diasporic Caribbeans such as herself early upon her arrival in the US. She realized that although she found herself in a different context, the misfortunes of her Blackness, to paraphrase Frank Bonilla, transferred to the US and added new layers, such as questions about national belonging as well as linguistic and ethnic discrimination.[43] As a result, she developed a renewed racial consciousness of what it meant to be Black in the US in order to understand and question the new codes of her hostland. Báez's new awareness allows her to negotiate "her ethnic, linguistic, and racial identity, navigating away from the official Dominican discourse that denies the African roots of Quisqueyan population," and to "recreate and deconstruct the American narrative, proposing instead an alternative history of migration that reveals the gaps, incongruence, and contradictions that have shaped her immigrant experience in the US."[44] As Báez explains, "When not understanding, we are feeling. And depending on our inner workings with equanimity this feeling can take us to inquiry in its various manifestations (research contemplation). We might learn from the experience. We might become *plenos* [whole] or closer to it."[45]

The journey of the young narrator and protagonist of *Dominican-ish* toward becoming *plena* requires that she go beyond contemplation to question the flawed and unjust dynamics of her surroundings. Báez's critique targets systemic discrimination against immigrants both in state laws and in popular culture. She highlights the political undertones in the mockery of Miñoso's "Baseball has been very very very good to me" and points to California's Proposition 187 of 1994, which set restrictions on undocumented immigrants' access to public education and health care systems.[46] The reference to this proposition wittily appears in these verses of *Dominicanish*: "my king of contradictions / the verbal addict / **monolingual linear lover** / 187 781 718 1 o 2 201."[47] Báez playfully combines legal codes and phone area codes linking discrimination toward undocumented immigrants and monolingualism moving from California to New York and New Jersey (718 and 201 are area codes in those states, respectively). Implicit in this fragment, which consists of meaningful transpositions of numbers, is California's Proposition 227 of 1998 decreeing the use of English only in public schools, a code against which *Dominicanish*, first published in 2000, must be read as a radically critical response.[48]

Dominicanish also exemplifies the behavior of a rebellious teenager who defies the rigid borders delineated by institutions and her communities to pigeonhole her identity. In the preface to the first edition of the text, Torres-Saillant stresses the insubordinate core of *Dominicanish*: "*Dominicanish* resists and combats the rigid definitions of culture." As the young narrator oscillates between two geographic spaces, New York and La Romana, the linguistic dyad becomes less appealing to her—"I ain't no bilingual nerd." During one of her trips to La Romana, she is asked to speak English as proof that she has learned the language: "*Ay habla un chin para nosotros ver si / tú sabes*" (Speak a little bit for us to see if / you know how). Upon her return to New York, the narrator notes, "And the North Americans laughed at my corny vocabulary." After being probed by her compatriots on the island and mocked by her peers in New York, she makes a conscious act to immerse herself in "the poetry of the senses. Poetry that / leads to acts of love. Like a prayer" as a survival mechanism to straddle, traverse, and blur the rigid borders imposed on her identity.[49]

The inclusion of the phrase "Like a prayer" may be a reference to Madonna's fourth album, *Like a Prayer*, and more precisely, to the widely known eponymous single, "Like a Prayer," a song and music video in which Madonna crosses the lines between the sacred and profane, appearing in the video dressed quite provocatively in a church with a chorus of Black American children (the Andraé Crouch Choir) singing alongside her.[50] Báez was cognizant of the many controversies that the song and video aroused after their release, and her inclusion of the phrase illustrates the connections between popular culture, identity formation, and the awakening of a new social consciousness that was happening in the US context surrounding the young narrator of *Dominicanish*. The song brings together Madonna and the Andraé Crouch Choir as a metaphorical union of two seemingly disparate groups: African American children dressed in proper church choir attire and a white woman wearing a risqué outfit expressing sexual desire for a Black saint turned man.

Just as the text of *Dominicanish* takes on a new life when it is performed and set in motion onstage, the music video conveys a deeper message of the song. Without watching the video, one will miss many of the nuances, and the song comes across as simply a racy, sacrilegious pop music hit. The video, though, emphasizes the political undertones of the song through a collage of symbols such as Martin Luther King Jr.'s picture and crosses burning in the background to allude to the civil rights movement and the abuses perpetrated by the KKK against Black communities in the US. This underlying meaning becomes more evident when the Black love interest is unrightfully incarcerated for assaulting and killing a white woman, whom he tried to defend from a group of white men who actually committed the crimes. Although there are no obvious parallels between the song and *Dominicanish*, Báez's crossing of the boundaries between Hindu prayers and mudras, Catholic traditions, political slogans, profane language, and sexually charged phrases in *Dominicanish* echo the transgressive ethos of the song. Both the "Like a Prayer" video and *Dominicanish* suggest that boundaries must be crossed to end structural, institutional, and systemic discrimination.

As *Dominicanish* continues, the narrator keeps questioning and refusing the mechanisms of exclusion that have delineated her identity. This becomes obvious in her views on institutionalized knowledge: "Higher education took me to places of pain and / pleasure History in black and white."[51] Confronted with the limitations of institutionalized knowledge, the narrator finds her teachers in African American soul, jazz, and salsa. Lawrence La Fountain-Stokes and García-Peña have both pointed out that African American jazz serves as an educational and pedagogical tool in *Dominicanish*.[52] Such pedagogical purpose is anchored in the fundamental role of jazz in the narrator's alignment with African American culture and vernacular language as well as in the development of her transcultural, translingual, and transracial consciousness. In New York City, she finds her "distinguished teachers" not in educational institutions, but in the sonic archive of African American soul and jazz music. García-Peña has argued that with the "lessons" of Ella Fitzgerald, Louis Armstrong, Billie Holiday, the Isley Brothers, Pearl Bailey, Earth Fantasy, and John Coltrane, Báez inserts herself into "an *other* history of political struggle" that affords her "a language to confront the colonial legacy of white supremacy that silenced her racexiled body from the historical archive of her home and host nations."[53]

To these observations, I add that by asserting that her teachers showed her "the other side of love," the narrator situates this encounter with music as paramount to affirming her Blackness, to learning "the ups and downs of the heart / the other side of love."[54] It was seminal in her journey toward learning a new language and finding her own groove in nonstandard English with a Dominican Spanish accent. In this regard, she speaks about her learning process of English and US American culture and politics through songs by the Isley Brothers:

> In that cover I found my teachers
> Los hermanos Tonga Isley
> los hermanos Isley
> The Isley Brothers
> Repeat after them
> my teachers the Isley Brothers
> **Repeated a whisper**
> whispered a little louder
> Sing a song sang a song
> **sang a whisper**
> the list grows the list grew
> grows grew growing[55]

The sonic archive of her "teachers" and the rich cultural, historical, and linguistic lessons embedded in each record she listened to were vital for the young narrator to learn to love and embrace herself as a young Black woman: "Discos del alma con afro. / Con afro black is beautiful. / Black is a color. / Black is my color. / My cat is black."[56]

Dominicanish's young narrator does indeed immerse herself in "the poetry of the senses," which leads her to tap into multiple levels of social consciousness that were foreign to her before her arrival in the US. Such is the case with her identification with US Black culture, identity, and history. She extends slogans such as "Black Is Beautiful" and "Fight the Power" into her context as a Black diasporic Latina in New York City. This insertion into US Black cultural and political revolution is also illustrated in the narrator's insistence on "**groovin' with soul**" and her interpellation to the reader/audience to "repeat after them repeat after me," immediately followed by her affirming that the cultural and political history of her teachers is also hers.[57] She states:

Now I'm part of my teacher's tour
Smoke and all the Garden
Smoke and all the Apollo
Smoke and all the Great Hall in San Francisco[58]

This move to inscribe herself in US Black cultural history, a space that was initially foreign to her while traversing diverse geographies, is seminal to inserting her Black Latina immigrant narrative into US Black cultural history. The move also indicates the narrator's rejection of cultural purity and acceptance of the diverse layers and intersections that make up the fabric of her identity as a Black, Spanish-speaking immigrant young woman crossing geographic and cultural borders:

Last Saturday my teachers sang in Soul Train
Now I don't care how my mouth look I like
what I'm Saying
Boy. Girls loves you she does she doesn't
A mor   And more[59]

In a similar vein, Ramón Rivera-Servera sees the narrator's acknowledgment of the impact of *Soul Train*, the iconic African American music and dance TV show, as a way to create a parallel between "the language learning process with the learning of movement."[60] "*Soul Train* was," in the words of professor and author Ericka Blount Danois, "one of the first national shows to showcase Black joy and our everyday lives on television."[61] Rivera-Servera argues further that Báez's "reference to *Soul Train* not only refers to the accessing of language through music, but is also a recognition of the world-making power of embodied culture; moving from a pleasurable identification with music, to an increased awareness of the power of language, to a full embodiment of the politics of radicalism" and that it can be read as an "identification with African-American culture that enables yet another bridging with other marginal communities."[62] Although I agree with these relevant interpretations, I also construe the presence of *Soul Train* in *Dominicanish* as an attempt to claim it as a Black space in the broader sense—a reminder that the celebration of Blackness is not exclusive to African Americans; it is also a celebration of diasporic and global Blackness.

Báez also pays tribute to Johnny Pacheco, "el maestro el artista," flutist, composer, bandleader, and cofounder with Jerry Masucci of Fania Records and a key figure in New York's Latinx music scene.[63] By inserting Pacheco alongside African American jazz and soul icons, Báez foregrounds the influences of Afro-descendant sonic archives and the ways they have shaped and influenced her conceptualizations of US latinidad and dominicanidad in the diasporic space. More specifically, following Paul Gilroy's description of Black identity as a continuous process of travel and exchanges across the Atlantic, I interpret Pacheco's inscription in *Dominicanish* as an illustration of the geographic and cultural vaivenes of Afro-diasporic subjects across the Black Atlantic.[64]

> Suerte que la 107 se arrulla con Pacheco
> Pacheco tumbo añejo
> Pacheco flauta Pacheco su nuevo tumbao. El
> Maestro el artista Tremendo Cache
> Compartido en cruz
> Juntos de nuevo como al detalle Tres de Café y
> dos de azúcar Con el swing del tumbao y
> Reculando como Ciguapa[65]

In the first verse of this fragment, the narrator situates Pacheco in East Harlem, also known as El Barrio, in Manhattan's Upper East Side, which has been populated at various times by Western Europeans, Nuyoricans, Dominicans, and Mexicans. However, the verses "Compartido en cruz / Juntos de nuevo" (Sharing in cross / Together again) immediately take us to Pacheco and Celia Cruz in Africa, as the narrator goes on to allude to their reunion in 1974 at the emblematic music festival at Stade du Hai in Kinshasa, Democratic Republic of the Congo (formerly Zaire), dovetailed with the historic Boxing Championship between George Foreman and Muhammad Ali. Celia Cruz and Johnny Pacheco, who had played together in previous years, shared the stage alongside other members of the Fania All Stars, a band composed of Afro-diasporic musicians, as well as African and African American stars such as Miriam Makeba, James Brown, B. B. King, Bill Withers, and the Crusaders. This event became a symbol of the celebration of Blackness and the unity of Black communities across the globe. Báez's reference to this particular concert condenses several bridgings: Cuba and the Dominican Republic; women and men musicians; Afro-Caribbean, African, and Afro-American artists; iconic Black musicians and the legendary political, activist, and humanitarian figure of Muhammad Ali. So the image of "Reculando como Ciguapa" (going backward as a Ciguapa), which refers to a Dominican mythological figure who has backward feet, suggests that moving backward is necessary to gather and put together missing pieces of identity.

What Báez does in these verses is reminiscent of George Lipsitz's idea that "historical events that we perceive as immediate and proximate have causes and consequences that span great distances."[66] In this vein, the verse *Tres de Café y dos de azúcar*, the title of one of Pacheco's albums with El Conde, conjures a sonic archive that highlights the song "Cositas buenas," which names all the good things that originated in Africa and found their way across the Atlantic to be transformed and adapted in new contexts and realities.[67] Paraphrasing Gilroy, the return to the African homeland as portrayed in this section of *Dominicanish* is redemptive and empowering, as it emphasizes a historical Black narrative that bridges and transcends national, temporal, and spatial boundaries, and as Gilroy also points out, it is a return, a movement backward, in which "the times are always contained in the rhythm."[68]

Dominicanish transcends geographic, cultural, and discursive borders. Entering the universe of *Dominicanish* is a journey through many borderlands to stories and histories that find a home in its pages and in the diverse theaters in which it has been performed. Báez's atypical voice in the Dominican and Latinx literary and theatrical scene makes subjects, stories, and histories that have been relegated to the margins of transnational Dominican and Latinx imaginaries visible, legible, and audible. *Dominicanish* brings various languages, cultures, rhythms into contact with one another, opening the possibility of a heterogeneous, inclusive, and fluid model of dominicanidad and latinidad. It becomes what Anzaldúa calls "border arte" that disrupts the neat separations between cultures through the mixing of language and culture.[69]

In weaving stories, we find a migrant subjectivity that, in its first encounter with unknown cultural and linguistic codes, navigates "the poetry of the senses" to overcome the many challenges of translocation in the "crooked city," what Méndez cogently describes as "an unfixed space, representative of the state of uncertainty and foreignness that are matter for the affective creolization that traverses the immigration process."[70] Throughout the piece, the reader-spectator is confronted with how the young narrator learns, negotiates, and transforms the codes that govern the newly discovered spatiality: New York, the "Crooked City," "Zip coded batey," a revamped version of home that ultimately becomes a new space in which to perform her translingual, transcultural, and transethnic identity in the borderlands of La Romana and New York.[71] The stories and histories of *Dominicanish* are intertwined with Black and Latinx sonic archives that "form and inform" Josefina Báez's cultural, linguistic, racial, and social consciousness traversing the borderlands between La Romana and New York to create transnational bridges where the collision of multiple times, geographies, sounds, histories, and languages culminates with a metaphor that represents the synergy of elements that the young narrator construed as oppositional in the beginning of the text, as illustrated in the last verses of *Dominicanish*: "God bless the child travelin' light / **Here I am chewing English / and spitting Spanish.**"[72]

STORYTELLING FROM EL NIÉ: THE VOICES OF LAS MUJERES OF *LEVENTE NO. YOLAYORKDOMINICANYORK*

Similarly to *Dominicanish*, *Levente no. Yolayorkdominicanyork* centers knowledge creation in and from the margins of official institutionalized knowledge and shows how diasporic Dominicans "reconfigure their conception of cultural identity reevaluating the issues of class, gender, and race" and challenge "the assumptions contained in official definitions of Dominicanness conveyed through the traditional textbooks."[73] Báez sets the stage for a space that goes beyond el aquí y el allá, where the collective experiences of multiple generations of immigrant and US-born women of Dominican heritage and from other US Latinx ethnic groups take center stage. These women characters inhabit the space called El Nié (neither the vagina nor the anus, neither here nor there), an apartment building with an ambiguous location—an interstice, a borderland where, to borrow from Anzaldúa, women reject "dominant paradigms, predefined concepts that exist unquestionable, unchallengeable, [and] are transmitted to us through culture."[74] García-Peña builds on Anzaldúa's conceptualization of the borderlands as barbed wire and defines El Nié as follows:

El Nié is an uncomfortable place that hurts and makes the subject bleed, creating an open wound of historical rejection: "una herida abierta." Yet this discomfort also offers the possibility of finding a poetics of dominicanidad ausente, from which to interject both US and Dominican histories. It is in El Nié that the contra*dictions* of dominicanidad are embraced and redefined, allowing the Dominican subject to emerge as an agent of his or her own history and identity/ies, finding hope, harmony, and even bliss within this very uncomfortable space of contra*diction*.[75]

Dominicanidad is not conceptualized from above in *Levente no*. It is an ongoing project conceptualized, embodied, and enunciated by everyday women who inhabit "la isla de mujeres" (island of women) that is El Nié.[76] The shift in social, gender, and racial dynamics that results from migratory movements to the United States enables the characters of *Levente no.* to reframe the embodied experiences of multiple generations of women, thus decentering hegemonic and patriarchal narratives of Dominican and US identities that deem the voices of working-class diasporic women invisible.

In the last section of *Levente no.*, "Apuntes del Nié" (Notes from El Ni é), the narrator asserts that the women of El Nié "dice(n) en lo que escrito lo que a él (ellos) usualmente se le(s) oye decir. Él la ha creado. Ella lo ha criado. Ella lo recrea"[77] (say in what is written what he [they] is usually heard saying. He has created her. She has raised him. She re-creates him). In other words, *Levente no.* is a revisionist space where women are no longer the product of incomplete stories told by men; women (re)create and narrate their own stories and choose the tools with which to tell of their experiences, describe their bodies, and contextualize their existence in the borderlands between Hispaniola and New York. The women who inhabit El Nié are builders; they build new cartographies of dominicanidad where the voices and "la historia de los que están siempre fuera de la Historia" (the history of those of us who are always outside of History) "contra*dict*, confront, and revise the passivity that dominates the hegemonic Archive of Dominicanidad."[78]

In the opening pages of the text, Quisqueya Amada Taína Anaísa Altagracia, also known as La Kay, protagonist and sometimes narrator, exclaims, "I am pure history."[79] She commands the reader, "Mira. Seat. Seat and listen."[80] There is a sense of urgency to having her voice and the plurality of voices of El Nié become audible and legible through the often-discordant mix of sounds and rhythms that reverberate from *Levente no.*

Levente no. centers marginalized voices, celebrating popular culture and privileging borderland orality and aurality of women, sounds, and experiences that have been relegated to the margins of official national and cultural discourses in the United States and the Dominican Republic.[81] Sound in *Levente no.* is also essential to understanding the impact of the intersections between race, class, gender, and ethnicity on the dynamic process of identity formation presented in the text. The emphasis on the linguistic and cultural hybridity as well as the vital role of the sonic in describing and challenging the multiple experiences of "surviving the borderlands" attain, as Miguel D. Mena suggests, "el máximo estado de hibridación hasta el que ha llegado hasta ahora la literature dominicana" (the highest state of hybridity reached in Dominican literature today) in *Levente no. Yolayorkdominicanyork.*[82]

Fernanda Bustamante likewise describes *Levente no.* as "un texto híbrido que habla sobre la hibridez, sirviéndose de un código escritural híbrido, desdiferenciado-diaspórico, y que pone de manifiesto las complejidades de la pluralidad tanto a modo conceptual como estético, haciendo uso de la polifonía la saturación, la repetición, la fragmentación"[83] (a hybrid text that talks about hybridity, making use of a hybrid, undifferentiated-diasporic scriptural code, and that reveals the complexities of plurality both conceptually and aesthetically, making use of polyphony, saturation, repetition, fragmentation). The hybrid nature of *Levente no.* is perceptible in both the form and content of the text. It transgresses the borders between literary genres; it is a collage of text for performance, poetic prose, verse novel, and fragments of real-life conversations. In the preface, the text is described as follows: "A novel in Dominicanish. / A poem with grajo. / A commentary. Not a visa for a dream."[84] It is also a mélange of diverse experiences of Dominican immigrant women and subsequent generations of Dominicans born in the United States, which, as I explain later in this chapter, is central to foregrounding the heterogeneous character of extrainsular dominicanidad through the diverse bodies and experiences of the women of El Nié.

Levente no. is a sonic text in which a collage of sounds (voices, noise, music) becomes alive and sonic memories mingle with current musical trends, where "la calle habla" (the street speaks) and "el ser y su extraordinaria canción cotidiana, bailada a diferentes tempos, [son] vitales en la sinfonía de la vida"[85] (the being and its extraordinary daily song, danced to different tempos, [are] vital in the symphony of life). *Levente no.* centers everyday voices and a hybrid sonic archive in which opera, boleros, merengue, bachata, hip-hop, reggaetón, and dembow collide and collude is essential to highlight the key role of sound in sustaining some sort of group identity as well as "contesting and negotiating identities and constructing new ones."[86] La Kay, for example, defines herself through the many music genres and rhythms that are inscribed in her body and personal history:

Me my hot hip hop steps.
Me mambo violento.
Mambo de calle.
Mambo rabioso.
Mi mambo sabroso.
Reggaetón.
Dembow, dembow, dembow.
Boleros not even in a dream.
Me my mami chula salsa swing.
Me chercha Royalty.
Merengue queen.

Bachata princess.
Me Queen of the Can.
Domini can that is.
Me, my bachata perreo.[87]

Here Dominican jargon and the deployment of Afro-diasporic popular music offer a heterogeneous, dynamic, and fluid definition of dominicanidad.

Levente no. puts English, Spanish, Spanglish, and Dominicanish, as well as US American and Dominican culture, in collusion rather than collision.[88] In it, the sonic archives of various generations of Dominicans coalesce, creating a holistic, inclusive, and more comprehensive definition of dominicanidad through sound. In this sense, Báez's text contradicts official narratives that have obliterated the histories of dominicanyorks, especially the embodied experiences of Dominican immigrant women and the strategies they have employed to extend the boundaries of gender, class, race, ethnicity, and sexuality. The redemptive tone of *Levente no.* sets the speaking tongue free from the chains of conventional linguistic repression, and *la lengua* of a parade of women who have endured historical silence is unleashed in the building of El Nié.

Although the title may very well suit different generations of Dominicans of all genders born or raised in New York City, the term *levente*, as used by the author, is specific to women. At a public reading in 2011 at Manhattan College, Báez described *levente* as "alguien que está siempre en movimiento, de un lado para otro"; "una mujer leve"[89] (someone who is always in motion, from one place to the other; an easy woman). The term refers to a community of women who are in constant migration, both literally and metaphorically. The women of El Nié are mostly migrants of Dominican descent, daughters and descendants of the Dominican exodus who are in constant negotiation with their cultural identity, geographic space, language, sexuality, and the traditions inherited from an island that sometimes is el aquí and other times is el allá.

The remaining two parts of the title add layers that set the tone and underlying theme of Báez's text for performance. The *no* negates the second definition of *levente*, "una mujer leve." In other words, it anticipates that the women protagonists of the text are no longer "easy women"; they are women reinventing themselves, women who are in control of their bodies and language. The last word, *Yolayorkdominicanyork*, aims to include an array of Dominican women and the many derivatives that may originate from Dominican migration to New York, as reflected in the following passage:

York Dominican, Dominican York, York
Dominican York, Dominicayorkness,
DominicanYorknity, Dominicanyorking,
Yorkdominicania, Dominicanyorkiando,
Dominicanyorkinidad.[90]

The women characters who inhabit the "isla-pueblo-barrio-mundo-
edificio"[91] (the island-village-neighborhood-world-building) are the
center of a third space that transcends demarcations of el aquí y el allá.
Inhabiting what Báez describes as "la tribu de la tangente" (the tangent
tribe) allows her characters to become agents of their personal and collective histories and identities.[92] Their detours and deflections from the
rigid delimitations of what here and there entail lead them to find comfort in escaping to an undefined and unconformable space that affords
them the freedom to negate imposed and uniform definitions of Dominican diasporic experiences. All these may be read as a reflection on the
condition of Báez as a diasporic poet herself. In a 2010 interview with
Victoriano-Martínez, Báez describes what it means for her to inhabit the
borderlands between New York City and the Dominican Republic:

> Yo me siento muy cómoda en el lugar no definido. Soy de la tribu
> de la tangente. Aún cuando yo digo aquí es la 107, ésa no es la
> 107 de un afroamericano, no es la de un blanco, cuando yo digo
> allá es la República Dominicana, es un allá que no es el allá de un
> dominicano tutumpote, blanquito y en yipeta ni el allá de un hai-
> tiano. Aquí y allá, sí, pero no se llega a ninguno de los dos sitios.[93]

> (I feel very comfortable in the undefined place. I'm from the tan-
> gent tribe. Even when I say here is 107, that is not the 107 of an
> African American, it is not that of a white person, when I say over
> there it is the Dominican Republic, it is an over there that is not
> the over there of a bigwig Dominican, white and in an SUV, nor
> the there of a Haitian. Here and there, yes, but you don't get to
> either of the two places.)

The diverse narratives portrayed in *Levente no.* are useful to understand
migration processes as neither linear nor homogeneous. Báez's characters
emerge from the author's insistence on the role of tangents in rejecting
fixed categories or avoiding the comfort of preestablished and static definitions of geography and identity to "reflect the fluid cultural contours that
frame the life of the [Dominican diasporic] community."[94] In *Levente no.*,

Báez embraces the multiplicity of experiences of Dominican women who live in the same building but each grapple with their immigrant/diasporic condition in disparate ways. Many faces and voices travel through from the text: Doña Altagracia, Miledis, and Celeste, first-generation immigrants who engage in the informal economy as a survival strategy; litigious Mireya, who makes a living off her lawsuits; a Dominican professional who just arrived at El Nié and feels superior to the other inhabitants of the building; a young woman of Dominican-Haitian descent who studied at an Ivy League university; and two Dominicans born and raised in the United States who are more assimilated to US American culture. All these women grapple with their *cotidianidad* (everyday life) while reinventing their identities as part of a borderland community.

It is important to highlight that these are not romanticized portrayals of the women who live in El Nié. Rather, they are aware of their imperfections, and the best attribute they have is "que nos decimos las cosas en la cara y con el corazón"[95] (that we say things to our faces and with our hearts). In other words, the women of El Nié are self-critical; they do not shy away from pointing out their complexities. They know that El Nié is a real place with real daily problems where "the Cinderella shit ain't happening."[96] These characteristics imbue the text with a level of humanity that resonates with the realities of the diasporic Dominican community in New York City. Moreover, the freedom of expression about women's issues and sexuality in El Nié erases the blurry borders between what can and cannot be said, felt, explored, critiqued, and shared by women (see fig. 4.1). Paraphrasing Anzaldúa, in El Nié, *se rompen los candados de la boca* (the locks of the mouth are broken) and women become *deslenguadas* (foulmouthed).[97] The women of El Nié are not afraid to use profanity in English and Spanish and often use it to explain their relationship with their bodies and sexuality, including "fuck," *mamagüebo* (cocksucker), *mañaneros* (morning sex), *cocomordam* (vagina that bites), and *ñema* (cock).

Vanessa Pérez Rosario notes that the works of twenty-first-century Latina writers in New York City expand the corpus exploring Latina identity, sexuality, transnational migration, race, family dynamics, and politics. Pérez Rosario also points out that since the turn of this century, Latina writers have felt "the freedom to move away from identity politics—as earlier generations of writers also do in their more recent works—and write about themes that continue to be silenced among Latinos, such as Latinas and sexuality, and blackness as a political identity." Their works consider the impact of transnationalism and globalization in the lives of Latina women and girls in the US and their home countries, as well as how "they create spaces to remember the past and, through the imagination, create

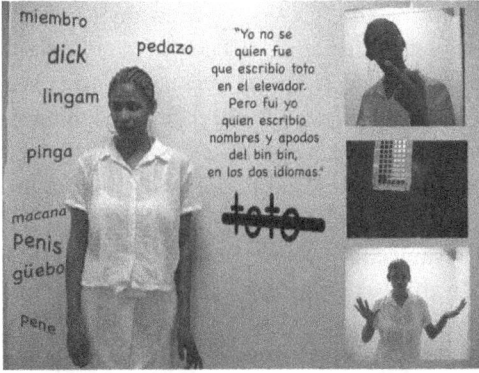

FIGURE 4.1. *Image with texts from* Levente no. Yola-yorkdominicanyork *by Adriana Vásquez-Ornelas.*

new possibilities for Latinas in the twenty-first century."[98] This significant shift in literary representations of diasporic Dominican women positions *Levente no.* as a transgressive and redemptive space where women discuss their "people and world affairs," speak freely, and celebrate their sexual agency:

> La flaca del 6J, la que jode con los jodedores de la esquina. Y cuando ella jode, la línea J completa lo sabe. La cama salta, ataca. La cama baila. Y la música a mil. Y todas cantamos "Sigue flaca, sigue, sigue" www.laflaca punto com.[99]

> (La flaca from 6J, the one who fucks the drug dealers from the corner. And when she fucks, the whole J floor knows it. The bed jumps, attacks. The bed dances. And the music at full volume. And we all sing "Keep going, flaca, keep going, keep going" www. laflaca punto com.)

The choral phrase, "Sigue flaca, sigue, sigue," references the infamous chorus "No pares, sigue, sigue" of the merenhouse/merenrap hit "El Tiburón" by the New York-based merengue house band Proyecto Uno.[100] I read the deployment of this line as establishing a parallel between the defiant ethos of the song and the residents of El Nié. In *Constructing Black Selves: Caribbean American Narratives and the Second Generation*, Lisa McGill posits that it is difficult to situate the geographic location of the character Magic Juan in "El Tiburón": "neither the chorus nor the listener is certain whether his character's home is *aquí* or *allá*, New York City or Santo Domingo."[101] Thus Magic Juan also inhabits a sort of Nié. Additionally, *el tiburón* (the shark) represents, as McGill notes, "the cultural hegemonic power that tries to hinder the character's border crossing," to no avail, pointing to the metaphorical triumph of the Dominican diasporic community to affirm a borderless and culturally hybrid experience.[102] In *Levente no.*, "La flaca del 6J" is the one making the moves and sleeping with all the men she wants. Further, her sexual agency is supported by her *vecinas* (neighbors), who are cheering her on. By ending the quote with La Flaca's URL, Báez is directing the reader to an exclusively personal fictional address on the World Wide Web, which is, as we know, a digital geography, a place where physical location becomes irrelevant and women gain agency by having access to global technologies. In this case, the web is an example of that indefinite topology that Báez calls El Nié.

Another instance of the unsettling effects of diasporic readings of otherwise male-centered, chauvinistic songs could be *Levente no.*'s inclusion of Wilfrido Vargas's 1985 hit "El Jardinero." At first glance, the presence of this song could be construed as a reproduction and reaffirmation of hierarchical gender structures through lyrics that glorify a male voice claiming that "todas las muchachas siempre van donde yo voy" (all women always go where I go) and that the woman he is pursuing will fall into his arms, madly in love with him.[103] Yet a closer look at the context in which it appears in *Levente no.* indicates that its presence in the text is used to contest hegemonic masculinity, what Raewyn Connell describes as "the configuration of gender practice which embodies the currently accepted answer to the problem of the legitimacy of patriarchy, which guarantees (or is taken to guarantee) the dominant position of men and the subordination of women."[104]

In the passage where La Kay describes her godson as a young boy who knows all the scientific Latin names of flowers, and says that when she sings portions of "El Jardinero" for him, "se le ve una sonrisa. Y le abre los brazos a la Gorda [La Kay]"[105] (one can see him smiling. And he opens his arms to la Gorda [La Kay]), she claims that he is a special flower in the garden of El Nié since he is different from other boys: "esa alma grande que vive en ese cuerpo que no hace lo que hacen los otros muchachos de esa edad"[106] (that big soul who lives in that body that does not do what other boys his age do). In this sense, El Nié offers the possibility of alternative masculinities that do not reproduce hegemonic patterns of masculine behavior, linked, in the Dominican case, to (neo)trujillian masculinity.

Further, in relation to the novel *Papi*, analyzed in chapter 1, invoking Wilfrido Vargas and "El Jardinero" is yet another way to center dominicanyorkness and appeal to the influences of Haitian and African American culture in Dominican popular music. As Austerlitz and Lipsitz have pointed out, the song is a version of Haitian *konpa* music that blends merengue, synthesizers, horns, and rap.[107] In other words, it is a representation of the cultural blending that happens in the borderlands between rayanos and dominicanyorks.[108] In *Levente no.*, Josefina Báez honors that cultural blending in the borderlands, which is a formal musical aspect of the song "El Jardinero."

In *Caribe Two Ways: Cultura de la migración en el Caribe insular hispánico*, Yolanda Martínez-San Miguel approaches dominicanyorks and their return to the home island through "Volvió Juanita," an emblematic merengue song for Dominican émigrés by Milly, Jocelyn y Los Vecinos.[109] In her analysis, Martínez-San Miguel explains that the song centers the experience of women migrants returning to the island through the character of Juanita. By analyzing some of the verses of the piece that situate the island as Juanita's *pueblo* (hometown) and *patria* (homeland), Martínez-San Miguel establishes a correspondence between Juanita's dominicanidad and an identifiable location: "su pueblo," "su patria." Grounded in nostalgic attachments to the island nation, the song, according to Martínez-San Miguel, "construye el regreso como una experiencia que restaura o preserva unos modos particulares de manifestarse y de ser que se asocian con la permanencia de la identidad dominicana" (constructs return as an experience that restores or preserves particular ways of manifesting and being that are associated with the permanence of Dominican identity).[110]

Levente no. offers an alternative perspective to describe the relationship of Dominican women migrants with the homeland through references to "Volvió Juanita." The presence of the song in the text does not appeal to nostalgia; instead, Báez revisits the song to point to a shift in the way Dominican diasporic women construe the idea of return to the homeland, "Porque sería terrible para el país que a todos los que estamos afuera nos dé con ir"[111] (because it would be terrible for the country if all of us who are abroad would happen to want to return). Báez subverts a sonic narrative that appeals to migrants' nostalgia to contest the notion of dominicanidad as exclusive to the island nation. Further, in the following passage, Báez dismantles the binary between here and there by emphasizing that the opinions of those who decide to inhabit El Nié have not been considered in narratives of Dominican migration. In the words of the narrator:

En esas cosas que presentan en la televisión, de
la tanta falta que nos hace el allá, que hablan
llorando-juanita-va tu negro querido, nunca le
han preguntado a alguien que viva en el Ni é.
Esa es una historia viejísima que ya cambió

hace ratón y queso. Pregúntame a mí. Yo estoy
bien. Aquí, allá y en Peking.[112]

(In those things they show on television, of
how much they miss it over there, when they talk
crying-juanita-there goes your darling, never
have they asked someone who lives in Ni é.
That is a very old story that changed
a long time ago. Ask me. I'm
good. Here, there and in Peking.)

As Báez refutes stereotypes of nostalgic Dominicans in New York in
Levente no., the women of El Nié also deconstruct patriarchal narratives
embedded in universal cultural imaginaries to contest gendered violence against Black women. One example of this is the transformation of
Georges Bizet's opera *Carmen* in *Levente no.* The protagonist, Carmen,
appears in El Nié as a transfigured ethnic migrant Black woman. Similar
to Bizet's Carmen, the Carmen portrayed in *Levente no.* flirts with and
seduces various men, but in Báez's version, Carmen fights back when men
try to hurt her and can rely on the support of her neighbors. Unlike in the
opera, the Carmen of El Nié does not die at the hands of a violent former
lover. Rather, the tragic ending of the classical opera is turned into a story
of survival in El Nié: "Aquí en el Ni e' se re-escribe la novela"[113] (Here
in the Ni é, the novel is rewritten). After sustaining a physical fight with
Rakli, one of the men Carmen is involved with, she meets Joseph O'Hara,
a cop, who falls madly in love with her. As their relationship unfolds,
Joseph becomes jealous and tries to control Carmen. Rather than being
submissive, she carries on with her daily life while remaining aware of the
tools she will need to resist the potential outburst of her lover.

Summoning Audre Lorde's reflections in her essay "Age, Race, Class,
and Sex," the Carmen of *Levente no.* is very much aware that her life has
been "stitched with violence and with hatred, that there is no rest," and
that "violence weaves through the daily tissues of our [Black women's]
living."[114] Rather than perpetuating old structures of oppression, *Levente
no.* shows Black women's survival in which, paraphrasing Lorde, women
choose each other in hopes of finding alternatives to dismantle the master's narratives that have dominated their stories.[115] When Joseph's anger
escalates, the narrator goes up to Carmen's apartment to remind him that
"aquí no aceptamos maltrato ni mucho menos la muerte de la Carmen.
Que arranque en fa'. Pero la violencia no va"[116] (here we do not accept
abuse, much less the death of Carmen. He can take off. But violence is

not accepted). Thus the story of Carmen is one of success and hope of change in community and communion among women who protect each other at "the edge of each other's battles."[117] The adaptation of Carmen's story elucidates how El Nié centers the agency and survival of Black migrant women. In this space, women can express and embody their sexuality freely without suffering fatal repercussions or becoming victims of domestic violence.

Levente no. mixes musical genres that span from Bizet's opera to merengue, salsa, bachata, soul, dembow, and reggaetón. Because of the extent and condensation of music genres, the sonic landscape of *Levente no.* represents the "highest state of hybridity" mentioned in the words of Mena that I invoked earlier in this section. Aware that the sonic richness of the text is material for a book monograph itself, I examine but a few examples in this chapter that convey how transnational sonic archives retell and create new narratives of Dominican migrant women. The text and the instances included here depict "el ser y su extraordinaria canción cotidiana, bailada a diferentes tempos, vitales en la sinfonía de la vida"[118] (the being and its extraordinary everyday song, danced at different tempos, vital in the symphony of life).

Thus the diverse sounds that permeate the walls of El Nié bridge musical borderlands, *derriban muros*, "rompen cualquier ritmo comenzado" (break any rhythm that has already begun), and take "las etiquetas impuestas o creadas y haciendo con ellas espacios transitorios-fronteras-vida-NiÉ"[119] (the imposed or created labels transforming them into transitory spaces-borders-life-NiÉ) to reinscribe women into scripts of borderless constructions of dominicanidad. These sounds, mostly in the form of music, also contribute to the relatability of the stories narrated in *Levente no.*, which open up the experiences of other migrant populations because, as the narrator explains, "Estas historias no son exclusivas de ellos/nosotros/yo, por nacionalidad."[120] (These stories are not exclusive to them/us/me, by nationality.) *Levente no.* is therefore a written archive of aural and sonic dominicanidad that extends to broader readings of latinidad. The text exhorts us to think beyond walls, separations, and binaries and to engage in "collective ways of being."[121] In other words, it embraces plurality. Toward the end of *Levente no.*, though, the tone becomes notably more reflective, inquisitive, and introspective. Sounds begin to fizzle; there is an anticipation of the imperative need of contemplation and return to oneness. This tone is resumed in and dominates the ethos of *Comrade, Bliss Ain't Playing*, the last of the three texts of the trilogy that make up this chapter.

On November 18, 2017, the Latino ministry of Riverside Church opened its doors to over fifty congregants who attended the first public reading of *Comrade, Bliss Ain't Playing* in the heart of Manhattan. The setting included three labyrinths (see figs. 4.2 and 4.3). At the entrance was an immense labyrinth, arranged for all guests to encounter silence and a communal space for reflection. In the center of the room was a second, blue-and-white labyrinth, where Josefina Báez and musician Carlos Snaider stood and sat during their performance. Behind them was an altar with the third labyrinth, decorated with a cornucopia of artichokes, pomegranates, bread, and butter. This trilogy of labyrinths—one for the greater community, one for the performers, and one on the altar—served as the setting for the hour-long staged reading, which combined string instruments with poetry, Southeast Asian rhythms, fragments of three songs from Caribbean popular music traditions (bolero, bachata, and merengue), West African udu and Balinese bells, prayer, incantations, and silence. As music, Báez's words, and crucial moments of silence filled the space, the audience was veiled in an aura of communal love. As one of the lucky attendees that night, I wallowed in the joy of experiencing radical love in the making. Between sounds and silence, it was a demonstration of how "the inner space invades the outer place" and "in the precise moment of love, there is silence."[122]

In the written version of *Comrade, Bliss Ain't Playing*, the narrator says, "My life's film had been scheduled to be seen in three times," and explains that *Bliss* is the second viewing, while *Dominicanish* and *Levente no.* are the first and third viewings, respectively.[123] In my analysis of Báez's trilogy, I instead approach *Bliss* as the third "viewing" that closes the trilogy of Báez's foundational texts. In this introspective journey, described by the author as her most revolutionary text,[124] readers and spectators are invited to an inward voyage, a lifelong reflection, and a celebration of transformative love and the power of silence that, in my view, closes the circle of the trilogy with grace and a greater sense of maturity.

Bliss is "a song of a particular politics," of everyday life, a poem guided by the rhythm of life in which the poetic voice "learns to transform the small 'i' into the total Self. *Se hace moldeadora de su alma: Según la concepción que tiene de sí misma, así será.*"[125] (She becomes a shaper of her soul: According to the conception she has of herself, so will it be.) In the poem, a mature woman, whose path toward loving herself and others has been determined by constant self-care, acceptance of difference, and aware-

FIGURE 4.2. *Josefina Báez and musician Carlos Snaider standing on a cloth labyrinth during the first public reading of* Comrade, Bliss Ain't Playing *in New York City.*

FIGURE 4.3. *Staging of* Comrade, Bliss Ain't Playing, *with a second labyrinth in the center of the room and a third labyrinth on the altar decorated with food.*

ness of the importance of prioritizing herself and her well-being, engages effectively with others and calls attention to the struggles and needs of her surrounding communities. García-Peña tells us that the fearless multiplication of the "I, I, I, I" in *Bliss* "suggests a collective history that rather than based on the erasure of the subject for the creation of the community, is grounded in the individual experiences of the subject from which then the collective emerges."[126] I argue that the meditation and the transitions between the individual and the collective can be inferred from the place and value of silence in the poem. Thus the poem is constantly swaying between silence and words in a dynamic where self-reflection in silence becomes vital to create effective and strong bridges between the individual and others.

In her essay titled "The Transformation of Silence into Language and Action," Lorde exhorts us to recognize our vital role in that transformation.[127] She also sees silence as immobilizing, hence the need to break it and turn it into action. One of the paradoxes of mystic poetry is that silence converges with words; poets say by retreating to silence and create silence by uttering words. Following the tradition of mystic poetry, in *Bliss*, silence and sound coalesce and empower each other. Sound and silence are the material elements of the poetic voice. As the poet reminds us, silence is "the beginning and end of my voice."[128] Silence is her own personal choice; in silence, she says, "I exercise all of my power," and ultimately silence becomes her power.[129] Silence empowers the poetic voice committed to engage in a relevant dialogue that transcends platitudes, slogans, and structural inequalities and to seek collective change through awareness. After moments of silence, the reader-spectator is immersed in graceful verses loaded with poignant critiques of the limitations of social structures that are not committed to addressing matters of universal human rights, child labor, women's health, migration, homelessness, capitalism, commodification of spirituality, and the dangers of globalization.[130] Departing from Lorde's conceptualization of silence as immobilizing, in *Bliss*, silence becomes the source of power to articulate the poet's inner struggles with illness, separation from her lover, and near-death experiences, as well as universal matters affecting her immediate and wider communities (see fig. 4.4).

In her foreword to the text, Aida Heredia asserts, "Bliss ain't playing when it summons us to harmonize our lives not with a blessed place out there but with one that reverberates within us as always in relation to the Other."[131] Báez's closing words are illustrative of this dynamic: "My words have become wiser than my deeds. / The only way to balance this sad affair, / yes I hear you / Silence."[132] The voice of this third and final stage is that of a mature woman who reconstructs her identity as she goes, as the voyage continues. Báez posits the notion of a fluid identity in continuity. Rather than being a finished project, identity in *Bliss* is, as Stuart Hall proposes, a product that is always in process, never completed, and under constant transformation and movement.[133] The poetic voice describes herself as a body made up of previous and all experiences. A body made/re-created

FIGURE 4.4. *Image of Josefina Báez by Giovanni Savino.*

in and through movement.[134] She notes that her identity is an amalgam of the places she has been and will be, as the following verses illustrate:

> Yes, yes like everybody else,
> I am from where I was born. I am from where I am right now.
> I am from all the places that I have been.
> I am from all the places that I will be.
> But above all, I am that place gathering
> Selected, subjective poetry
> on my own trail.
> I am that I am.[135]

Similarly, in accordance with Hall, identity in *Bliss* is a process that originates from within, reverberates to the outside, and is constructed in and through difference, through the relationship with the "Other."[136] In this sense, *Bliss* can be construed as a radical embrace of difference, the source of a love politics that, borrowing from Jennifer Nash, "has been amplified to orient the self *toward* difference." Throughout the poem, the poetic voice recognizes "the possibility of a politics organized not around the elisions (and illusions) of sameness, but around the vibrancy and complexity of difference."[137] The various manifestations of love presented in *Bliss* (self-love, radical ethics of care, and romantic love) center new forms of relationality in which "life now plays with light; / dances with differences and agreements in the land of the possible" and love "is the topmost and only engine," which transforms human relations and is the gateway to galvanizing human beings across differences.[138]

In *Comrade, Bliss Ain't Playing*, we find a migrant subject on her path to becoming and accepting the many dichotomies that make up her humanity: "company, solitude, / fasting, eating, / public and private moments; / certainties and doubts; / laughter and tears; / thoughts and actions; / life and death."[139] The focus is on her inner self; the journeys into her spirit are the foundation of her being. In *Bliss*, the invitation to inhabit silence summons us to see that energy has gone out of resisting the noise created by the collision of cultures, languages, and spaces. The many voices of *Levente no.* turn into one that, by acknowledging the many times she wanted to speak, challenge, protest, and act, remained invisible and mute until "a light shone through her veil of silence."[140] Báez's silence is her responsible choice. It is a public, collective protest reminding us that silence does not mean passivity as much as expressiveness, especially for people of color in the United States, to whom silence is another form of self-love, self-preservation, resistance, and at times, nonverbal privilege. The historical silences imposed on borderland subjects can be transformative and empowering, especially when their aim is to heal and generate joy in community and communion.

Báez's conceptualization of silence accounts for notable changes in her exploration of poetic language from *Dominicanish* to *Bliss*. The poet is no longer "chewing English and spitting Spanish" or "laughing in Dominicanish." Rather, she engages in a process of renegotiation of identity that transcends language, culture, time, and space. There is a disengagement from binaries; the poetic voice is a border crosser who is no longer resisting the seemingly opposing elements that make up her identity. This is clearly illustrated when the opposition between Spanish and English is resolved and destabilized at the beginning of the text, where Báez opens with a translation into English of a prayer that her mother would only say in Spanish: "God, I do not know where any member of my family is. / But you do. / That comforts me. Maria Pérez vda. Báez (my mother)."[141]

This shift may have surprised readers and critics of Báez's works before *Bliss*. For example, Méndez notes that her choice to write the text in English was "an unsettling point of departure for an audience that knows Báez's works or persona." He adds, "We seem to be immersed in another moment entirely, one in which the energy has gone out of resisting the colonial English presence inside the English tongue."[142] Méndez accurately identifies a change in her creative process. However, I would argue that Báez's use of English can hardly be seen as a surrender to "colonial English." *Bliss* is one of her most political texts, in which she contests binaries, radically embraces difference, and brings attention to capitalist global structures that have negatively affected her surrounding communities. She critiques how her identity has been construed, perceived, probed, and even erased in the United States. She resists "the colonial English presence" by writing in English, thus reaching out and connecting with a readership that otherwise would not have been aware of her experiences as a migrant subject. Finally, I would add that although the poetic exploration of language in *Bliss* differs from that in *Dominicanish* and *Levente no.*, Báez's use of English maintains some of the particularities that have characterized her works (intonation, syntax, cadence, and accent). She writes in her idiosyncratic poetic English, which becomes even more evident when she reads her poetry in public.

In *Queering Mestizaje*, Alicia Arrizón explains that Báez's corpus "calls for a Latinidad that not only subverts hegemonic knowledge, but also recognizes identity as an awareness of the cultural meanings of various representational options by the subjects' cross-cultural encounter." She emphasizes that "it is precisely these interdisciplinary possibilities offered by performance art that allow Báez and other Latina/o performance artists to enter the 'scene of representation,' not as the otherwise absent or objectified 'other,' but as transgressors of the social and economic containment that often displaces their sense of Latinness, self and community."[143] Beginning with her first experiments with poetry and theater in New York, Báez became a careful observer of the Latinx immigrant experience. Her process is embedded in her works, as she is a dislocated migrant subject creating multiple Ni és that make legible her migratory experience and those of Dominican immigrant women. Báez's trilogy reveals the many worlds that, as María Lugones suggests, "we can travel to lovingly and travelling to them is part of loving at least some of their inhabitants."[144] The three texts are long-life songs, jukeboxes filled with diverse sounds, especially popular music, which, in Lipsitz's words, "can mark the present as history, helping us understand where we have been and where we are going."[145] They are also bridges that connect divergent and contradictory aspects of diasporic life.

While writing the final pages of the main text, I remembered that Josefina Báez often says that "everything we are attracted to is a part of us" and that "we must listen to be able to say."[1] It became clear to me that my desire to create connections between popular music and literature comes from the fact that both have been a part of me since childhood. It was thanks to a lifetime of listening to music aquí y allá that I became a sort of *vellonera ambulante* (walking jukebox), constantly reverberating with lyrics of songs from a variety of musical genres: merengue, salsa, hip-hop, reggaetón, US American pop rock, Latin American pop and rock, reggae, bolero, and balada. My scholarship is a continuation of my passion for listening. In *Bridging Sonic Borders*, I reencountered the sounds that have shaped me as a dominicanyork Latina and scholar in literary works that have been my lifeline since I began my graduate work. As we reach the end of the journey, I hope that readers have come to understand how the evocations of sonic memories, images, and musical icons in literary texts bridge the experiences of Dominicans and dominicanyorks across both geographic and temporal borders. Exploring the sonic elements (popular music, noise, silence) in the texts analyzed in this book encourages us to rethink how reading can be affected by sonic memories, experiences, and historical events that, in the cases discussed, are linked to popular music and their icons.

Rita Indiana's *Papi* may influence how readers listen to and experience merengues from the 1970s and 1980s. For me, listening to Fernando Villalona after reading *Papi* raised a different awareness about how he had appealed to me as a child and a young woman growing up between the Dominican Republic and New York. He was no longer the merengue singer and band leader that I occasionally watched on TV or listened to at family gatherings; he and his music made me feel at home when nostalgia invaded me after I moved permanently to the United States.

I also learned that merengue is polyvalent for writers from that same generation. This became evident through reading Rita Indiana and Rey Andújar. Although both authors refer to songs and icons from the golden age of merengue, their use of this music genre carries different meanings that enrich the ways we listen and help us understand that the Dominican diasporic experience—even in cohort groups—is not homogeneous. Whereas Indiana pays homage to merengue de ruptura and pinpoints its nostalgic appeal for Dominicans in the diaspora, Andújar reminds us that merengue is still a heterosexist domain that excludes queer people. My engagement with the works of Elizabeth Acevedo and Raquel Cepeda in chapter 3 tell a different story: although they belong to different generations, both deploy hip-hop to empower Black Latina girls and women. In their texts, hip-hop becomes an instrument of survival for the first US-born generation of Black Dominican Latinas in New York City. These cases evince the continuities and discontinuities in the uses of popular music in Dominican/dominicanyork literature. Thus the dissonances, contradictions, and similarities presented throughout the book illustrate the relevance of popular music in rethinking dominicanidad as a plurality of experiences.

While I was writing this book, several music events took place in New York City that showcased Dominican/dominicanyork musicians from a variety of genres. In 2020, Dominican-based singer and composer Riccie Oriach participated in the Latin Alternative Music Conference, held virtually. On August 13, 2023, Vicente García, Prince Royce, and Yendry performed at Central Park's SummerStage series, culminating the celebration of New York's Dominican Day Parade for the Orgullo Dominicano event. Two months earlier, on June 24, the emblematic United Palace opened its doors to the first-ever Mujeres Del Movimiento concert, produced by MTV Live and hosted by Dominican journalist and dembow historian Jennifer Mota. The sold-out concert featured some of the most prominent women in dembow: La Perversa, Yailin La Más Viral, La Insuperable, Melymel, Chelsy, Queen Parker, and Lismar.

In a Twitter post on April 5, 2023, Mota wrote, "My legacy will be tied to historic moments. That's enough for me. Honored to announce 'Mujeres Del Movimiento' created by a Dominican woman for Dominican women—everyone is invited to celebrate, support and honor them tho!"[2] Mota's legacy was linked to a historic moment for Dominican women in dembow. She listened to these women and, alongside producer Diana Dotel, carved a space to make them audible and visible beyond the confines of the Dominican island nation. This event created sonic memories deeply tied to Dominican identity in the borderlands between the

Dominican Republic and New York City. I see Mujeres Del Movimiento as a parallel phenomenon to "the gender-inflected texture of Dominican-American literature" I have analyzed throughout the book.[3] This concert continues substantiating the central role of Dominican women as producers of alternative discourses of Dominican cultural identity that bridge the borderlands between Hispaniola and New York.

Circling back to Báez's idea that "everything we are attracted to is a part of us," I was personally affected by the series of baseball games between Las Águilas Cibaeñas and Los Tigres del Licey on November 10–12, 2023, at Citi Field in Queens, ballpark of the New York Mets. Being a proud *liceista* (Licey fan) and baseball fan, I perused the pictures and videos that friends and family members who had attended posted on Instagram. I was surprised to note that I really did not care that the Licey lost all three games. Instead, I focused on two details: first, that the event had taken place in the stadium of the Mets, where the first Dominican-born Major League Baseball (MLB) player, Osvaldo "Ozzie" Virgil, was made honorary coach by the MLB for a game against the Atlanta Braves on September 26, 2018, and second, that popular music enlivened the historic encounter of these two national baseball rivals with the live performances of three iconic figures of merengue, Fernando Villalona, Rubby Pérez, and Héctor Acosta "El Torito." My instinctive linkage of Ozzie's recognition at the same stadium that housed thousands of Dominicans from November 10 to 12 and the sounds of the hit songs of the three merengueros (two of them from the 1980s) reminded me that there is plenty of fertile ground to cover on the relationships between dominicanidad, sports, and popular music.

In a phone conversation with one of my older siblings, who attended the last game, I asked, "What happened when Fernandito sang 'Dominicano soy'?" She responded, "El estadio se fue abajo." (The stadium was shaken.) Then I asked, "Did you feel an air of nostalgia?" She answered, "Sí, of course, you know how we [Dominicans] get when we are at a game, with noise, listening to Fernandito, and with alcohol." Her response brought me back to Indiana's and Mateo's appeals to the nostalgia that merengue evokes in the diaspora and the need those of us who live in El Nié have to be constantly reminded of our dominicanidad and to assert it collectively through the famous verse "Dominicano soy." It also reminded me that noise is yet another way to find a path toward discovering, or perhaps dealing with, parts of our identities that we have been taught to exclude, bury, and deny.

As I reflect on these recent historic music events involving Dominican popular music, I think back to Romeo Santos's groundbreaking 2014 concerts at Yankee Stadium. Santos was the second Latinx music artist to perform in this venue (the first was the Fania All Stars in 1973), and he played two consecutive sold-out shows. Rather than citing this as an instance of Dominican exceptionalism in New York's Latinx music industry, I consider this milestone as reflecting the appeal of Dominican popular music in Latinx diasporic communities in New York City. Similarly to the Orgullo Dominicano concert in Central Park and the Mujeres Del Movimiento concert at the United Palace, Santos's monumental success tells a different story about the mass appeal and visibility of Dominican music in New York City than most of those that I have examined in this book through literature. Rey Andújar's "Terror," for instance, substantiates the marginal existence of Dominicans in US Latinx music. Andújar's depiction of Luis "Terror" Días is not that of a successful artist with sold-out concerts; instead, the music icon is a specter, a phantom in New York City's music scene. I look forward to seeing how literature responds to the most recent hypervisible and hyperaudible contributions of Dominicans to Latinx music in the United States in future writings by Dominican/dominicanyork authors.

The multimedia performance project "Tu nombre verdadero" (Your real name) by Rita Indiana and Noelia Quintero Herencia, which debuted on April 14, 2023, in the Clemente's Flamboyán Theater, marks another instance of music and its intersections with literature to conceptualize renewed scripts of Dominican identity from New York City. In Indiana's first piece created and produced in New York City, where she currently resides, she explores death and illness during the COVID-19 pandemic. In her words, "The performance is a way to guide 'our ghosts' to a better place and process our memories of them."[4] The piece blends sounds of her childhood and poetic language. Like her previous literary and music works, "Tu nombre verdadero" does not shy away from mixing music genres often thought of as divergent to meditate on identity by revisiting sonic memories to weave a personal and collective history of transnational and global dominicanidad.

As I reach the end of this book, I return to Báez's words: "We must listen to be able to say." In her works, we can see the many intertwined relations and contradictions among sound, word, noise, listening, talking, and silence that encompass the processes of becoming and unbecoming. These are the elements of her versatile and persistent poetic search, spanning from narrating migratory experiences as a multisensorial exercise in which colloquial words and quotidian, musical, loud, accelerating, and cacophonic sounds take precedence in the constant reframing of identity to a retreat and an invitation to silence in *Bliss*. In this, the last text of Báez's trilogy that I analyzed in chapter 4, sounds fizzle and are engulfed by the growing prominence of silence, marking the inception and the conclusion of her voice.

During my recent visit to the Josefina Báez Papers at Columbia University, I pondered the idea of silence while I examined the contents of the collection. In the midst of the overwhelming silence of the library, I sifted through the boxes of Báez's archives. There I found pictures of Dominican parades, recordings of her performances, a reference to Johnny Pacheco on a page in one of her notebooks, and photographs of her dance movements and choreographies, which, at a standstill, convey the rhythms of the music that have since fallen silent and capture the expressive bodily gestures that evoke the melodies that have now faded away. It was as if all these images in the archives dwelled in a kind of "sonic Nié," in the fertile yet ambiguous space between sound and silence, memory and loss, perception and imagination—in that liminal realm that epitomizes the very experience of reading. Reading sounds and music in literature, which has been my endeavor in this book, cannot escape, and is actually nurtured by, those uncertain grounds.

ACKNOWLEDGMENTS

When I started my journey toward becoming a scholar, I was petrified of writing a book-length manuscript but also ecstatic. I was afraid of getting lost in words and isolating myself from my surroundings. While writing my dissertation and then this book, however, I learned that writing is anything but a lonely process. On the contrary, I always found myself in the physical and spiritual company of dear friends and colleagues; my life partner, Rubén; and my cherished pets. I also found accompaniment in the voices, sounds, and musical memories that have shaped me as a human and scholar. I will be forever grateful for having the opportunity to write *Bridging Sonic Borders* alongside unique living beings and surrounded by phenomenal music.

Writing a book comes with many financial and emotional costs. The generous financial support from diverse units at the University of Georgia has been seminal to completing my manuscript. The grants received from the Willson Center for Humanities and Arts, the Franklin College of Arts and Sciences' First Book Subvention Program, the Department of Romance Languages, and the Latin American and Caribbean Studies Institute permitted me to complete this book and to conduct research in New York City and the Dominican Republic; helped with travel costs to conference venues, where I received valuable feedback from peers; and allowed me to dedicate time exclusively to the advancement and successful completion of my book. While at SUNY New Paltz, I received funds to spend a summer consulting archives in the Dominican Republic. I am incredibly thankful for the intellectual, financial, and community support from the Dominican Studies Institute and the Global Dominicanidades working group. They have been crucial to the crystallization of this project. My endless appreciation goes to my friends, family, and dear life partner, who have also contributed in one way or another to cover the financial costs of writing a book and have sent and made me meals to keep me nourished while I wrote this book.

The amazing Sarah Aponte, Jhensen Ortiz, and Jessy Pérez of the Dominican Studies Institute gave me their unwavering and unconditional support while I was conducting archival research. Gracias, de corazón, for all you do to enhance Dominican studies. I am very grateful to Dra. Ramona Hernández for being a beacon and an example to follow. I was fortunate to meet Pablo Mella and Quisqueya Lora on many trips to the Dominican Republic. Gracias por abrir las puertas a tantos de nosotros, académicos de la diáspora y por todo el apoyo que nos brindan. I was privileged to have taken this journey alongside writers and artists involved in this project. Gracias infinitas a la gran maestra, cocreator, and source of it all, Josefina Báez. My gratitude goes to Francis Mateo, Carla Franchesca, Frank Báez, Giselle Rodríguez Cid, Jorge Suberví, Ángel Ulerio, Adán Vasquez, Guillermo Zouain, Giovanni Savino, Adrianna Vásquez-Ornelas, Rey Andújar, Alex Guerrero, and Scherezade García for their kindness, disposition, and generosity.

I would be remiss not to acknowledge my fellow dominicanistas, Caribbean, and Latinx studies scholars who have accompanied and mentored me in one way or another and have been in dialogue with my work: Ginetta Candelario, Silvio Torres-Saillant, Raj Chetty, Arturo Victoriano-Martínez, Fernanda Bustamante, Rachel Afi Quinn, Elena Valdes, Carlos Decena, Néstor Rodríguez, Lissette Acosta-Corniel, Danny Méndez, Maja Horn, Angelina Tallaj, Wendy Muñiz, Lourdes Torres, Marisel Moreno, Vanessa Pérez Rosario, Lawrence LaFountain-Stokes, Licia Fiol-Matta, Urayoán Noel, and Laura Redruello. Thanks to April Mayes, Yolanda Martínez-San Miguel, Mabel Cuesta, and Jossiana Arroyo for the insightful feedback and thought-provoking questions about my work in the 2019 Global Dominicanidades Workshop and Hispanic Caribbean Intersections: Race, Sexuality and Cultural Production. A special shout-out to my dear friend, mentor, and interlocutor, Beth Manley. Beth, thank you por tanto. This book is as much yours as mine. Gracias. Mil gracias a Esther Hernández-Medina for constantly reminding me that I am worth it and for being such a fantastic collaborator. I have found stimulating and supportive friends and colleagues in various writing groups and fellowships: UGA's Lilly Teaching Fellows, the Teaching Academy, UGA Humanities Council's Nancy Felson Writing Group, Haiti-DR LASA Section Writing Group, and Social Distance Writing Group. Justin, Julie, Linda, Beth, Tom, Dan, Robin, Óscar, Roseanne, Karissa, Alexandra, and Avi, thank you for making the Social Distance Writing Group feel like a second home to me.

I have been fortunate to have phenomenal mentors: Elena Martínez,

Marlene Gottlieb, Óscar Montero, Marta Ana Diz, José del Valle, gracias por su apoyo incondicional durante mis estudios de subgrado y posgrado. Thanks go to my fellow graduate student comrades, Michele Nascimento Kettner, Zaida Godoy, Berenice Darwich, Laura Villa, Luana Ferreira, José Antonio "Cheché" Lozada, and Astrid Roldán. I am incredibly grateful to Miguel Martínez for being mi panita in the journey toward getting my PhD. Miguelín, gracias mil for helping me navigate the torrid waters of academia and always being a phone call away to guide me, listen to me, and talk about Caribbean music.

To my fantastic editor, Kerry Webb, and her remarkable assistant, Christina Vargas, as well as the whole staff team of University of Texas Press, thank you for guiding me through publishing my first book and for all your support in this process! I am obliged to the trailblazing series editors, Nicole Guidotti-Hernández and Lorgia García-Peña, for believing in this project and showing through example the importance of ethnic studies and feminist praxis in academia. Ustedes son dos matatanas y qué gran honor es para mí publicar este libro bajo su mentoría. Lorgia, el resto is indeed "la selva." Thank you for the many communities you keep building in communion and rebellion. Megan Bayles was immensely helpful in being such a careful, insightful reader of my work.

I sincerely appreciate being part of the Department of Romance Languages at UGA. Thank you to every colleague who embraced me since my arrival in Athens, Georgia, in 2018. I thank Ángel Nicolás Lucero, un hermano, colega y ángel que me regaló Mendoza via Athens. Gracias por llegar conmigo hasta la meta final. I am profoundly indebted to Betina Kaplan, whose hands have literally held me in my most challenging professional and personal times, and to Lesley Feracho, for her constant support and care and for lending an ear when the hallways of academia have been inhospitable for women of color. Many thanks to Betsy Wright, for her unwavering support of my work and her wise advice, and to Luis Correa-Díaz, Emily Sahakian, Timothy Gupton, and Stacey Casado, for rooting for me since day one. Nora Benedict generously shared resources to complete the final stages of my book. My deepest gratitude goes to my department head, Dana Bultman, for believing in me, guiding me, and cheering me on to accomplish my dreams and goals. Alicia, Nuño, Paola, Alberto, Milvet, Fuad, thank you for your constant support and for making Georgia feel at home. Cecília and Frans, I am grateful for your kindness and generosity.

I consider myself lucky to share paths with colleagues in other departments at the University of Georgia who have become extended family and have supported me in various capacities: Cassia Roth, Éric Morales Franceschini, Rebecca Matthews, and Rielle Navisky. Many thanks to my colleagues and friends at SUNY New Paltz: Anne Roschelle, Alex Cox, Cruz Bueno, Isidoro Janeiro, Rachel Sommerstein, Jess Pabón, César Barros, Kiersten Greene, Nathan Clerici, Dean Laura Barrett, and Roberto Velez-Velez. I feel especially privileged to have come to know the students I have worked with throughout my career. I kid you not when I say you all make this worth it!

Thanks also go to my fellow ayombians, Jei Bi, Aris, Ela, Carlos, Jhensen, Mayra, Vania, Pilar, Inma, and Andrea, for being my comrades and for the many blessings I receive from you always. Gracias to my childhood friend Angely, por siempre apostar a mí. Gracias Francisco, Kiwry, and Aneudy for always believing in me and defying every stereotype. Infinitas gracias a Leo Cotlar y Paula Reynaldi, for constantly checking in on me. Pao, Eduardo, Yolin y Bella, muy agradecida con cada uno de ustedes por el cariño y cuidados desde mi llegada a Athens. Mabe, gracias por ser un alma generosa, por todo el cariño que he recibido de ti y por siempre estar ahí.

No tengo cómo agradecerle a la vida por el gran regalo de una hermana con la que tengo tanto que compartir. Manita, sé que nunca pronuncié la g en tu nombre como debería ser, but you know that this sisterhood has nothing to do with labels and everything to do with genuine love. Gracias por dejarme entrar en tu vida, en la de mi adorado sobri-gato y en la de tu compañera, la gran amante del chocolate con un corazón gigante. I am grateful daily for mis tres pilares, Ileana, Andrea, and Cristina, for over two decades of friendship, for *always* being there, for celebrating every little milestone, and for holding me when life has gotten rough. And my utmost gratitude goes to Chris and Clare Potter—my career would not have happened without your constant encouragement and support. To my tíos Moises and Nicolás and all their friends who became tíos políticos, for opening up the world of music at a very young age. To tía Noemí and tío Pache, for being the doorway to my beloved New York. To the many sobrinos who have come into my life through my blood sisters and the many friends who have become hermanas. And to my parents, Rosa Ana de la Rosa and Ahmmed Pérez, and my siblings for teaching me to love unconditionally, to be tolerant, and to embrace differences. Gracias a mi abuela, María Altagracia Marte Uribe, for shaping me into the woman I am today and for her scarce yet joyful moments of clarity.

I am grateful for my maño amado, Rubén, for holding up the mirror and showing me what I often can't see. Te amo, maño. Thank you for opening the doors into your family. Ana, suegra querida, gracias por todas las velitas y abrazos virtuales. Thank you for bringing Rubén, Diana, and

Sergio into a world that needs more people like them, like you. My dear kitties, Frida and Julia, who came into our lives via my sister, La Beba, in 2015, thank you for showing me that sunbathing while listening to music is underrated. My beloved Gabo, a gift from my parents in the darkest of times in my life, thank you for being a shining light and reminding me that taking breaks is also underrated.

NOTES

INTRODUCTION. BRIDGING SONIC LITERARY BORDERS BETWEEN THE DOMINICAN REPUBLIC AND NEW YORK CITY

1. Daisy Cocco De Filippis, "Dominican Writers at the Crossroads: Reflections of a Conversation in Progress," *Latino Review of Books* 2, no. 2 (1996): 4.
2. Throughout the book, I lowercase *dominicanidad* and *latinidad* when I do not make direct associations with hegemonic structures. In the cases where I do make such links, I capitalize these terms.
3. Fernanda Bustamante Escalona, *A ritmo desenfadado: Narrativas dominicanas del nuevo milenio* (Santiago, Chile: Editorial Cuarto Propio, 2014), 35. Unless otherwise noted, all translations are my own.
4. María Josefina Saldaña-Portillo, "Epilogue: Latina/o Literature: The Borders Are Burning," in *The Cambridge History of Latina/o Literature*, ed. John Morán González and Laura Lomas (New York: Cambridge University Press, 2018), 741.
5. Lorgia García-Peña, *The Borders of Dominicanidad: Race, Nation, and Archives of Contradiction* (Durham, NC: Duke University Press, 2016), 14.
6. Frances R. Aparicio, *Listening to Salsa: Gender, Latin Popular Music, and Puerto Rican Cultures* (Middletown, CT: Wesleyan University Press, 1998), 5.
7. Juan Flores, *The Diaspora Strikes Back: Caribeño Tales of Learning and Turning*, Cultural Spaces Series (New York: Routledge, 2009), 170.
8. Lorraine E. Ben-Ur, "Hacia la novela del Caribe: Guillermo Cabrera Infante y Luis Rafael Sánchez," in *Luis Rafael Sánchez: Crítica y bibliografía*, ed. Daisy Caraballo Abréu and Néloda Hernández Vargas (Río Piedras: Editorial de la Universidad de Puerto Rico, 1985), 209.
9. Héctor López, *La música caribeña en la literatura de la postmodernidad* (Mérida, Venezuela: Fondo Editorial "Ramón Palomares," 1998), 9.
10. For more on this, see Lorgia García-Peña, "Dominican Ethnic Identities, National Borders, and Literature," and Silvio Torres-Saillant and Nancy Kang, "Currents in Dominican American Literature," both in *The Oxford Encyclopedia of Latina and Latino Literature*, vol. 1, ed. Louis G. Mendoza (New York: Oxford University Press, 2020), 475–489, 489–506.
11. Michael P. Smith and Luis E. Guarnizo, eds., "The Locations of Transnationalism," in *Transnationalism from Below* (New Brunswick, NJ: Transaction Publishers, 1998), 9.

12. Laird Bergad, *The Dominican Population of the New York Metro Region, 1970–2020*, Latino Data Project, Report 91, Center for Latin American, Caribbean, and Latino Studies, City University of New York, August 2022, https://academicworks.cuny.edu/cgi/viewcontent.cgi?article=1105&context=clacls_pubs. The seminal works by the following authors reflect on the cultural exchanges that result from Hispanic Caribbean migration to the US: Jorge Duany, *Blurred Borders: Transnational Migration between the Hispanic Caribbean and the United States* (Chapel Hill: University of North Carolina Press, 2011); Flores, *Diaspora Strikes Back*; Luis E. Guarnizo, "Los Dominicanyorks: The Making of a Binational Society," *Annals of the American Academy of Political and Social Science* 533 (1994): 70–86; Jose Itzigsohn, Carlos Dore Cabral, Esther Hernández-Medina, and Obed Vazquez, "Mapping Dominican Transnationalism: Narrow and Broad Transnational Practices," *Ethnic and Racial Studies* 22, no. 2 (1999): 316–339; Peggy Levitt, *The Transnational Villagers* (Berkeley: University of California Press, 2001); Patricia R. Pessar, *A Visa for a Dream: Dominicans in the United States* (Boston: Allyn and Bacon, 1995); Nancy Foner, ed., *New Immigrants in New York* (New York: Columbia University Press, 2001); Sherri Grasmuck and Patricia R. Pessar, *Between Two Islands: Dominican International Migration* (Berkeley: University of California Press, 1991).

13. Flores, *Diaspora Strikes Back*, 170.

14. Yolanda Martínez-San Miguel, *Caribe Two Ways: Cultura de la migración en el Caribe insular hispánico* (San Juan, PR: Ediciones Callejón, 2003), 47.

15. Lorena Alvarado, "Listening to Literature: Popular Music, Voice, and Dance in Latina/o Literary Imagination, 1980–2010," in *The Cambridge History of Latina/o American Literature*, ed. John Morán González and Laura Lomas (New York: Cambridge University Press, 2018), 583–601.

16. Médar Serrata, ed., *El sonido de la música en la narrativa dominicana: Ensayos sobre identidad, nación y performance* (Santo Domingo, DR: Instituto de Estudios Caribeños, 2012).

17. Silvio Torres-Saillant, "Dominican-American Literature: Immigrants, Exiles, and Ethnics," in *The Routledge Companion to Latino/a Literature*, ed. Suzanne Bost and Frances R. Aparicio (New York: Routledge, 2013), 432.

18. Aparicio, *Listening to Salsa*; George Lipsitz, *Footsteps in the Dark: The Hidden History of Popular Music* (Minneapolis: University of Minnesota Press, 2007).

19. María Elena Cepeda, *Musical ImagiNation: U.S.-Colombian Identity and the Latin Music Boom* (New York: New York University Press, 2010).

20. Flores, *Diaspora Strikes Back*, 169.

21. See Martínez-San Miguel, *Caribe Two Ways*, 323. Extending the readings of migration scholars who have deemed New York an extension of the Caribbean, Martínez-San Miguel argues that "Nueva York se convierte entonces en una extensión geográfica, económica y simbólica del Caribe hispánico, que reconfigura las definiciones clásicas de la experiencia insular para incorporarla a una cartografía alternativa delimitada por la cultura de desplazamientos." (New York then becomes a geographic, economic, and symbolic extension of the Hispanic Caribbean that reconfigures the classic definitions of the island experience to incorporate it into an alternative cartography delimited by the culture of displacement.) *Caribe Two Ways*, 325.

22. Paul Austerlitz, *Merengue: Dominican Music and Dominican Identity* (Philadel-

phia: Temple University Press, 1997); Sydney Hutchinson, "Merengue Típico in Santiago and New York: Transnational Regionalism in Neo-Traditional Dominican Music," *Ethnomusicology* 50, no. 1 (2006): 37–72; Sydney Hutchinson, *Tigers of a Different Stripe: Performing Gender in Dominican Music* (Chicago: University of Chicago Press, 2016).

23. Deborah Pacini Hernández, "*La lucha sonora*: Dominican Popular Music in the Post-Trujillo Era," *Latin American Music Review / Revista de Música Latinoamericana* 12, no. 2 (1991): 105–123.

24. Jonathan Sterne, *The Audible Past: Cultural Origins of Sound Reproduction* (Durham, NC: Duke University Press, 2003); Jonathan Sterne, *The Sound Studies Reader* (New York: Routledge, 2012).

25. Leonardo Cardoso, *Sound-Politics in São Paulo* (New York: Oxford University Press, 2019).

26. Josefina Báez, *Dominicanish: A Performance Text* (New York: I.Om.Be, 2000).

27. Gloria Anzaldúa, *Light in the Dark / Luz en lo Oscuro: Rewriting Identity, Spirituality, Reality* (Durham, NC: Duke University Press, 2015), 79.

28. Anzaldúa, *Light in the Dark*, 81.

29. Austerlitz, *Merengue*.

30. Merengue típico cibaeño, also known as merengue *liniero* (which originates from the border region between Haiti and the Dominican Republic), is a folk style of merengue from the north-central region of the Dominican Republic.

31. Carlos Ulises Decena, *Tacit Subjects: Belonging and Same-Sex Desire among Dominican Immigrant Men* (Durham, NC: Duke University Press, 2011).

32. Omaris Z. Zamora, "Before *Bodak Yellow* and Beyond the Post-Soul: Cardi B Performs AfroLatina Feminisms in the Trance," *Black Scholar* 52, no. 1 (2022): 54.

33. García-Peña, *Borders of Dominicanidad*, 173.

34. Esther Hernández-Medina, "Josefina Báez y El Nié," *Acento*, January 3, 2023, https://acento.com.do/opinion/josefina-baez-y-el-nie-9169365.html.

CHAPTER 1. MERENGUE MAKES IT TO LOS PAÍSES— WITH A TWIST

1. In Dominican slang, *los países* usually refers to New York or other large cities or destination countries for Dominican immigration.

2. Flores, *Diaspora Strikes Back*, 4.

3. See Martínez-San Miguel, "'Con mi música pa' otra parte': Desplazamientos simbólicos dominicanos," in *Caribe Two Ways*, 263–322; Silvio Torres-Saillant, *El retorno de las yolas: Ensayos sobre diáspora, democracia y dominicanidad* (Santo Domingo, DR: Librería Trinitaria y Editora Manatí, 1999); Angelina Tallaj, "A Country That Ain't Belong to Me: Dominicanyorks, Identity and Popular Music," *Guttman Community College Publications and Research* No. 93 (New York: CUNY Academic Works, 2006), https://academicworks.cuny.edu/nc_pubs/93; Lorna Torrado, "Desplazamientos bailables: Revisión histórica en la producción musical de Rita Indiana Hernández," in *Rita Indiana: Archivos*, ed. Fernanda Bustamante (Santo Domingo, DR: Ediciones Cielo Naranja, 2017), 331–350; Syd-

ney Hutchinson, "Listening Sideways: The Transgenre Work of Rita Indiana," in *Tigers of a Different Stripe*, 173–210.

4. Flores, *Diaspora Strikes Back*, 4.
5. Flores, *Diaspora Strikes Back*, 158.
6. Francis Mateo, in discussion with the author, March 2014 and July 2020.
7. Catalina Maria Johnson, "Interview: Rita Indiana at LAMC 2011," Gozamos Chicago, July 25, 2011, YouTube video, 00:40, https://www.youtube.com/watch?v=VWkb68Ka75c.
8. The column was first published under the name "Archipiélago Pájaro," and when the scope became more academic, the title changed to "Salón Abierto." The column was published less regularly until summer 2020, when it reemerged in the context of COVID-19 as "La maldita columna." It is published regularly on the *Acento* website.
9. Smith and Guarnizo, *Transnationalism from Below*, 5.
10. Flores, *Diaspora Strikes Back*, 160.
11. Flores, *Diaspora Strikes Back*, 17; López, *La música caribeña*, 9.
12. Silvio Torres-Saillant and Ramona Hernández, "Dominicans: Community, Culture, and Collective Identity," in *One out of Three: Immigrants in New York in the Twenty-First Century*, ed. Nancy Foner (New York: Columbia University Press, 2013), 230. Hernández and Torres-Saillant note that although Washington Heights "is still a heavily Dominican neighborhood," since 1990 the number of Dominicans moving to the Bronx has increased (230). In the same chapter, they quote a 2010 report for the Latino Data Project showing a significant shift in numbers of Dominicans moving there, resulting in the Bronx becoming the county with the largest Dominican population in New York State.
13. Lyn Di Iorio Sandín, *Killing Spanish: Literary Essays on Ambivalent U.S. Latino/a Identity* (New York: Palgrave Macmillan, 2009), 12–13.
14. García-Peña, *Borders of Dominicanidad*, 173.
15. Walter Benjamin, *Charles Baudelaire: A Lyric Poet in the Era of High Capitalism*, trans. Harry Zohn (London: New Left Books, 1973), 54.
16. Francis Mateo, *Ubre Urbe* (self-pub., 2013), 13.
17. José David Saldívar, *Border Matters: Remapping American Cultural Studies* (Berkeley: University of California Press, 1997), 14.
18. Mateo, *Ubre Urbe*, 38–39.
19. Francis Mateo, "Cañemo Revival Blues," Cielo Naranja, 2010, http://www.cielonaranja.com/francismateo.htm
20. Mateo, "Cañemo Revival Blues."
21. Mateo, "Cañemo Revival Blues."
22. Mirca Madianou and Daniel Miller, *Migration and New Media: Transnational Families and Polymedia* (New York: Routledge, 2013), 1.
23. This global phenomenon is extensively recorded in Andoni Alonso and Pedro J. Oiarzabal, eds., *Diasporas in the New Media Age: Identity, Politics, and Community* (Reno: University of Nevada Press, 2010); Jessica Retis and Roza Tsagarousianou, eds., *The Handbook of Diaspora, Media and Culture* (Hoboken, NJ: Wiley-Blackwell, 2019).
24. Mateo, "Cañemo Revival Blues."
25. Hutchinson, "Merengue Típico," 56.
26. Mateo, "Cañemo Revival Blues."

27. Mateo, in discussion with the author, July 2020.

28. Michel Foucault, "Nietzche, Genealogy, History," in *The Foucault Reader*, ed. Paul Rabinow (New York: Pantheon Books, 1984), 81.

29. Mateo, "Cañemo Revival Blues."

30. Veronica Bayetti-Flores cogently defines this music style as "the joyous collision of merengue with hip-hop, dancehall, and reggae popularized by dominicanos in New York." Veronica Bayetti-Flores, "A Look Back at Merenhouse, the Most Lit Pari Music of All Time," Remezcla.com, December 17, 2017, https://remezcla.com/lists/music/merenhouse-merenrap-tribute/. For further and more comprehensive information on this style and other musical trends that emerged in the Dominican borderlands between New York City and the DR, see "A History of Dominican Music in the United States," an essential virtual project on the evolution of Dominican music in the US, spearheaded by the CUNY Dominican Studies Institute. "A History of Dominican Music in the United States," accessed July 22, 2021, http://dominicanmusicusa.com/narratives/1990s-new-musical-trends/4#_ftnref1.

31. Rossy Díaz, *Rumbas Barriales: Aproximaciones al análisis del merengue de Calle* (Santo Domingo, DR: Editorial Seña, 2011), 22.

32. Hutchinson, "Merengue Típico," 40.

33. Mateo, "Cañemo Revival Blues."

34. Mateo, "Cañemo Revival Blues."

35. Lipsitz, *Footsteps in the Dark*, xii.

36. Silvio Torres-Saillant and Ramona Hernández, *The Dominican Americans* (Westport: Greenwood Press, 1998), 137.

37. Hutchinson, "Listening Sideways," 174.

38. Rita Indiana Hernández, "El legado," *Vetas* 17 (March 1996); "La caída," *Vetas* 19 (June 1996); "La división," *Vetas* 19 (June 1996).

39. For more on Rita Indiana's international popularity in the Latin American, Caribbean, and Latinx alternative music scenes, see "'Dios Salve a la Montra': 6 Reversiones de Rita Indiana que debes escuchar," *Discolai*, March 24, 2017, https://discolai.com/2017/03/24/dios-salve-a-la-montra-6-reversiones-de-rita-indiana-que-debes-escuchar/.

40. Before Rita Indiana y los Misterios, Rita Indiana was involved in two music-oriented projects, Casiful and Miti Miti. For detailed information about both projects, see Celiany Rivera-Velázquez, "The Importance of Being Rita Indiana-Hernández," in *Globalizing Cultural Studies: Ethnographic Interventions in Theory, Method, and Policy*, ed. Cameron McCarthy (New York: Peter Lang, 2007), 205–227; Hutchinson, "Listening Sideways."

41. Rita Indiana, "Guest DJ Rita Indiana," interview by Jasmine Garsd and Félix Contreras, *alt.Latino*, NPR, April 7, 2011, https://www.npr.org/sections/altlatino/2011/04/16/135151650/this-week-on-alt-latino-guest-dj-rita-indiana.

42. Hutchinson, "Listening Sideways," 210.

43. Fernando Valerio-Holguín, "El orden de la música popular en la literatura dominicana," *Céfiro: A Journal of the Céfiro Graduate Student Organization* 8.1–8.2 (2008): 101.

44. Indiana, "Guest DJ."

45. Rita Indiana Hernández, *Ciencia succión* (Santo Domingo, DR: Amigo del hogar, 2001). The short stories from this collection were recently compiled in Rita

Indiana, *Cuentos y poemas (1998–2003)* (Santo Domingo, DR: Ediciones Cielo Naranja, 2017).

46. For more on this, see Médar Serrata, introduction to *El sonido de la música en la narrativa dominicana: Ensayos sobre identidad, nación y performance*, ed. Médar Serrata (Santo Domingo, DR: Instituto de Estudios Caribeños, 2012), 11–19.

47. For example, Johnson, "Interview: Rita Indiana"; "Papi: Entrevista a Rita Indiana, escritora y músico," El Centre de Cultura Contemporánia de Barcelona, September 23, 2011, YouTube video, 6:52, https://www.youtube.com/watch?v=STiwYxwyEQM.

48. Fernanda Bustamante Escalona, "Rita Indiana Hernández: Una escritura que retuerce los márgenes y los paradigmas de representación identitaria," in Bustamante Escalona, *Rita Indiana*, 284.

49. Hutchinson, "Listening Sideways," 177.

50. Néstor E. Rodríguez, "Rita Indiana Hernández y la novísima narrativa dominicana," Cielo Naranja, 2005, http://www.cielonaranja.com/nestorchochueca.htm.

51. Miguel D. Mena, "El dominicano, sus imaginarios," in *Poética de Santo Domingo II: Identidad, poder, territorios*, 2nd ed. (Santo Domingo, DR: Ediciones Cielo Naranja, 2013), 17.

52. Seminal research on *Papi* has been compiled in Bustamante Escalona, *Rita Indiana*. The novel's second edition and publication in 2010 by Periférica, which has published three other novels by the author (*Nombres y animales*, *La mucama de Omicunlé*, and *Hecho en Saturno*), extended the range of Rita Indiana's literary audience to Spain. *Papi* also became available to English-speaking audiences and academic circles after its translation by Achy Obejas in 2016.

53. Tallaj, "Country That Ain't," 18. In her essay, ethnomusicologist Tallaj speaks of the demonization of this transnational subgroup in the Dominican Republic.

54. Odalís Pérez, *La ideología rota: El derrumbe del pensamiento pseudonacionalista dominicano* (Santo Domingo, DR: Centro de Información Afroamericano, 2002), 35.

55. See chapter 3 of this book.

56. Smith and Guarnizo, *Transnationalism from Below*, 23.

57. Miguel D. Mena places the work of Rita Indiana within a literary corpus that emerged toward the end of the 1990s and transcended the geographic limits of the island. He defines postinsular writing as "trascendencia de la Isla, de una historia en macro, preferencia por los espacios del sujeto en su cotidianidad, y o por los pasillos del pasado o el predominio del afuera, del otro, de 'lo otro'" (transcendence of the Island, of a macrohistory, a preference for spaces inhabited by subject in their daily life, and/or in the corridors of the past or the predominance of the outside, of the other, of "the other"). "Ciudades revisadas: La literatura posinsular dominicana," *Revista Iberoamericana* 79, no. 243 (April–June 2013): 356.

58. See Deborah Pacini Hernández, *Bachata: A Social History of a Dominican Popular Music* (Philadelphia: Temple University Press, 1995); Peter Manuel, *Caribbean Currents: Caribbean Music from Rumba to Reggae* (Philadelphia: Temple University Press, 1995); Austerlitz, *Merengue*.

59. These two major events in 1965 had a direct impact on the cultural, social, and political transformation of the Dominican nation-state and propelled mass migration from the island to the United States. The passage of the Immigration

and Nationality Act lifted the nationality quota system that had been instituted in 1921 (and revised in 1924) and prompted a radical shift in the demographics of immigrants to the US, namely from Asian, Latin American, and Caribbean countries, and the US military intervention in the Dominican Republic culminated in the Dominican Civil War of 1965.

60. Manuel, *Caribbean Currents*, 124.

61. Balaguer was far less restrictive about immigration than Trujillo had been. Further, Balaguer encouraged the emigration of his political opponents, as well as dispossessed farmers who could not find a means of subsistence through internal migration from rural to urban spaces. See Manuel, *Caribbean Currents*, 126.

62. Juan Duchesne-Winter, "*Papi*, La profecía: Espectáculo e interrupción en Rita Indiana Hernández," *Revista de Crítica Literaria Latinoamericana* 34, no. 67 (2008), 292.

63. Rita Indiana, *Papi* (Cáceres, Spain: Periférica, 2011), 9.

64. Indiana, *Papi*, 9.

65. Rosana Díaz-Zambrana, "¿Una alternativa a la novela del dictador? Paternalismo, nación y posmodernidad en *Papi* de Rita Indiana Hernández," in Bustamante, *Rita Indiana*, 108.

66. Indiana, *Papi*, 10.

67. Christian Krohn-Hansen, "Masculinity and the Political among Dominicans: The Dominican Tiger," in *Machos, Mistresses, Madonnas: Contesting the Power of Latin American Gender Imagery*, ed. Marit Melhuus and Kristi Anne Stolen (London: Verso, 1996), 108.

68. Maja Horn, *Masculinity after Trujillo: The Politics of Gender in Dominican Literature* (Gainesville: University of Florida Press, 2014), 116.

69. Indiana, *Papi*, 81.

70. Horn, *Masculinity after Trujillo*, 120.

71. Indiana, *Papi*, 13.

72. Indiana, *Papi*, 12.

73. Indiana, *Papi*, 22.

74. Horn, *Masculinity after Trujillo*, 119. Here I am following Lauren Derby's definition of *tíguere* where she describes the ways Trujillo meets some of the characteristics of this Dominican subjectivity: "Trujillo embodied the tigre (tiger; pron. tiguere), the quintessential Dominican underdog who gains power, prestige, and social ascendance through a combination of extra-institutional wits, force of will, sartorial style, and cojones (balls). The tigre seduces through impeccable attire, implacable charm, irresistible sexuality, and a touch of violence." "The Dictator's Seduction: Gender and State Spectacle during the Trujillo Regime," *Callaloo* 23, no. 3 (2000), 1116. Of note, and related to the parallelism that I draw between Trujillo's and papi's aesthetics, is the emphasis on the sartorial style favored by Trujillo. For further reading on tíguere and *tigueraje*, see Lipe Collado, *El tíguere dominicano: Ensayo* (Santo Domingo, DR: Editora Panamericana, 1992); Krohn-Hansen, "Masculinity and the Political"; Christian Krohn-Hansen, *Political Authoritarianism in the Dominican Republic* (New York: Palgrave Macmillan, 2009), 147–156.

75. Indiana, *Papi*, 22.

76. Wendy D. Roth, *Race Migrations: Latinos and the Cultural Transformation of Race* (Stanford, CA: Stanford University Press, 2012), 14.

77. Pessar, *Visa for a Dream*, xii.
78. García-Peña, *Borders of Dominicanidad*, 3.
79. Pacini Hernández, "La lucha sonora," 116.
80. This framework is in dialogue with George Lipsitz's thoughts on the role of a bachata song in the reconfiguration of Dominican nationalism. *Footsteps in the Dark: The Hidden History of Popular Music* (Minneapolis: University of Minnesota Press, 2007), 135.
81. Pacini Hernández, "La lucha sonora," 116.
82. Pacini Hernández, "*La lucha sonora*," 116; Martínez-San Miguel, *Caribe Two Ways*, 298.
83. Bustamante Escalona, "Rita Indiana Hernández," 284.
84. Indiana, *Papi*, 41.
85. Lipsitz, *Footsteps in the Dark*, xix.
86. Indiana, *Papi*, 43–44.
87. Celiany Rivera-Velázquez, "A una década de la importancia de ser Rita Indiana: La incursión en videoarte, sonido, y performance de la montra del Caribe hispano," in Bustamante Escalona, *Rita Indiana*, 310.
88. *Pajón* is used to denote "cabello abundante y alborotado" (abundant and unruly hair) in Carlos Esteban Deive, *Diccionario de Dominicanismos* (Santo Domingo, DR: Ediciones Librería La Trinitaria, 2006), 151. Pajón has been used pejoratively to describe Afro natural hair in Dominican society. Current hair movements such as "Yo amo mi pajón" have reclaimed the word to remove the social stigma from natural hair. For more on this, see Ginetta E. B. Candelario, *Black behind the Ears: Dominican Racial Identity from Museums to Beauty Shops* (Durham, NC: Duke University Press, 2007); Jacqueline Lyon, "Pajón Power: Styling Citizenship and Black Politics in the Dominican Natural Hair Movement," Ethnic and Racial Studies 43, no. 12 (2020): 2120–2139; Saudi García, "An Afro Dominican Guide," *La Galería: Voices of the Dominican Diaspora*, accessed October 31, 2020, http://lagaleriamag.com/an-afro-dominican-guide-part-i/.
89. Rachel Afi Quinn, *Being la Dominicana: Race and Identity in the Visual Culture of Santo Domingo* (Urbana: University of Illinois Press, 2021), 4.
90. For more information on the impact of immigration to the United States in the conceptualization of Dominican racial identity, see these seminal works: Torres-Saillant, "Tribulations of Blackness"; Torres-Saillant, *Introduction to Dominican Blackness*; Silvio Torres-Saillant and Ramona Hernández, *The Dominican Americans* (Westport, CT: Greenwood Press, 1998); Candelario, *Black behind the Ears*; García-Peña, *Borders of Dominicanidad*; Roth, *Race Migrations*.
91. I adapt the use of the term "sonic blackness" from Nina Sun Eidsheim, "Marian Anderson and 'Sonic Blackness' in American Opera," *American Quarterly* 63, no. 3 (2011), 653.
92. Indiana, *Papi*, 42.
93. Mena, "El dominicano, sus imaginarios," 17.
94. Gloria Anzaldúa, *Borderlands / La Frontera: The New Mestiza*, 3rd ed. (San Francisco: Aunt Lute Books, 1987), 81.
95. Lipsitz, *Footsteps in the Dark*, 151.
96. Torrado, "Desplazamientos bailables," 339.
97. García-Peña, *Borders of Dominicanidad*, 18.
98. Indiana, *Papi*, 44–47.

99. Anzaldúa, *Borderlands / La Frontera*, 79.

100. See Rita De Maeseneer, "¿Cómo dejar de narrar el (neo)trujillato?," in *Aproximaciones a la literatura dominicana*, vol. 2, *1980-2005*, ed. Rei Berroa (Santo Domingo, DR: Banco Central de la República Dominicana, 2008), 221-237; Rita De Maeseneer, *Seis ensayos sobre narrativa dominicana contemporánea* (Santo Domingo, DR: Banco Central de la República Dominicana, 2011); Rita De Maeseneer, "Bregando con la autoridad: Papi," in Bustamante Escalona, *Rita Indiana*, 117-126. See also Díaz-Zambrana, "¿Una alternativa?" In these essays, the authors note a series of typical characteristics of dictator novels, including references to historical tyrants, violence, corruption, masculinity, and excessive sexuality. *Papi* has been compared to *El otoño del patriarca* by Gabriel García Márquez, *El señor presidente* by Miguel Ángel Asturias, and *La fiesta del chivo* by Mario Vargas Llosa, among others.

101. De Maeseneer, "¿Cómo dejar de narrar?" In Spanish, the suffix *-ato* has multiple uses often attached to masculine nouns. In the cases of Trujillato and Balaguerato, it indicates the periods in Dominican history consumed by the governmental reigns of Rafael Leónidas Trujillo (1930-1961) and Joaquín Balaguer (1960-1962; 1966-1978; 1986-1996).

102. De Maeseneer, "¿Cómo dejar de narrar?," 229.

103. The 1965 US military intervention also brought the expansion of internal markets, the proliferation of urban life and activity, and the widespread growth of the Dominican education system. In addition, newspapers and magazines during this period multiplied, and broadcast media was developed and innovated. In 1962, there was one radio station per every 72,000 Dominicans on the island; by the early 1990s, the number had grown to one station per 29,000 listeners. Radio broadcasting became one of the media outlets with the greatest national breadth and audience. Similarly, by 1995, the island already had seven national television channels and several cable channels, and video stores were becoming fashionable. Hence mass media acquired a fundamental role in the construction of Dominican cultural identity, partly as a result of the historical-political events of 1965.

104. Néstor García Canclini, "Noticias recientes sobre la hibridación," *Revista Transcultural de Música* 7 (2003).

105. Torres-Saillant, *El retorno de las yolas*, 38.

106. Mena, "Ciudades revisadas," 349.

107. The queer experience in a transnational setting has been centered in recent works by Dominican and Dominican-American writers such as Pedro Antonio Valdez, Rita Indiana, Frank Báez, Ana-Maurine Lara, Elizabeth Acevedo, and Isabel Spencer. Before this new corpus, an effort was made to compile queer Dominican texts in what became the first national collection of gay literature, Mélida García and Miguel de Camps Jiménez, eds., *Antología de la Literatura Gay en la República Dominicana* (Santo Domingo, DR: Editora Manatí, 2004). Although this anthology was a key step toward the recognition of an almost invisible sector in Dominican letters and scholarship, most of the included texts frame their characters within a sexual identity based on hegemonic constructions, rather than positioning them as transgressive voices. Jacqueline Jiménez Polanco, ed., *Divagaciones bajo la luna: Voces e imágenes de lesbianas dominicanas / Musing under the Moon: Voices and Images of Dominican Lesbians* (Santo Domingo, DR:

Idegraf Editora, 2006) compiles the work of twenty-four Dominican lesbian women writers who reside on the island, as well as in diasporic communities in the United States, Mexico, and Colombia. The voices of the women in this anthology overtly challenge patriarchy and question the systems that consider lesbians invisible. The general premise of the compilation is to challenge the oppression of and pervasive discrimination against queer Dominican women.

108. See Rita de Maeseneer and Fernanda Bustamante, "Cuerpos heridos en la narrativa de Rita Indiana Hernández, Rey Emmanuel Andújar y Junot Díaz," *Revista Iberoamericana* 79, no. 243 (2013): 395–414.

109. Lawrence La Fountain-Stokes, "Queer Diasporas, Boricua Lives: A Meditation on Sexile," *Review: Literature and Arts of the Americas* 41, no. 2 (2008): 296. La Fountain-Stokes borrows the concept of "sexile" from Puerto Rican sociologist Manolo Guzmán, who defines the term as "the exile of those who had to leave their nations of origin on account of their sexual orientation." Manolo Guzmán, "'Pa La Escuelita Con Mucho Cuidaó y por la Orillita': A Journey through the Contested Terrains of the Nation and Sexual Orientation," in *Puerto Rican Jam: Essays on Culture and Politics*, ed. Frances Negrón Muntaner and Ramón Grosfoguel (Minneapolis: University of Minnesota Press, 1997), 227.

110. Consuelo Martínez-Reyes, "Hispanic Caribbean Sexiles," *Oxford Research Encyclopedia of Literature*, November 20, 2018. https://oxfordre.com/literature/view/10.1093/acrefore/9780190201098.001.0001/acrefore-9780190201098-e-393.

111. In the story, the narrator oscillates between feminine and masculine pronouns and adjectives when speaking about la loca. Throughout my analysis, I use the singular *they* when making references to the character to avoid gender binarism.

112. Rey Andújar, "Merengue," in *Saturnalia / Saturnario*, trans. Kolin Jordan (Chicago: Siete Vientos, 2013), 95.

113. Andújar, "Merengue," 87–95.

114. Andújar, "Merengue," 88, 90, 91.

115. Andújar, "Merengue," 87.

116. In his seminal work on Puerto Rican masculinity, Rafael Ramírez concludes that homosexuality does not constitute a denial of masculinity. According to Ramírez, "Homosexuality can be an integral part of the construction of masculinity." In addition, he argues that homosexuality is synonymous with homoeroticism—that is, "erotic attraction and sexual acts between persons of the same sex." *What It Means to Be a Man: Reflections on Puerto Rican Masculinity* (New Brunswick, NJ: Rutgers University Press, 1999), 80, 79.

117. For a more detailed analysis of the ideological role of the Catholic Church in the trujillista national project, see Juan Félix Pépen, *La cruz señaló el camino: Influencia de la iglesia en la formación y conservación de la nacionalidad dominicana* (Ciudad Trujillo: Duarte, 1954); Germán Ornes, *Trujillo: Little Caesar of the Caribbean* (New York: Thomas Nelson and Sons, 1958); Alfau Durán, *Trujillo and the Roman Catholic Church in Santo Domingo* (Ciudad Trujillo, DR: Editora Handicap, 1960).

118. Howard Wiarda argues that the Catholic Church had lost strength in the wake of the Treaty of Basel in 1795 and that it was not until the Trujillo era that it regained power and reorganized as an entity in the Dominican Republic. *Dictatorship and Development: The Methods of Control in Trujillo's Dominican Republic* (Gainesville: University of Florida Press, 1968), 141.

119. See Austerlitz, *Merengue*, on merengue and the Dominican nation. Regarding Caribbean dance and culture, see also Ángel G. Quintero Rivera, *Cuerpo y cultura: Las músicas "mulatas" y la subversión del baile* (Madrid: Iberoamericana, 2009).
120. Krohn-Hansen, *Political Authoritarianism*, 4.
121. Andújar, "Merengue," 91–92.
122. For more on this, see Emelio R. Betances, "En busca de un nuevo papel en la sociedad," in *La iglesia católica y la política del poder en América Latina: El caso dominicano en perspectiva comparada* (Santo Domingo, DR: Editorial Funglode, 2017), 173–232.
123. Andújar, "Merengue," 88.
124. Andújar, "Merengue," 90.
125. Andújar, "Merengue," 88.
126. Andújar, "Merengue," 94.

CHAPTER 2. FROM SANTO DOMINGO TO NEW YORK CITY

1. See Odalís Pérez, *Literatura dominicana y memoria cultural: Ritmos y tiempos de la alteridad* (Santo Domingo, DR: Editora Manatí, 2005); Bustamante Escalona, *A ritmo desenfadado*.
2. Rodríguez, "Rita Indiana Hernández."
3. See also Mena, "El dominicano, sus imaginarios," 17.
4. Rita Indiana Hernández, *La estrategia de Chochueca* (San Juan, PR: Editorial Isla Negra, 2003), 46.
5. Andrea A. Lunsford, "Toward a Mestiza Rhetoric: Gloria Anzaldúa on Composition and Postcoloniality," *JAC* 18, no. 1 (1998): 16.
6. See Ramón Antonio (Arturo) Victoriano-Martínez, "Memoria y espacios en Santo Domingo," Cielo Naranja, accessed August 23, 2020, http://www.cielonaranja.com/victorianomemoria.htm; Miguel D. Mena, "¿La ciudad hostil?," Cielo Naranja, 2002, http://www.cielonaranja.com/hostil_mena.htm. El Polígono Central became the economic and business center of the capital in the mid-1990s after Resolution No. 94/98 of the Ayuntamiento del Distrito Nacional (1996). It comprises some of the most affluent neighborhoods in the city, demarcated by arterial avenues of the capital such as Abraham Lincoln, Winston Churchill, 27 de febrero, and John F. Kennedy. For more information, see Blas R. Jiménez, *Afrodominicano por elección, negro por nacimiento: Seudonesayos* (Santo Domingo, DR: Editora Manatí, 2008), 71; Miguel D. Mena, "Distopías urbanas, el Polígono Central," Cielo Naranja, 2017, http://www.cielonaranja.com/menapoligono.html.
7. The concept of the nation as an "imagined community" is theorized in Benedict Anderson, *Imagined Communities: Reflections on the Origins and Spread of Nationalism*, rev. ed. (London: Verso, 2006). Anderson writes that the nation is "*imagined* because the members of even the smallest nation will never know most of their fellow-members, meet them, or even hear them, yet in the minds of each lives the image of their communion" (6).
8. Joaquín Balaguer rose to power during an unstable political moment. After Rafael Leónidas Trujillo died, there were several provisional governments. The assumed threat of the spread of Communism and the fear that the country would follow

in Cuba's footsteps provoked a military coup against president-elect Juan Bosch in 1963 and the abolition of the constitution that same year. As a result of these events, Movimiento Revolucionario leaders began a battle on June 14 that culminated in many of them dying or being imprisoned. The population's discontent provoked a group of soldiers, led by Francisco Caamaño Deñó and Rafael Tomás Fernández Domínguez, to fight to reinstitute the constitution. A civil war began in the Dominican capital on April 25, 1965. Three days later, a North American invasion began that supported the national reconstruction efforts against the restoration of constitutionality, so much so that Balaguer's victory in 1966 was supported by North American troops. The advisor and leader of the Partido Reformista Social Cristiano (Christian Social Reform Party) was one of the core ideologues of the "Trujillo city." Therefore, the period known as doce años (twelve years) strengthened and perpetuated Dominican conservativism instituted by the Trujillo regime.

9. Darío Tejeda, *La pasión danzaria: Música y baile en el Caribe a través del merengue y la bachata* (Santo Domingo, DR: Academia de Ciencias de República Dominicana, 2002), 113.

10. Miguel D. Mena, ed., *Luis Días, ¡Échale gas!* (Santo Domingo, DR: El jardín de las delicias, 1999), 9. Luis "Terror" Días elaborated on the origins of his name in a 2009 interview with Patricia Solano and Edith Febles: "De la época de Balaguer, que era la época de terror que vivíamos cuando éramos estudiantes. En el '72, '73, ser estudiante ya era ser sospechoso, ya tu eras 'un elemento,' y si te oponías al régimen tenías que andar escondiéndote, brincando patios, una zozobra constante, y todo ese terror yo me lo eché arriba poniéndome el nombre." (It is from the Balaguer era, which was a time of terror when we were students. In '72 and '73, being a student was already suspicious, you were already 'an element,' and if you opposed the regime you had to hide yourself, hopping fences to get away, a constant anxiety, and I took all that terror on by making it my name.) Patricia Solano, "Luis Días explica algunas de sus canciones," Cielo Naranja, 2009, http://www.cielonaranja.com/ldpatricias.htm.

11. Miguel D. Mena, "Mi delirio," in Mena, *Luis Días*, 15. Convite emerged during a foundational moment of the Dominican nation marked by the remnants of the second North American invasion, civil disputes for national sovereignty, repressions, and the death of revolutionary leader Francisco Caamaño Deñó. The group included Dagoberto Tejeda, José Rodríguez, Ana María Guzmán, Miguel Mañaná, Iván Domínguez, José Castillo, Chemo, José Enrique Trinidad, and Luis "Terror" Días.

12. José Rodríguez, "Años germinales en Convite," in Mena, *Luis Días*, 20.

13. Mena, "Mi Delirio," 14. See also Austerlitz, *Merengue*. In chapter 6, the ethnomusicologist asserts that this aspect of Convite was opposed to the exclusion and denigration of Afro-descendant culture in official discourse.

14. Gilles Deleuze and Félix Guattari, "Introduction: Rhizome," in *A Thousand Plateaus: Capitalism and Schizophrenia* (Minneapolis: University of Minnesota Press, 1987), 3–28.

15. Diógenes Céspedes, "Entrevista con Luis Días," in Mena, *Luis Días*, 113.

16. Céspedes, "Entrevista con Luis Días," 113.

17. López, *La música caribeña*, 9.

18. López, *La música caribeña*, 9.

19. Céspedes, "Entrevista con Luis Días," 115.
20. Aurora Arias, "¿Por qué la música en mis cuentos?" (paper presented at the Latin American Roundtable Artist Conference, New York, October 24, 2011), 2. The author provided a copy of her manuscript to me after her presentation, and the page numbers cited in the endnotes correspond to this version. The conference minutes were later published in 2014.
21. Arias, "¿Por qué la música?," 6.
22. This urbanization project began at the end of the 1950s, the culminating years of the dictatorship. The acronym represents the name of the institution that finished the construction project: the Instituto Nacional de la Vivienda (National Housing Institute).
23. Arias, "¿Por qué la música?," 3.
24. See Néstor Rodríguez, "Un-imagining the Dominican Nation," in *Divergent Dictions: Contemporary Dominican Literature* (Coconut Creek, FL: Caribbean Studies Press, 2011), 63–98; Rita de Maeseneer, "Aurora Arias y sus cronotopías subversivas," in *Seis ensayos sobre narrativa dominicana contemporánea* (Santo Domingo, DR: Banco Central de la República Dominicana, 2011), 123–151.
25. For the remainder of the chapter, I will refer to Luis "Terror" Días as Terror to be faithful to the use of this nickname in the texts analyzed.
26. Miguel D. Mena, "Drake's, Raffles, Poco-Loco," in Mena, *Luis Días*, 65.
27. Aurora Arias, "Poco Loco," in *Fin de mundo y otros relatos* (San Juan, PR: Universidad de Puerto Rico, 2000), 2.
28. Simon Frith, "Music and Identity," in *Questions of Cultural Identity*, ed. Stuart Hall and Paul du Gay (London: Sage Publications, 1996), 122–123.
29. Pablo Vila, "Narrative Identities and Popular Music," in *Music and Youth Culture in Latin America: Identity Construction Processes from New York to Buenos Aires* (New York: Oxford University Press, 2014), 33.
30. Arias, "Poco Loco," 71.
31. Arias, "Poco Loco," 71.
32. Arias, "Poco Loco," 71.
33. Emily Maguire, "'Hace[r] encantadora la idea del desencanto': Luis 'Terror' Días en los cuentos de Aurora Arias," in *El sonido de la música en la narrativa dominicana: Ensayos sobre identidad, nación y performance*, ed. Médar Serrata (Santo Domingo, DR: Instituto de Estudios Caribeños, 2012), 158.
34. It is notable that Trujillo based his electoral campaign on merengue with the goal of winning over rural voters. As a candidate, he traveled across many regions accompanied by famous merengue artists who literally sang his praises. Once he occupied the presidency, he promoted merengue as a national symbol to the extent that it became indissolubly tied to Dominican identity.
35. Arias, "Poco Loco," 72.
36. *Payola* is a contraction of the English word *pay* and the commercial brand Victrola. The word syntactically means "pay for play"—that is, to make a payment in exchange for the possibility of being played on radio stations with greater listenership. Kim Kelly, "A Brief History of American Payola," *Vice*, February 14, 2016, https://www.vice.com/en/article/a-brief-history-of-american-payola/.
37. See Pacini Hernández, "*La lucha sonora.*"
38. Aurora Arias, "Invi's Paradise," in *Invi's Paradise y otros relatos* (Montreal: Concordia University, 1998), 12.

39. Néstor E. Rodríguez, *Escrituras de desencuentro en la República Dominicana* (México City: Siglo XXI Editores, 2005), 28.

40. Arias, "Invi's Paradise," 11.

41. Arias, "Invi's Paradise," 20.

42. Céspedes, "Entrevista con Luis Días," 105–106.

43. Arias, "Invi's Paradise," 27–28.

44. Maguire, "'Hace[r] encantadora," 156.

45. Néstor E. Rodríguez, "Terror y sus maneras de hacerse el muerto," *80 Grados*, July 8, 2011, http://www.80grados.net/terror-y-sus-maneras-de-hacerse-el-muerto/.

46. Here I am invoking Silvio Torres-Saillant's ruminations on the spaces that ought to be considered when thinking of the Caribbean: "To fathom the Caribbean, then, one has to train one's eyes on three primary spaces: the insular, the continental and the diasporic and none today can be dispensed with in a serious attempt to understand holistically the cluster of societies involved." *An Intellectual History of the Caribbean* (New York: Palgrave Macmillan, 2006), 21. Martínez-San Miguel also proposes considering New York as an extension of the Caribbean in *Caribe Two Ways*.

47. Rey Andújar, "Terror," in *Saturnalia / Saturnario*, trans. Kolin Jordan (Chicago: Siete Vientos, 2013), 32.

48. Andújar, "Terror" 32.

49. See Silvio Torres-Saillant, *El retorno de las yolas: Ensayos sobre diaspora, democracia y dominicanidad*, 2nd ed. (Santo Domingo: Editorial Universitaria Bonó, 2019), 38. Looking at emigration as a form of expatriation forced on individuals who face financial difficulties in their homelands, Torres-Saillant argues, "Sépase que la gente normalmente no abandona su tierra de manera voluntaria. Se desgaja de su cálido terruño, sus paisajes familiares, su lengua, su cultura y sus amores compelida por la urgencia material. Emigra quien no puede quedarse. Se van aquellos a quienes la economía nacional les ha cerrado las puertas. Aunque sus recursos analíticos no siempre les permitan discernir las fuerzas sociales que moldean su decisión de partir, los que se van realmente son expulsados: nuestra emigración es una expatriación." (Know that people do not normally leave their land voluntarily. They detach themselves from their warm homeland, their familiar landscapes, their language, their culture, and their loved ones, compelled by material urgency. Those who cannot stay emigrate. Those to whom the national economy has closed the doors leave. Although their analytical resources do not always allow them to discern the social forces that shape their decision to leave, those who leave are actually expelled: our emigration is an expatriation.) Torres-Saillant's arguments denote the forms of disenfranchisement that propel emigration from the home island. Central to the analysis in this section is the idea that those who cannot stay emigrate, as is the case with the characters in and narrator of "Terror."

50. Andújar, "Terror," 35.

51. Andújar, "Terror," 35.

52. Andújar, "Terror," 35.

53. Andújar, "Terror," 34.

54. Andújar, "Terror," 34.

55. García-Peña, *Borders of Dominicanidad*.

56. Andújar, "Terror," 36, 33, 36.

57. Andújar, "Terror," 36.

---

58. Andújar, "Terror," 36–37.

59. On "sexile," see Lawrence La Fountain-Stokes, *Queer Ricans: Cultures and Sexualities in the Diaspora* (Minneapolis: University of Minnesota Press, 2009).

60. Andújar, "Terror," 40.

61. Mayra Santos Febres, "Caribe y travestismo," in *El artista caribeño como guerrero de lo imaginario*, ed. Rita De Maeseneer and An Van Hecke (Madrid: Iberoamericana, 2005), 43.

62. Lawrence Lafountain-Stokes, *Translocas: The Politics of Puerto Rican Drag and Trans Performance* (Ann Arbor: University of Michigan Press, 2021).

63. Andújar, "Terror" 43, 41.

64. Andújar, "Terror," 42–43.

65. García-Peña, *Borders of Dominicanidad*, 4.

66. Josefina Báez, "Lista del Terror," Cielo Naranja, December 2009, http://www.cielonaranja.com/ldjosefinabaez.htm.

67. Josefina Báez, *Levente no. Yolayorkdominicanyork* (New York: I.Om.Be, 2011).

68. Báez, "Lista del Terror."

69. Thomas van Buren and Leonardo Iván Domínguez, "Transnational Music and Dance in Dominican New York," in *Dominican Migration: Transnational Perspectives*, ed. Ernesto Sagás and Sintia Molina (Gainesville: University Press of Florida, 2004), 246.

70. Van Buren and Domínguez, "Transnational Music and Dance," 245.

71. Van Buren and Domínguez, "Transnational Music and Dance," 245.

72. Quisqueya en el Hudson is a series of Dominican folk music festivals that began in 1996 in the Dominican enclave of Washington Heights in Manhattan and ran until 2004. Although it is not clear what year Báez may be alluding to in this passage of *Levente no. Yolayorkdominicanyork*, it may be one of Luis "Terror" Días's performances in 1997 or 2004.

73. Báez, *Levente no. Yolayorkdominicanyork*.

74. Vila, "Narrative Identities," 35.

75. Vila, "Narrative Identities," 35–36.

76. For more on the ways we can see sound in literature and the visual, see Sam Halliday, *Sonic Modernity: Representing Sound in Literature, Culture, and the Arts* (Edinburgh: Edinburgh University Press, 2013), introduction and chap. 3.

77. Báez, "Lista del Terror."

78. Juan Duchesne-Winter, prologue to *La estrategia de Chochueca*, 3rd ed. (San Juan, PR: Editorial Isla Negra, 2006), 7.

79. I am referring to the works of Aurora Arias, Pedro Antonio Valdez, and most recently, Rita Indiana, Rey Andújar, Frank Báez, Juan Dicent, Karol Starocean, and Miguel Yarull.

80. Michel de Certeau, *The Practice of Everyday Life*, trans. Steven Rendall (Berkeley: University of California Press, 1984), 95.

81. See Victoriano, "Memoria y espacios."

82. Bustamante Escalona, "Rita Indiana Hernández," 260.

83. Rodríguez, *Divergent Dictions*, 109–128.

84. Lorna Torrado, "Sinfonía del desencanto: La destrucción de Ciudad Trujillo en Rita Indiana Hernández," in *El sonido de la música en la narrativa dominicana: Ensayos sobre identidad, nación y performance*, ed. Médar Serrata (Santo Domingo, DR: Instituto de Estudios Caribeños, 2012), 249.

85. Hernández, *La estrategia de Chochueca*, 54.

86. María Teresa Vera-Rojas, "¡Se armó el juidero! Cartografías imprecisas, cuerpos disidentes, sexualidades transgresoras: Hacia una lectura queer de Rita Indiana Hernández," in Bustamante Escalona, *Rita Indiana*, 212.

87. Torrado, "Sinfonía del desencanto," 249.

88. Hernández, *La estrategia de Chochueca*, 15.

89. Torrado, "Sinfonía del desencanto," 243.

90. This historic musical gathering took place in different parts of the country between November 25 and December 1, 1974. It brought together key local and international figures from the Canción Protesta/Nueva Canción, such as Dominican groups Los Virtuosos de Cuco Valoy, el Combo Show de Johnny Ventura, Convite, Nueva Forma, and Expresión Joven, among others. Among the international participants and attendees were Mercedes Sosa, Danny Rivera, Noel Nicola, Lucecita Benítez, Ana Belén, Víctor Manuel, and Los Guaraguao. For more information about the impact of this event, see Eduardo Díaz Guerra and Gustavo Ubrí Acevedo, *Memorias de la cayena: A cuarenta años de 7 días con el pueblo* (Santo Domingo, DR: Ministerio de Cultura, 2004); Alfonso Quiñones, "'7 días con el Pueblo,' un evento que cambió la canción," *Diario Libre*, November 26, 2004, https://www.diariolibre.com/revista/7-das-con-el-pueblo-un-evento-que-cambi-la-cancin-XADL52550.

91. For the full manifesto and more information on the event, see "7 días con el pueblo: Politics and Music," El Taller Latino Americano, January 8, 2020, https://tallerlatino.org/blog/2020/1/8/7-das-con-el-pueblo-politics-and-music-the-woodstock-of-the-dominican-republic.

92. Hernández, *La estrategia de Chochueca*, 64.

93. Hernández, *La estrategia de Chochueca*, 63.

94. Hernández, *La estrategia de Chochueca*, 63.

95. Hernández, *La estrategia de Chochueca*, 64.

96. Antonio Benítez-Rojo, *The Repeating Island: The Caribbean and the Postmodern Perspective* (Durham, NC: Duke University Press, 1992), 27.

97. Hernández, *La estrategia de Chochueca*, 19.

98. Hernández, *La estrategia de Chochueca*, 19.

99. See Pacini Hernández, "*La lucha sonora.*"

100. Hernández, *La estrategia de Chochueca*, 66.

101. See Rita Indiana's columns published in *El País*. In two of them, "Nueva narrativa" (New narrative) and "Tu afro no cabe en la foto" (Your afro doesn't fit in the photo), she addresses Afro-Caribbean culture and problematizes the relationship between dominicanidad and Blackness. Rita Indiana, "Nueva narrativa," *El País*, January 27, 2014, https://elpais.com/elpais/2014/01/27/eps/1390830451_271183.html; Rita Indiana, "Tu afro no cabe en la foto," *El País*, July 28, 2014, https://elpais.com/elpais/2014/07/28/eps/1406564419_461753.html.

102. Torrado, "Desplazamientos bailables," 345.

103. Hernández, *La estrategia de Chochueca*, 29–30.

104. Hernández, *La estrategia de Chochueca*, 30.

105. See Rodríguez, *Divergent Dictions*, chaps. 1 and 2.

106. García-Peña, *Borders of Dominicanidad*, 13.

107. See Torres-Saillant, *Introduction to Dominican Blackness*, 38.

108. Hernández, *La estrategia de Chochueca*, 19.

109. Hernández, *La estrategia de Chochueca*, 19.

110. Hernández, *La estrategia de Chochueca*, 19.

111. Ray Pratt, *Rhythm and Resistance: Explorations in the Political Uses of Popular Music* (New York: Praeger, 1990), 12.

112. Néstor Rodríguez, "Dos artículos sobre *La estrategia de Chochueca*," in Bustamante Escalona, *Rita Indiana*, 36.

113. Hernández, *La estrategia de Chochueca*, 13.

114. Quintero Rivera, *Cuerpo y cultura*, 10.

115. Hernández, *La estrategia de Chochueca*, 71–72.

CHAPTER 3. REFRAMING AFRO-LATINA NARRATIVES OF GIRLHOOD AND WOMANHOOD

1. The Notorious B.I.G., "Big Poppa," track 13 on *Ready to Die*, Bad Boy Records and Arista Records, 1994, compact disc.

2. Aparicio, *Listening to Salsa*, 5.

3. Silvio Torres-Saillant, "The Latino Autobiography," in *Latino and Latina Writers*, ed. Alan West-Durán (New York: Charles Scribner's Sons, 2004), 63.

4. April Mayes, "Black Feminist Formations in the Dominican Republic since *La Sentencia*," in *AfroLatin American Politics*, ed. Kwame Dixon and Ollie Johnson III (New Brunswick, NJ: Rutgers University Press, 2019), 139–160.

5. Mayes, "Black Feminist Formations," 153, 152.

6. Raquel Cepeda, *Bird of Paradise: How I Became Latina* (New York: Atria Books, 2013), 62.

7. Luisa María González, "Digging through the Past to Reconcile Race and Latinx Identity in Dominican-American Women's Memoirs," in *Latinidad at the Crossroads: Insights into Latinx Identity in the Twenty-First Century*, ed. Amanda Ellen Gerke and Luisa María Rodríguez (Boston: Brill, 2021), 47.

8. Joan Morgan and Brittney Cooper, "Keynote with Joan Morgan and Dr. Brittney Cooper at the Hip Hop Literacies Conference 2014," College of Education and Human Ecology, Ohio State University, February 28, 2014, 5:37–6:02, https://www.youtube.com/watch?v=my9pLqUwfK4.

9. Here I use "dominiyorkian," following Cepeda's terminology to self-identify as a dominicana from New York City. This is the only instance where I use this term; throughout the rest of the book, I use the more commonly known demonym *dominicanyork*.

10. Aisha Durham, Brittney C. Cooper, and Susana M. Morris, "The Stage Hip-Hop Feminism Built: A New Directions Essay," *Signs: Journal of Women in Culture and Society* 38, no. 3 (2013): 722–723.

11. Zamora, "Before *Bodak Yellow*," 54.

12. Báez, *Dominicanish*, 55–59.

13. For more on García, see Pedro A. Regalado, "The Washington Heights Uprising of 1992: Dominican Belonging and Urban Policing in New York City," *Journal of Urban History* 45, no. 5 (2019): 961–986; David Gonzalez and Jane Fritsch, "Shared Streets, Crossed Paths, and a Death," *New York Times*, July 12, 1992, 2, 28; Amanda Alcántara, "How the Diaspora Made Its Name through Activism and Community Organizing: The Dominican-American Dream," *La Galería: Voices of the Dominican Diaspora* 1 (2018): 65–71.

14. George Lipsitz, *Time Passages: Collective Memory and American Popular Culture* (Minneapolis: University of Minnesota Press, 2001), 109.

15. Suzanne Bost, *Shared Selves: Latinx Memoir and Ethical Alternatives to Humanism* (Urbana: University of Illinois Press, 2020), 11.

16. Anzaldúa, *Borderlands / La Frontera*, 19.

17. Throughout the book, I lowercase *dominicanidad* and *latinidad* when I do not make direct associations with hegemonic structures. In the cases where I do make such links, I capitalize these terms.

18. Gaye Theresa Johnson, *Spaces of Conflict, Sounds of Solidarity: Music, Race, and Spatial Entitlement in Los Angeles* (Berkeley: University of California Press, 2013).

19. Lourdes Torres, "The Construction of the Self in U.S. Latina Autobiographies," in *Third World Women and the Politics of Feminism*, ed. Chandra Talpade Mohanty, Ann Russo, and Lourdes Torres (Bloomington: Indiana University Press, 1991), 272.

20. Torres, "Construction of the Self," 272.

21. Christina Lam, "Bearing Witness: Alternate Archives of Latinx Identity in Raquel Cepeda's *Bird of Paradise: How I Became Latina*," *Studies in American Culture* 43, no. 1 (2020): 26–27.

22. Agustín Laó-Montes, "Afro-Latinidades and the Diasporic Imaginary," *Iberoamericana* 5, no. 17 (2015): 118.

23. Trent Masiki, "Post-Soul Latinidad: Black Nationalism in *Mama's Girl* and *Bird of Paradise: How I Became Latina*," *Latino Studies* 20, no. 4 (2022): 486.

24. For more on this, see Robert W. Snyder, "Crack Years," in *Crossing Broadway: Washington Heights and the Promise of New York City* (New York: Cornell University Press, 2015), 158–195.

25. Lam, "Bearing Witness," 27.

26. Cepeda, *Bird of Paradise*, 269.

27. Lam, "Bearing Witness," 34.

28. Cepeda, *Bird of Paradise*, 8.

29. Cepeda, *Bird of Paradise*, 5.

30. See Juanita Heredia, *Transnational Latina Narratives in the Twenty-First Century: The Politics of Gender, Race, and Migrations* (New York: Palgrave McMillan, 2009), 61–62.

31. Social scientist Benjamin Bailey studies the relationship between Spanish and ethno-racial identity in his essay "Black and Latino: Dominican Americans Negotiate Racial Worlds," in *Mixed Messages: Multiracial Identities in the "Color-blind" Era*, ed. David L. Brunsma (Boulder, CO: Lynne Rienner, 2006), 285–300. After looking at the interactions between Dominican Americans and their peers from Dominican and other ethnic clusters, Bailey observes that although Spanish language can be used by Latinas/os to distinguish themselves from Blacks, in some cases assuming it as part of one's identity "highlights both the agency of an individual to resist the hegemonic racial structuring of society and the subjective nature of identity constitution, as his identity is achieved through congruent self-ascription and other ascription" (294).

32. Cepeda, *Bird of Paradise*, 51.

33. Cepeda, *Bird of Paradise*, 259.

34. Cepeda, *Bird of Paradise*, 33.

35. Cepeda, *Bird of Paradise*, 84.
36. Sophie Maríñez, "The Quisqueya Diaspora: The Emergence of Latina/o Literature from Hispaniola" in *The Cambridge History of Latina/o American Literature*, ed. John Morán González and Laura Lomas (New York: Cambridge University Press, 2018), 562.
37. Cepeda, *Bird of Paradise*, 60.
38. Cepeda, *Bird of Paradise*, 84.
39. Cepeda, *Bird of Paradise*, 279.
40. Maríñez, "Quisqueya Diaspora," 563.
41. Torres-Saillant, *Introduction to Dominican Blackness*, 52.
42. Ana M. Lara, "Uncovering Mirrors: Afro-Latina Lesbian Subjects," in *The Afro-Latin@ Reader: History and Culture in the United States*, ed. Miriam Jiménez Román and Juan Flores (Durham, NC: Duke University Press, 2010), 305.
43. Israel Reyes, *Embodied Economies: Diaspora and Transcultural Capital in Latinx Caribbean Fiction and Theater* (New Brunswick, NJ: Rutgers University Press, 2022), 9.
44. Cepeda, *Bird of Paradise*, xvii.
45. Reyes, *Embodied Economies*, 9.
46. Roth, *Race Migrations*.
47. Torres-Saillant, *Introduction to Dominican Blackness*, 54.
48. Torres-Saillant, *Introduction to Dominican Blackness*, 54. A similar trend is noticed in Jose Itzigsohn and Carlos Dore-Cabral, "Competing Identities? Race, Ethnicity, and Panethnicity among Dominicans in the United States," *Sociological Forum* 15, no. 2 (2000): 232–247; Sherezada "Chiqui" Vicioso, "Discovering Myself: Un Testimonio," in *The Afro-Latin@ Reader: History and Culture in the United States*, ed. Miriam Jiménez Román and Juan Flores (New York: Duke University Press, 2010), 262–265.
49. Alejandro Portes, "The New Latin Nation: Immigration and the Hispanic Population of the United States," in *A Companion to Latino Studies*, ed. Renato Rosaldo and Juan Flores (Hoboken, NJ: Blackwell, 2007), 22.
50. Cepeda, *Bird of Paradise*, 151.
51. For more on this, see Tanya Katerí Hernández, "The New Census Proposal May Likely Undercount Black People by Ignoring Afro-Latinos. We Can't Let That Happen," *Grio*, March 16, 2023, https://thegrio.com/2023/03/16/the-new-census-proposal-may-likely-undercount-black-people-by-ignoring-afro-latinos-we-cant-let-that-happen/. For more information on the current development of these changes, consult Rachel Marks, Nicholas Jones, and Karen Battle, "What Updates to OMB's Race/Ethnicity Standards Mean for the Census Bureau," *Random Samplings* (blog), US Census Bureau, April 8, 2024, https://www.census.gov/newsroom/blogs/random-samplings/2024/04/updates-race-ethnicity-standards.html.
52. Cepeda, *Bird of Paradise*, 255.
53. Frank Bonilla, "Beyond Survival: Por qué seguiremos siendo puertorriqueños," in *The Puerto Ricans: Their History, Culture, Society*, ed. Adalberto López (Rochester, VT: Schenkman, 1980), 464.
54. Raquel Cepeda, interview by Dr. Brenda Greene, *Writers on Writing*, 91.5 WNYE FM, New York, May 2, 2014.
55. Cepeda, *Bird of Paradise*, 45.

56. Oboler, *Ethnic Labels, Latino Lives.*

57. Roth, *Race Migrations,* 155.

58. Itzigsohn and Dore-Cabral, "Competing Identities?," 232.

59. Cepeda, *Bird of Paradise,* 84.

60. Cepeda, *Bird of Paradise,* 46, 54.

61. Cepeda, *Bird of Paradise,* 46.

62. Torres, "Construction of the Self," 275.

63. See Torres-Saillant, "Latino Autobiography." Here Torres-Saillant deems Latino autobiography the most important form in Latino literature, given its impact on "US Hispanic writing from the outset of tradition" (65).

64. Cepeda, *Bird of Paradise,* xv.

65. Tanya L. Saunders, "The Cuban Remix: Rethinking Culture and Political Participation in Contemporary Cuba" (PhD diss., University of Michigan, 2008); Tanya L. Saunders, *Cuban Underground Hip Hop: Black Thoughts, Black Revolution, Black Modernity* (Austin: University of Texas Press, 2015); Raquel Z. Rivera, *New York Ricans from the Hip Hop Zone* (New York: Palgrave Macmillan, 2003).

66. Masiki, "Post-Soul Latinidad," 491.

67. Lorgia García-Peña, *Translating Blackness: Latinx Colonialities in Global Perspective* (Durham, NC: Duke University Press, 2022), 8.

68. García-Peña, *Translating Blackness,* 6.

69. See Tricia Rose, *Black Noise: Rap Music and Black Culture in Contemporary America* (Hanover, CT: Wesleyan University Press, 1994); Robert Thompson, "Hip Hop 101," in *Droppin' Science: Critical Essays on Rap Music and Hip Hop Culture,* ed. William Eric Perkins (Philadelphia: Temple University Press, 1996), 211–219; Raquel Z. Rivera, "Hip-Hop, Puerto Ricans, and Ethnoracial Identities in New York," in *Mambo Montage: The Latinization of New York,* ed. Agustín Laó-Montes and Arlene Dávila (New York: Columbia University Press, 2001), 235–262; Raquel Z. Rivera, "Between Blackness and *Latinidad* in the Hip Hop Zone," in *A Companion to Latino Studies,* ed. Juan Flores and Renato Rosaldo (Hoboken, NJ: Wiley-Blackwell, 2011), 351–362.

70. Rose, *Black Noise,* 22.

71. Saunders, *Cuban Remix,* 235.

72. The Crunk Feminist Collective, "Hip Hop Generation Feminism: A Manifesto," March 10, 2010, https://www.crunkfeministcollective.com/2010/03/01/hip-hop-generation-feminism-a-manifesto/.

73. See Rose, *Black Noise,* xii–21.

74. Cepeda, *Bird of Paradise,* 70.

75. Cepeda, *Bird of Paradise,* 70.

76. Public Enemy, "Prophets of Rage," *It Takes a Nation of Millions to Hold Us Back* (Def Jam Records, 1985).

77. Gustavo Pérez-Firmat, *Life on the Hyphen: The Cuban-American Way* (Austin: University of Texas Press, 2012), 6.

78. Public Enemy, "Prophets of Rage."

79. Rivera, "Hip-Hop, Puerto Ricans," 236. See also Linda Chávez, *Out of the Barrio: Toward a New Politics of Hispanic Assimilation* (New York: Basic Books, 1991).

80. In some cases, her identity is questioned by her Latina/o counterparts, who assume because of the appearance of her father's wife that she is white and thus not a true Latina. In other instances, she is challenged by other Afro-diasporic

groups for liking hip-hop and aligning with "Black" behavior or cultural expressions.

81. Johnson, *Spaces of Conflict*, xv.
82. Cepeda, *Bird of Paradise*, 61–62.
83. Juan Flores, *From Bomba to Hip-Hop: Puerto Rican Culture and Latino Identity* (New York: Columbia University Press, 2000), 17.
84. Cepeda, *Bird of Paradise*, 110.
85. Rivera, *New York Ricans*, 99.
86. Cepeda, *Bird of Paradise*, 71.
87. Masiki, "Post-Soul Latinidad," 486–487.
88. Some of the foundational hip-hop figures who appear in the memoir are Public Enemy, Melle Mel, Russell Simmons, Wu-Tang Clan, LL Cool J, and N.W.A, among others.
89. Cepeda, *Bird of Paradise*, 68, 154.
90. Cepeda, *Bird of Paradise*, 103.
91. Elizabeth Acevedo, *The Poet X: A Novel* (New York: HarperTeen, 2018), 41.
92. Durham, Cooper, and Morris, "Stage Hip-Hop Feminism Built," 722.
93. See Macarena Martín Martínez, "Afro-Caribbean Women Reclaiming Their Bodies and Sexuality: Nicki Minaj and Cardi B's Ambivalent Self Portrayals," *Popular Culture as Transformative Action: Videoclips, Performances, and Speeches in US Popular Culture, PopMeC Research Blog*, November 17, 2020, https://popmec.hypotheses.org/3304.
94. Macarena Martín Martínez, "Corporeal Activism in Elizabeth Acevedo's *The Poet X*: Towards a Self-Appropriation of US Afro-Latinas' Bodies," *Revista de Estudios Norteamericanos* 25 (2021): 1–23.
95. Omaris Z. Zamora, "Black Latina Girlhood Poetics of the Body: Church, Sexuality and Dispossession," *Post 45: The Body of Contemporary Latina/o/x Poetry* (September 20, 2020): 1–15.
96. Mark Dery, "Public Enemy: Confrontation," in *That's the Joint! The Hip-Hop Studies Reader*, ed. Murray Forman and Mark Anthony Neal (New York: Routledge, 2004), 409.
97. Esther Álvarez López, "Identity, De-colonization and Cosmopolitanism in (Afro)Latina Artists' Spoken Word Performances," in *Latinidad at the Crossroads: Insights into Latinx Identity in the Twenty-First Century*, ed. Amanda Ellen Gerke and Luisa María Rodríguez (Boston: Brill, 2021), 86.
98. Álvarez López, "Identity, De-colonization and Cosmopolitanism," 103.
99. Durham, Cooper, and Morris, "Stage Hip-Hop Feminism Built," 725.
100. See Martín Martínez, "Corporeal Activism," 8–9.
101. Acevedo, *Poet X*, 58–59.
102. Acevedo, *Poet X*, 96.
103. Acevedo, *Poet X*, 82–83.
104. For more on this, see Martín Martínez, "Corporeal Activism"; Zamora, "Black Latina Girlhood Poetics."
105. Acevedo, *Poet X*, 105, 283, 357.
106. Audre Lorde, *Sister Outsider: Essays and Speeches* (Trumansburg, NY: Crossing Press, 1984), 37–38.
107. Lorde, "Poetry Is Not a Luxury," 38.
108. Acevedo, *Poet X*, 355.

109. Aparicio, *Listening to Salsa*, 121–124.

110. Martín Martínez, "Corporeal Activism," 17, 19.

111. Crunktastic [Brittney Cooper], "Disrespectability Politics: On Jay-Z's Bitch, Beyonce's 'Fly' Ass, and Black Girl Blue," *Crunk Feminist Collection* (blog), Crunk Feminist Collective, January 19, 2012, http://www.crunkfeministcollective.com/2012/01/19/disrespectability-politics-on-jay-zs-bitch-beyonces-fly-ass-and-black-girl-blue/.

112. Acevedo, *Poet X*, 82.

113. See Theresa Renee White, "Missy 'Misdemeanor' Elliott and Nicki Minaj: Fashionistin' Black Female Sexuality in Hip-Hop Culture—Girl Power or Overpowered?," *Journal of Black Studies* 44, no. 6 (2013): 607–626; Carmen Rios, "Nicki Minaj's Feminism Isn't about Your Comfort Zone: On 'Anaconda' and Respectability Politics," *Autostraddle*, August 25, 2014, https://www.autostraddle.com/nicki-minajs-feminism-isnt-about-your-comfort-zone-on-anaconda-and-respectability-politics-251866/; Jamilah Lemieux, "Nicki Minaj's Butt Is Not Your Daughter's Problem," *Ebony*, July 29, 2014, http://www.ebony.com/entertainment-culture/nicki-minajs-butt-is-not-your-daughters-problem-503#axzz38slZjGrm; Mychal Denzel Smith, "Nicki Minaj's Butt and the Politics of Black Women's Sexuality," *Feministing* (blog), July 29, 2014, http://feministing.com/2014/07/29/nicki-minajs-butt-and-the-politics-of-black-womens-sexuality/; Luchina Fisher, "Nicki Minaj Doesn't Get All the 'Talk' about Her Racy 'Anaconda' Video," ABC News, October 20, 2014, https://abcnews.go.com/blogs/entertainment/2014/10/nicki-minaj-doesnt-get-all-the-talk-about-her-racy-anaconda-video; Martín Martínez, "Afro-Caribbean Women."

114. Sophie Kleeman, "Nicki Minaj's New 'Anaconda' Video Is Here—And It's a Huge Letdown," *Mic*, August 29, 2014, https://www.mic.com/articles/96698/nicki-minaj-s-new-anaconda-video-is-here-and-it-s-a-huge-letdown.

115. Acevedo, *Poet X*, 180.

116. Acevedo, *Poet X*, 181.

117. Martín Martínez, "Afro-Caribbean Women," 7.

118. Adam Bradley, "The Artists Dismantling the Barriers between Rap and Poetry," *New York Times*, March 4, 2021, https://www.nytimes.com/2021/03/04/t-magazine/rap-hip-hop-poetry.html.

119. Acevedo, *Poet X*, 205.

120. Acevedo, *Poet X*, 205.

121. Beyoncé Knowles, "Ring the Alarm," directed by Sophie Mueller, Sony Music Studios, October 3, 2009, YouTube video, https://www.youtube.com/watch?v=eY_mrU8MPfI.

122. Daphne A. Brooks, "'All That You Can't Leave Behind': Black Female Soul Singing and the Politics of Surrogation in the Age of Catastrophe," *Meridians* 8, no. 1 (2008): 182.

123. Acevedo, *Poet X*, 142–143.

124. Acevedo, *Poet X*, 145.

125. Durham, Cooper, and Morris, "Stage Hip-Hop Feminism Built," 722.

126. Aparicio, *Listening to Salsa*, 5.

127. Durham, Cooper, and Morris, "Stage Hip-Hop Feminism Built," 727.

128. bell hooks, *The Will to Change: Men, Masculinity, and Love* (New York: Washington Square, 2004), xvi.

129. Gloria Anzaldúa, Preface to *This Bridge We Call Home: Radical Visions for Trans-*

formation, ed. Gloria E. Anzaldúa and Ana Louise Keating (New York: Routledge, 2002), 3.

130. Kendrick Lamar, "Poetic Justice," track 6 on *Good Kid, M.A.A.D City*, Top Dawg Entertainment, Interscope Records, 2012, compact disc.

131. Lamar, "Poetic Justice."

132. Anthony B. Pinn and Christopher M. Driscoll, "Introduction: K.Dotting the American Cultural Landscape with Black Meaning," in *Kendrick Lamar and the Making of Black Meaning*, ed. Christopher M. Driscoll, Monica R. Miller, and Anthony B. Pinn (New York: Routledge, 2023), 5.

133. Acevedo, *Poet X*, 349.

CHAPTER 4. STORYTELLING FROM THE BORDERLANDS

1. Daisy Cocco De Filippis, "Las tertulias de las escritoras dominicanas en Estados Unidos: Una historia," *Camino Real: Estudios de las hispanidades norteamericanas* 4 (2011): 53.

2. Cocco De Filippis, "Las tertulias," 53.

3. On doing "theory in the flesh," see Cherríe Moraga, "Entering the Lives of Others: Theory in the Flesh," in *This Bridge Called My Back: Writings by Radical Women of Color*, 40th anniv. ed., ed. Cherríe Moraga and Gloria Anzaldúa (Albany: State University of New York Press, 2021), 19.

4. García-Peña, *Borders of Dominicanidad*.

5. Josefina Báez, message to author, July 24, 2023.

6. García-Peña, *Borders of Dominicanidad*, 188.

7. Torres-Saillant and Hernández, *Dominican Americans*, 131.

8. This has been extensively discussed in Lorgia García-Peña, "Performing Identity, Language, and Resistance: A Study of Josefina Báez's Dominicanish," *Wadabagei: A Journal of the Caribbean and Its Diaspora* 11, no. 3 (2008): 28–45; Sophie Maríñez, "Poética de la relación en *Dominicanish* de Josefina Báez," *La Torre* 10, no. 35 (2005): 149–160; Néstor Rodríguez, "De La Romana a Washington Heights: El azar trashumante de Josefina Báez," *Revista Surco Sur* 2, no. 4 (2011): 71–74; Ramón Arturo Victoriano-Martínez, *Rayanos y Dominicanyorks: La Dominicanidad del siglo XXI* (Pittsburgh: Instituto Internacional de Literatura Iberoamericana, 2014).

9. Emilia Durán Almarza, "Ciguapas in New York: Transcultural Ethnicity and Transracialization in Dominican American Performance," *Journal of American Studies* 46, no. 1 (2012): 139. See also Camilla Stevens, *Aquí and Allá: Transnational Dominican Theater and Performance* (Pittsburgh: University of Pittsburgh Press, 2019); Emilia Durán Almarza, *Performeras del Dominicanyork: Josefina Báez y Chiqui Vicioso* (Valencia, Spain: Universitat de Valencia, 2010); Emilia Durán Almarza, "Staging Transculturation: Border Crossings in Josefina Báez's Performance Texts," in *Caribbean without Borders*, ed. Ileana Cortés Santiago, Raquel Puig, and Dorsia Smith (Cambridge: Cambridge Scholars, 2009), 161–174.

10. Torres-Saillant and Hernández, *Dominican Americans*, 131.

11. Diana Taylor, *The Archive and the Repertoire: Performing Cultural Memory in the Americas* (Durham, NC: Duke University Press, 2003), 2–3.

12. Cocco De Filippis, "Las tertulias," 63–64.

13. Throughout the chapter, I use the terms *Dominican American* and *dominican-york*. Although the former has been used in a wider sense to designate Dominicans living in the United States, and they are often used interchangeably, I turn to the demonym *dominicanyork* to account for the socially and culturally specific conditions and realities of Dominican immigration to New York City post–1961. Further, Josefina Báez is a self-proclaimed dominicanyork to whom affirming this identity is central to reflect on the social, cultural, economic, and political impact of New York City in the fluid construction of dominicanidad. Thus when referring to her and her oeuvre, I use *dominicanyork*.

14. Anzaldúa, *Borderlands / La Frontera*, 102, 101.

15. Josefina Báez, "Notas personales de Josefina Báez," in *First Draft of Handbook of Performance Autology* (self-pub., 1989), 19.

16. Aparicio, *Listening to Salsa*, 5.

17. Alvarado, "Listening to Literature," 583.

18. Daisy Cocco de Filippis, "Palabras para rescatar existencias: De diáspora, nacionalidad, escritura y marginalidad," in *La literatura dominicana al final del siglo: Diálogo entre la tierra natal y la diáspora* (New York: CUNY Dominican Studies Institute City College of New York, 1999), 7.

19. Torres-Saillant and Hernández, *Dominican Americans*, 133.

20. Báez, *Dominicanish*, 37.

21. Anzaldúa, *Borderlands / La Frontera*, 43.

22. Josefina Báez, *Comrade, Bliss Ain't Playing* (New York: Self-pub., 2008), 55–61.

23. García-Peña, *Borders of Dominicanidad*; Miguel D. Mena, "Y con ustedes Josefina Báez: De La Romana al infinito," Cielo Naranja, accessed May 10, 2023, http://www.cielonaranja.com/menajosefinabaez.htm.

24. García-Peña, *Borders of Dominicanidad*, 4.

25. Josefina Báez, interview by author, June 30, 2016.

26. García-Peña, *Borders of Dominicanidad*; Durán Almarza, *Performeras del Dominicanyork*; Camilla Stevens, "'Home Is Where Theater Is': Performing Dominican Transnationalism," *Latin American Theater Review* 44, no. 1 (2010): 29–48; Lawrence La Fountain-Stokes, "Speaking Black Latino/a/ness: Race, Performance, and Poetry in Tato Laviera, Willie Perdomo and Josefina Báez," in *The AmeRícan Poet: Essays on the Work of Tato Laviera*, ed. Stephanie Alvarez and William Luis (New York: Center for Puerto Rican Studies Press, 2014), 240–257; Roberto Irizarry, "Traveling Light: Performance, Autobiography and Immigration in Josefina Báez's *Dominicanish*," *Gestos* 42 (2006): 81–96.

27. Frances R. Aparicio, "Popular Music," in *The Routledge Companion to Latina/o Literature*, ed. Suzanne Bost and Frances R. Aparicio (New York: Routledge, 2013), 229.

28. Aparicio, "Popular Music," 236.

29. Durán Almarza, *Performeras del Dominicanyork*, 66–67.

30. Báez, *Dominicanish*, 22.

31. García-Peña, "Performing Identity," 30.

32. Danny Méndez, *Narratives of Migration and Displacement in Dominican Literature* (New York: Routledge, 2012), 157.

33. Victoriano-Martínez, *Rayanos y Dominicanyorks*, 167.

34. Báez, *Dominicanish*, 21.

35. Stevens, "'Home Is Where Theater Is,'" 42; Báez, *Dominicanish*, 49.
36. Méndez, *Narratives of Migration*, 178.
37. Gloria Anzaldúa, "How to Tame a Wild Tongue," in *Borderlands / La Frontera*, 75–86.
38. See Stevens, *Aquí and Allá*, 152; Victoriano-Martínez, *Rayanos y Dominican-yorks*, 166–167.
39. Victoriano-Martínez, *Rayanos y Dominicanyorks*, 167.
40. Báez, *Dominicanish*, 26.
41. For more on Miñoso's trajectory as a Black Latino baseball player in the MLB, see Joel Coen, dir., *Baseball's Been Very, Very Good to Me: The Minnie Minoso Story*, PBS, 2014, 51:33, https://www.pbs.org/video/wttw-documentaries-baseballs-been-very-very-good-me-minnie-minoso-story/.
42. Roth, *Race Migrations*.
43. Bonilla, "Beyond Survival," 464.
44. Durán Almarza, "Staging Transculturation," 165; García-Peña, "Performing Identity," 30.
45. Josefina Báez, message to author, July 29, 2023.
46. For more information on Proposition 187, visit the virtual research guide by Herman Luis Chavez and María Guadalupe Partida, "1994: California's Proposition 187," *A Latinx Resource Guide: Civil Rights Cases and Events in the United States*, Library of Congress, August 17, 2020, https://guides.loc.gov/latinx-civil-rights/california-proposition-187.
47. Báez, *Dominicanish*, 39.
48. Although this law was in effect for close to two decades, it was repealed in 2016, and bilingual education was reestablished in California public schools. For the text of Proposition 227, see Legislative Analyst's Office, June 1998, https://lao.ca.gov/ballot/1998/227_06_1998.htm. For a holistic idea of the impact of the law on the instruction of English learners, see the study conducted by Patricia Gándara et al., *The Initial Impact of Proposition 227 on the Instruction of English Learners* (Berkeley: University of California Linguistic Minority Research Institute, 2000), https://escholarship.org/uc/item/491925b7.
49. Báez, *Dominicanish*, 13, 31–32.
50. Madonna, "Like a Prayer," track 1 on *Like a Prayer*, Sire, Warner Bros., 1989.
51. Báez, *Dominicanish*, 48.
52. La Fountain-Stokes, "Speaking Black Latino/a/ness," 251; García-Peña, *Borders of Dominicanidad*, 190–191.
53. García-Peña, *Borders of Dominicanidad*, 191.
54. Báez, *Dominicanish*, 48.
55. Báez, *Dominicanish*, 26–27.
56. Báez, *Dominicanish*, 26.
57. Báez, *Dominicanish*, 34.
58. Báez, *Dominicanish*, 34.
59. Báez, *Dominicanish*, 28.
60. Ramón Rivera-Servera, "A Dominican York in Andhra," in *Caribbean Dance from Abakuá to Zouk: How Movement Shapes Identity*, ed. Susanna Sloat (Gainesville: University Press of Florida, 2005), 159.
61. Sam Sander, Anjuli Sastry Krbechek, Liam McBain, and Jordana Hochman, "There Was Nothing like 'Soul Train' on TV. There's Never Been Anything like

It Since," *It's Been a Minute*, NPR, September 28, 2021, https://www.npr.org /2021/09/14/1037118049/soul-train-hanif-abdurraqib.

62. Rivera-Servera, "Dominican York in Andhra," 159.

63. Báez, *Dominicanish*, 42.

64. Paul Gilroy, *The Black Atlantic: Modernity and Double Consciousness* (Cambridge, MA: Harvard University Press, 1993), 19.

65. Báez, *Dominicanish*, 42. I made the decision not to translate this passage in its entirety because most of its meaning would be lost in a translation that, in my view, would not do justice to the richness of these verses. Further, considering the multiple linguistic dimensions of *Dominicanish*, I do not consider this translation necessary. My hope is that my analysis of the fragment facilitates the understanding of non-Spanish-speaking readers, and I do translate some of the individual lines in my discussion.

66. Lipsitz, *Footsteps in the Dark*, viii.

67. Johnny Pacheco and El Conde, "Cositas buenas," track 2 on *Tres de leche y dos de azúcar*, Fania Records, 1973.

68. Gilroy, *Black Atlantic*, 4, 1.

69. Anzaldúa, *Light in the Dark*, 49.

70. Méndez, *Narratives of Migration*, 148.

71. Báez, *Dominicanish*, 42, 45.

72. Báez, *Dominicanish*, 49.

73. Torres-Saillant and Hernández, *Dominican-Americans*, 145.

74. Anzaldúa, *Borderlands / La Frontera*, 58.

75. García-Peña, *Borders of Dominicanidad*, 173.

76. Báez, *Levente no*.

77. Báez, *Levente no*.

78. Báez, *Levente no*.; García-Peña, *Borders of Dominicanidad*, 175.

79. Báez, *Levente no*. Fernanda Bustamante Escalona does an in-depth analysis of the name Quisqueya Amada Taína Anaísa Altagracia, a.k.a. La Kay, proposing that it represents the multiple codes and cultural, ethnic, and religious legacies that traverse the body of the protagonist-narrator. Further, Bustamante notes that Quisqueya and Taína hark to the Spanish colonization, while Anaísa and Altagracia are religious references that attest to the syncretic nature of Dominican religious practices and cultural identity. "'Aquí en el Ni e' se reescribe la novela': Celebración de la comunidad y la escritura diaspórica en voces de mujeres con conciencia mestiza, en *Levente no. Yolayorkdominicanyork* (2011), de Josefina Báez," in *Escribir la otra isla: República Dominicana en su literatura* (Netherlands: Almenara, 2021), 289.

80. Báez, *Levente no*.

81. Mena, "Y con ustedes Josefina Báez"; Bustamante Escalona, "Aquí en el Ni e," 298.

82. Miguel D. Mena, "El mejor libreto para la dominicanidad manhattanera: Josefina Báez," *Areito*, Suplemento Cultural del periódico *Hoy*, September 17, 2011, 2, https://issuu.com/editorahoy/docs/areito_20110917.

83. Bustamante Escalona, "Aquí en el Ni e," 301.

84. Báez, preface to *Levente no*. In the last verse, there is a direct reference to Juan Luis Guerra's "Visa Para un Sueño" (A visa for a dream), a popular merengue song that narrates the vicissitudes of Dominicans who stand in line at the US Consulate in the Dominican Republic hoping to obtain a visa to fulfill their

dreams of traveling to the US. For an in-depth description of the song, see Paul Austerlitz, "Merengue on the Global Stage," in *Merengue: Dominican Music and Identity* (Philadelphia: Temple University Press, 1997), 131–132.

85. Báez, *Levente no.*
86. Rolf Lidskog, "The Role of Music in Ethnic Identity Formation in Diaspora: A Research Review," *International Social Science Journal* 55, no. 219–220 (2017): 25. See also these related works: Eun-Young Jung, "Transnational Migrations and YouTube Sensations: Korean Americans, Popular Music, and Social Media," *Ethnomusicology* 58, no. 1 (2014): 54–82; Jennifer Kyker, "Listening in the Wilderness: The Audience Reception of Oliver Mtukudzi's Music in the Zimbabwean Diaspora," *Ethnomusicology* 57, no. 2 (2013): 261–285; Martin Stokes, "Music and the Global Order," *Annual Review of Anthropology* 33 (2004): 47–72.
87. Báez, *Levente no.*
88. Gustavo Pérez Firmat, *Life on the Hyphen: The Cuban-American Way* (Austin: University of Texas Press, 2012), 5.
89. Josefina Báez, "Josefina Báez: A Dominicanyork Artist: A Dialogue," public reading, Modern Languages and Literatures Department of Manhattan College, New York City, October 3, 2011.
90. Báez, *Levente no.*
91. Báez, *Levente no.*
92. García-Peña, *Borders of Dominicanidad*, 175.
93. Ramón A. Victoriano-Martínez, "'Tienes que conocer tu historia . . .': Una entrevista con Josefina Báez," *Karpa* 3, no. 2 (2010).
94. Torres-Saillant and Hernández, *Dominican-Americans*, 146.
95. Báez, *Levente no.*
96. Báez, *Levente no.*
97. Anzaldúa, "How to Tame a Wild Tongue."
98. Vanessa Pérez Rosario, "Latinas Write the New York City Diaspora," *Review: Literature and Arts of the Americas* 89 (2014): 164, 170.
99. Báez, *Levente no.*
100. For more information on Proyecto Uno and its trajectory, see CUNY Dominican Studies Institute, "Narrative: 1990s: New Musical Trends," *A History of Dominican Music in the United States*, accessed July 22, 2021, http://dominicanmusicusa .com/narratives/1990s-new-musical-trends/4#_ftnref1.
101. Lisa D. McGill, *Constructing Black Selves: Caribbean American Narratives and the Second Generation* (New York: New York University Press, 2005), 200.
102. McGill, *Constructing Black Selves*, 200–201.
103. Wilfrido Vargas, "El Jardinero," track 1 on *El Jardinero*, Karen Records, 1984.
104. Raewyn Connell, *Masculinities* (Berkeley: University of California Press, 1995), 77.
105. Báez, *Levente no.*
106. Báez, *Levente no.*
107. See Austerlitz, *Merengue*, 93; Lipsitz, *Footsteps in the Dark*, 145.
108. In *Rayanos y Dominicanyorks*, Arturo Victoriano attributes the parallels he establishes between the Dominicanyork and *lo rayano* to the fact that both evoke lives and experiences demarcated by borders that divide and unite two cultures. He argues that the Dominicanyork also shares with lorayano a long history of discrimination and that both conjure images of movement, border crossing, and nonbelongingness to a nation-state (146).

109. The merengue band Milly, Jocelyn y Los Vecinos was a family enterprise that disbanded in the mid-1990s. Raised in Washington Heights, the siblings and children of Dominican immigrants who made up the band grew up surrounded by the Dominican diasporic community and went on to infuse the lyrics of their songs with the experiences of their community. Milly Quezada had a trailblazing career and became "The Queen of Merengue." Milly and her sister Jocelyn represented a shift in merengue music in which women's voices became more prevalent and their perspectives permeated the genre, as illustrated in "Volvió Juanita." Los Vecinos, "Volvió Juanita," the first track on *Esta Noche!*, Algar Records, 1984.

110. Martínez-San Miguel, *Caribe Two Ways*, 290–291.

111. Báez, *Levente no.*

112. Báez, *Levente no.*

113. Báez, *Levente no.*

114. Audre Lorde, *Sister Outsider: Essays and Speeches* (Trumansburg, NY: Crossing Press, 1984), 119.

115. Lorde, *Sister Outsider*, 123.

116. Báez, *Levente no.*

117. Lorde, *Sister Outsider*, 123.

118. Báez, *Levente no.*

119. Báez, *Levente no.*

120. Báez, *Levente no.*

121. García-Peña, *Borders of Dominicanidad*, 195.

122. Báez, *Comrade, Bliss Ain't Playing*, 73, 95.

123. Báez, *Comrade, Bliss Ain't Playing*, 55.

124. See Cristiane Lira, "Josefina Báez não está de brincadera: Negociando a seu espaço através do Sagrado e da delicadeza," *Karpa* 6 (2013).

125. Báez, *Comrade, Bliss Ain't Playing*, 29; Anzaldúa, *Borderlands*, 105.

126. García-Peña, *Borders of Dominicanidad*, 188.

127. Lorde, *Sister Outsider*, 43.

128. Báez, *Comrade, Bliss Ain't Playing*, 29.

129. Lorde, *Sister Outsider*, 92; Báez, *Comrade, Bliss Ain't Playing*, 97.

130. Báez, *Comrade, Bliss Ain't Playing*, 95.

131. Aida Heredia, foreword to *Comrade, Bliss Ain't Playing*, by Josefina Báez, n.p. (New York: Self-published, 2008).

132. Báez, *Comrade, Bliss Ain't Playing*, 100.

133. Stuart Hall, "Cultural Identity and Diaspora," in *Identity, Community, Culture, Difference*, ed. Jonathan Rutherford (London: Lawrence and Wishart, 1990), 222.

134. Báez, *Comrade, Bliss Ain't Playing*, 34.

135. Báez, *Comrade, Bliss Ain't Playing*, 24–25.

136. Hall, "Cultural Identity and Diaspora," 222–237.

137. Jennifer Nash, "Practicing Love: Black Feminism, Love-Politics, and Post-intersectionality," *Meridians: Feminism Race Transnationalism* 19 (2020): 448–449.

138. Báez, *Comrade, Bliss Ain't Playing*, 88, 43. For more on the revolutionary power of love, see June Jordan, "Where Is the Love?," in *Some of Us Did Not Die* (New York: Basic Books), 275–283.

139. Báez, *Comrade, Bliss Ain't Playing*, 3.

140. Anzaldúa, *Light in the Dark*, 45.

141. Báez, *Comrade, Bliss Ain't Playing*, 1.

142. Danny Méndez, "The Intricacies of Bliss in Diaspora: Dominican Diasporic Subjectivities in Josefina Báez's *Comrade Bliss Ain't Playing*," *La Habana Elegante* 52 (2012).

143. Alicia Arrizón, *Queering Mestizaje: Transculturation and Performance* (Ann Arbor: University of Michigan Press, 2006), 45–46.

144. María Lugones, "Playfulness, 'World'-Travelling, and Loving Perception," *Hypathia* 52, no. 2 (1987), 17.

145. Lipsitz, *Footsteps in the Dark*, xii.

EPILOGUE

1. Josefina Báez, "Conversation on *Dominicanish*," public conversation, University of Georgia, Athens, October 30, 2023.

2. Jenni Mota (@jennifermotaval), "My legacy will be tied to a historic moment. That's enough for me," Twitter (now X), April 5, 2023, 1:00 p.m., https://twitter.com/jennifermotaval/status/1643659969131053069.

3. Torres-Saillant, "Dominican-American Literature," 432.

4. Isabelia Herrera, "In Her New Show, Rita Indiana Confronts All Kinds of Ghosts," *New York Times,* April 12, 2023, https://www.nytimes.com/2023/04/12/arts/music/rita-indiana-tu-nombre-verdadero.html.

Acevedo, Elizabeth. *The Poet X: A Novel*. New York: HarperTeen, 2018.

Alcántara, Amanda. "How the Diaspora Made Its Name through Activism and Community Organizing: The Dominican-American Dream." *La Galería: Voices of the Dominican Diaspora* 1 (2018): 65–71.

Alonso, Andoni, and Pedro J. Oiarzabal, eds. *Diasporas in the New Media Age: Identity, Politics, and Community*. Reno: University of Nevada Press, 2010.

Alvarado, Lorena. "Listening to Literature: Popular Music, Voice, and Dance in Latina/o Literary Imagination, 1980–2010." In *The Cambridge History of Latina/o American Literature*, edited by John Morán González and Laura Lomas, 583–601. New York: Cambridge University Press, 2018.

Álvarez López, Esther. "Identity, De-colonization and Cosmopolitanism in (Afro) Latina Artists' Spoken Word Performances." In *Latinidad at the Crossroads: Insights into Latinx Identity in the Twenty-First Century*, edited by Amanda Ellen Gerke and Luisa María Rodríguez, 84–107. Boston: Brill, 2021.

Anderson, Benedict. *Imagined Communities: Reflections on the Origins and Spread of Nationalism*. Rev. ed. London: Verso, 2006.

Andújar, Rey. "Merengue." In *Saturnalia / Saturnario*, trans. Kolin Jordan, 87–96. Chicago: Siete Vientos, 2013.

Andújar, Rey. "Terror." In *Saturnalia / Saturnario*, trans. Kolin Jordan, 31-43. Chicago: Siete Vientos, 2013.

Anzaldúa, Gloria. *Borderlands / La Frontera: The New Mestiza*. 3rd ed. San Francisco: Aunt Lute Books, 2007.

Anzaldúa, Gloria. "How to Tame a Wild Tongue." In *Borderlands / La Frontera*, 75–86.

Anzaldúa, Gloria. *Light in the Dark / Luz en lo Oscuro: Rewriting Identity, Spirituality, Reality*. Durham, NC: Duke University Press, 2015.

Anzaldúa, Gloria. Preface to *This Bridge We Call Home: Radical Visions for Transformation*, edited by Gloria E. Anzaldúa and Ana Louise Keating, 1–5. New York: Routledge, 2002.

Aparicio, Frances R. *Listening to Salsa: Gender, Latin Popular Music, and Puerto Rican Cultures*. Middletown, CT: Wesleyan University Press, 1998.

Aparicio, Frances R. "Popular Music." In *The Routledge Companion to Latina/o Literature*, edited by Suzanne Bost and Frances R. Aparicio, 229–239. New York: Routledge, 2013.

Arias, Aurora. "Invi's Paradise." In *Invi's Paradise y otros relatos*, 9–33. Montreal: Concordia University, 1998.

Arias, Aurora. "Poco Loco." In *Fin de mundo y otros relatos*, 67–76. San Juan, PR: Universidad de Puerto Rico, 2000.

Arias, Aurora. "¿Por qué la música en mis cuentos?" Paper presented at the Latin American Roundtable Artist Conference, New York, October 2011.

Arrizón, Alicia. *Queering Mestizaje: Transculturation and Performance*. Ann Arbor: University of Michigan Press, 2006.

Austerlitz, Paul. *Merengue: Dominican Music and Dominican Identity*. Philadelphia: Temple University Press, 1997.

Austerlitz, Paul. "Merengue on the Global Stage." In *Merengue: Dominican Music and Identity*, 123–134. Philadelphia: Temple University Press, 1997.

Báez, Josefina. *Comrade, Bliss Ain't Playing*. New York: Self-published, 2008.

Báez, Josefina. "Conversation on *Dominicanish*." Public conversation. University of Georgia, Athens, October 30, 2023.

Báez, Josefina. *Dominicanish: A Performance Text*. New York: I.Om.Be, 2000.

Báez, Josefina. "Josefina Báez: A Dominicanyork Artist: A Dialogue." Public reading. Modern Languages and Literatures Department of Manhattan College, New York City, October 3, 2011.

Báez, Josefina. *Levente no. Yolayorkdominicanyork*. New York: I.Om.Be, 2011.

Báez, Josefina. "Lista del Terror." Cielo Naranja, December 2009. http://www.cielonaranja.com/ldjosefinabaez.htm.

Báez, Josefina. "Notas personales de Josefina Báez." In *First Draft of Handbook of Performance Autology*. Self-published, 1989.

Bailey, Benjamin. "Black and Latino: Dominican Americans Negotiate Racial Worlds." In *Mixed Messages: Multiracial Identities in the "Color-Blind" Era*, edited by David L. Brunsma, 285–300. Boulder, CO: Lynne Rienner, 2006.

Bayetti-Flores, Veronica. "A Look Back at Merenhouse, the Most Lit Pari Music of All Time." Remezcla, December 17, 2017. https://remezcla.com/lists/music/merenhouse-merenrap-tribute/.

Benítez-Rojo, Antonio. *The Repeating Island: The Caribbean and the Postmodern Perspective*. Durham, NC: Duke University Press, 1992.

Benjamin, Walter. *Charles Baudelaire: A Lyric Poet in the Era of High Capitalism*. Translated by Harry Zohn. London: New Left Books, 1973.

Ben-Ur, Lorraine E. "Hacia la novela del Caribe: Guillermo Cabrera Infante y Luis Rafael Sánchez." In *Luis Rafael Sánchez: Crítica y bibliografía*, edited by Daisy Caraballo Abréu and Néloda Hernández Vargas, 207–222. Río Piedras: Editorial de la Universidad de Puerto Rico, 1985.

Bergad, Laird. *The Dominican Population of the New York Metro Region, 1970–2020*. Latino Data Project, Report 91. Center for Latin American, Caribbean, and Latino Studies, City University of New York. August 2022. https://academicworks.cuny.edu/cgi/viewcontent.cgi?article=1105&context=clacls_pubs.

Betances, Emilio R. "En busca de un nuevo papel en la Sociedad." In *La iglesia católica y la política del poder en América Latina: El caso dominicano en perspectiva comparada*, 173–232. Santo Domingo, DR: Editorial Funglode, 2017.

Bonilla, Frank. "Beyond Survival: Por qué seguiremos siendo puertorriqueños." In *The Puerto Ricans: Their History, Culture, Society*, edited by Adalberto López, 453–466. Rochester, VT: Schenkman, 1980.

Bost, Suzanne. *Shared Selves: Latinx Memoir and Ethical Alternatives to Humanism*. Urbana: University of Illinois Press, 2020.

Bradley, Adam. "The Artists Dismantling the Barriers between Rap and Poetry." *New York Times*, March 4, 2021. https://www.nytimes.com/2021/03/04/t-magazine/rap-hip-hop-poetry.html

Brooks, Daphne A. "'All That You Can't Leave Behind': Black Female Soul Singing and the Politics of Surrogation in the Age of Catastrophe." *Meridians* 8, no. 1 (2008): 180–204.

Bustamante Escalona, Fernanda. "Aquí en el Ni e' se reescribe la novela": Celebración de la comunidad y la escritura diaspórica en voces de mujeres con conciencia mestiza, en *Levente no. Yolayorkdominicanyork* (2010), de Josefina Báez." In *Escribir la otra isla: República Dominicana en su literatura*, 283–303. Leiden, Netherlands: Almenara, 2021.

Bustamante Escalona, Fernanda. *A ritmo desenfadado: Narrativas dominicanas del nuevo mileno*. Santiago, Chile: Editorial Cuarto Propio, 2014.

Bustamante Escalona, Fernanda, ed. *Rita Indiana: Archivos*. Santo Domingo, DR: Ediciones Cielo Naranja, 2017.

Bustamante Escalona, Fernanda. "Rita Indiana Hernández: Una escritura que retuerce los márgenes y los paradigmas de representación identitaria." In Bustamante Escalona, *Rita Indiana*, 259–289.

Candelario, Ginetta E. B. *Black behind the Ears: Dominican Racial Identity from Museums to Beauty Shops*. Durham, NC: Duke University Press, 2007.

Cardoso, Leonardo. *Sound-Politics in São Paulo*. New York: Oxford University Press, 2019.

Cepeda, María Elena. *Musical ImagiNation: U.S.-Colombian Identity and the Latin Music Boom*. New York: New York University Press, 2010.

Cepeda, Raquel. *Bird of Paradise: How I Became Latina*. New York: Atria Books, 2013.

Cepeda, Raquel. Interview by Dr. Brenda Greene. *Writers on Writing*. 91.5 WNYE FM, New York, May 2, 2014.

Céspedes, Diógenes. "Entrevista con Luis Días." In Mena, *Luis Días*, 2nd ed., 111–124.

Chavez, Herman Luis, and María Guadalupe Partida. "1994: California's Proposition 187." *A Latinx Resource Guide: Civil Rights Cases and Events in the United States*. Library of Congress. August 17, 2020. https://guides.loc.gov/latinx-civil-rights/california-proposition-187.

Chávez, Linda. *Out of the Barrio: Toward a New Politics of Hispanic Assimilation*. New York: Basic Books, 1991.

Cocco De Filippis, Daisy. "Dominican Writers at the Crossroads: Reflections of a Conversation in Progress." *Latino Review of Books* 2, no. 2 (1996): 2–7.

Cocco De Filippis, Daisy. "Las tertulias de las escritoras dominicanas en Estados Unidos: Una historia." *Camino Real: Estudios de las hispanidades norteamericanas* 4 (2011): 53–71.

Cocco De Filippis, Daisy. "Palabras para rescatar existencias: De diáspora, nacionalidad, escritura y marginalidad." In *La literatura dominicana al final del siglo: Diálogo entre la tierra natal y la diáspora*, 4–11. New York: CUNY Dominican Studies Institute, City College of New York, 1999.

Cohen, Joel, dir. *Baseball's Been Very, Very Good to Me: The Minnie Minoso Story*. PBS, 2014. https://www.pbs.org/video/wttw-documentaries-baseballs-been-very-very-good-me-minnie-minoso-story/.

Collado, Lipe. *El tíguere dominicano: Ensayo*. Santo Domingo, DR: Editora Panamericana, 1992.

Connell, Raewyn. *Masculinities*. Berkeley: University of California Press, 1995.

Crunkadelic. "Hip Hop Generation Feminism: A Manifesto." *Crunk Feminist Collection* (blog). Crunk Feminist Collective, March 10, 2010. https://www.crunkfeminist collective.com/2010/03/01/hip-hop-generation-feminism-a-manifesto/.

Crunktastic [Brittney Cooper]. "Disrespectability Politics: On Jay-Z's Bitch, Beyoncé's 'Fly' Ass, and Black Girl Blue." *Crunk Feminist Collection* (blog). Crunk Feminist Collective, January 19, 2012. http://www.crunkfeministcollective.com/2012/01/19 /disrespectability-politics-on-jay-zs-bitch-beyonces-fly-ass-and-black-girl-blue/.

CUNY Dominican Studies Institute. "Narrative: 1990s: New Musical Trends." *A History of Dominican Music in the United States*. Accessed July 22, 2021. http://domin icanmusicusa.com/narratives/1990s-new-musical-trends/4#_ftnref1.

Decena, Carlos Ulises. *Tacit Subjects: Belonging and Same-Sex Desire among Dominican Immigrant Men*. Durham, NC: Duke University Press, 2011.

de Certeau, Michel. *The Practice of Everyday Life*. Translated by Steven Rendall. Berkeley: University of California Press, 1984.

Deive, Carlos Esteban. *Diccionario de Dominicanismos*. Santo Domingo, DR: Ediciones Librería La Trinitaria, 2006.

Deleuze, Gilles, and Félix Guattari. "Introduction: Rhizome." In *A Thousand Plateaus: Capitalism and Schizophrenia*, 3–28. Minneapolis: University of Minnesota Press, 1987.

De Maeseneer, Rita. "Aurora Arias y sus cronotopías subversivas." In *Seis ensayos sobre narrativa dominicana contemporánea*, 123–151. Santo Domingo, DR: Banco Central de la República Dominicana, 2011.

De Maeseneer, Rita. "Bregando con la autoridad: Papi." In Bustamante Escalona, *Rita Indiana*, 117–126.

De Maeseneer, Rita. "¿Cómo dejar de narrar el (neo)trujillato?" In *Aproximaciones a la literatura dominicana*, vol. 2, *1980–2005*, edited by Rei Berroa, 221–237. Santo Domingo, DR: Banco Central de la República Dominicana, 2008.

De Maeseneer, Rita. *Seis ensayos sobre narrativa dominicana contemporánea*. Santo Domingo, DR: Banco Central de la República Dominicana, 2011.

De Maeseneer, Rita, and Fernanda Bustamante. "Cuerpos heridos en la narrativa de Rita Indiana Hernández, Rey Emmanuel Andújar y Junot Díaz." *Revista Iberoamericana* 79, no. 243 (2013): 395–414.

Derby, Lauren. "The Dictator's Seduction: Gender and State Spectacle during the Trujillo Regime." *Callaloo* 23, no. 3 (2000): 1112–1146.

Dery, Mark. "Public Enemy: Confrontation." In *That's the Joint! The Hip-Hop Studies Reader*, edited by Murray Forman and Mark Anthony Neal, 407–420. New York: Routledge, 2004.

Díaz, Rossy. *Rumbas Barriales: Aproximaciones al análisis del merengue de Calle*. Santo Domingo, DR: Editorial Seña, 2011.

Díaz Guerra, Eduardo, and Gustavo Ubrí Acevedo. *Memorias de la cayena: A cuarenta años de 7 días con el pueblo*. Santo Domingo, DR: Ministerio de Cultura, 2004.

Díaz-Zambrana, Rosana. "¿Una alternativa a la novela del dictador? Paternalismo, nación y posmodernidad en Papi de Rita Indiana Hernández." In Bustamante Escalona, *Rita Indiana*, 103–115.

Di Iorio Sandín, Lyn. *Killing Spanish: Literary Essays on Ambivalent U.S. Latino/a Identity*. New York: Palgrave Macmillan, 2009.

"'Dios Salve a la Montra': 6 Reversiones de Rita Indiana que debes escuchar." *Discolai*, March 24, 2017. https://discolai.com/2017/03/24/dios-salve-a-la-montra-6-reversiones-de-rita-indiana-que-debes-escuchar/.

Duany, Jorge. *Blurred Borders: Transnational Migration between the Hispanic Caribbean and the United States*. Chapel Hill: University of North Carolina Press, 2011.

Duchesne-Winter, Juan. "*Papi*, La profecía: Espectáculo e interrupción en Rita Indiana Hernández." *Revista de Crítica Literaria Latinoamericana* 34, no. 67 (2008), 289–308.

Duchesne-Winter, Juan. Prologue to *La estrategia de Chochueca*, 3rd ed., by Rita Indiana Hernández, 7–10. San Juan, PR: Editorial Isla Negra, 2006.

Durán, Alfau. *Trujillo and the Roman Catholic Church in Santo Domingo*. Ciudad Trujillo, DR: Editora Handicap, 1960.

Durán Almarza, Emilia. "Ciguapas in New York: Transcultural Ethnicity and Transracialization in Dominican American Performance." *Journal of American Studies* 46, no. 1 (2012): 139–153.

Durán Almarza, Emilia. *Performeras del Dominicanyork: Josefina Báez y Chiqui Vicioso*. Valencia, Spain: Universitat de Valencia, 2010.

Durán Almarza, Emilia. "Staging Transculturation: Border Crossings in Josefina Báez's Performance Texts." In *Caribbean without Borders*, edited by Ileana Cortés Santiago, Raquel Puig, and Dorsia Smith, 161–174. Cambridge: Cambridge Scholars, 2009.

Durham, Aisha, Brittney C. Cooper, and Susana M. Morris. "The Stage Hip-Hop Feminism Built: A New Directions Essay." *Signs: Journal of Women in Culture and Society* 38, no. 3 (2013): 721–737.

Eidsheim, Nina Sun. "Marian Anderson and 'Sonic Blackness' in American Opera." *American Quarterly* 63, no. 3 (2011): 641–671.

Fisher, Luchina. "Nicki Minaj Doesn't Get All the 'Talk' about Her Racy 'Anaconda' Video." ABC News, October 20, 2014. https://abcnews.go.com/blogs/entertainment/2014/10/nicki-minaj-doesnt-get-all-the-talk-about-her-racy-anaconda-video.

Flores, Juan. *The Diaspora Strikes Back: Caribeño Tales of Learning and Turning*. Cultural Spaces Series. New York: Routledge, 2009.

Flores, Juan. *From Bomba to Hip-Hop: Puerto Rican Culture and Latino Identity*. New York: Columbia University Press, 2000.

Foner, Nancy, ed. *New Immigrants in New York*. New York: Columbia University Press, 2001.

Foucault, Michel. "Nietzche, Genealogy, History." In *The Foucault Reader*, edited by Paul Rabinow, 76–100. New York: Pantheon Books, 1984.

Frith, Simon. "Music and Identity." In *Questions of Cultural Identity*, edited by Stuart Hall and Paul du Gay, 108–127. London: Sage, 1996.

Gándara, Patricia, Julie Maxwell-Jolly, Eugene García, Jolynn Asato, Kris Gutiérrez, Tom Stritikus, and Julia Curry. *The Initial Impact of Proposition 227 on the Instruction of English Learners*. Berkeley: University of California Linguistic Minority Research Institute, 2000. https://escholarship.org/uc/item/491925b7.

García, Mélida, and Miguel de Camps Jiménez, eds. *Antología de la Literatura Gay en la República Dominicana*. Santo Domingo, DR: Editora Manatí, 2004.

García, Saudi. "An Afro Dominican Guide." *La Galería: Voices of the Dominican Diaspora*. Accessed October 31, 2020. http://lagaleriamag.com/an-afro-dominican-guide-part-i/.

García Canclini, Néstor. "Noticias recientes sobre la hibridación." *Revista Transcultural de Música* 7 (2003).

García-Peña, Lorgia. *The Borders of Dominicanidad: Race, Nation, and Archives of Contradiction*. Durham, NC: Duke University Press, 2016.

García-Peña, Lorgia. "Dominican Ethnic Identities, National Borders, and Literature." In *The Oxford Encyclopedia of Latina and Latino Literature*, vol. 1, edited by Louis G. Mendoza, 475–489. New York: Oxford University Press, 2020.

García-Peña, Lorgia. "Performing Identity, Language, and Resistance: A Study of Josefina Báez's Dominicanish." *Wadabagei: A Journal of the Caribbean and Its Diaspora* 11, no. 3 (2008): 28–45.

García-Peña, Lorgia. *Translating Blackness: Latinx Colonialities in Global Perspective*. Durham, NC: Duke University Press, 2022.

Gilroy, Paul. *The Black Atlantic: Modernity and Double Consciousness*. Cambridge, MA: Harvard University Press, 1993.

Gonzalez, David, and Jane Fritsch. "Shared Streets, Crossed Paths, and a Death." *New York Times*, July 12, 1992.

González, Luisa María. "Digging through the Past to Reconcile Race and Latinx Identity in Dominican-American Women's Memoirs." In *Latinidad at the Crossroads: Insights into Latinx Identity in the Twenty-First Century*, edited by Amanda Ellen Gerke and Luisa María Rodríguez, 46–65. Boston: Brill, 2021.

Grasmuck, Sherri, and Patricia R. Pessar. *Between Two Islands: Dominican International Migration*. Berkeley: University of California Press, 1991.

Guarnizo, Luis E. "Los Dominicanyorks: The Making of a Binational Society." *Annals of the American Academy of Political and Social Science* 533 (1994): 70–86.

Guzmán, Manolo. "'Pa La Escuelita Con Mucho Cuidaʼo y por la Orillitaʼ: A Journey through the Contested Terrains of the Nation and Sexual Orientation." In *Puerto Rican Jam: Essays on Culture and Politics*, edited by Frances Negrón Muntaner and Ramón Grosfoguel, 209–228. Minneapolis: University of Minnesota Press, 1997.

Hall, Stuart. "Cultural Identity and Diaspora." In *Identity, Community, Culture, Difference*, edited by Jonathan Rutherford, 222–237. London: Lawrence and Wishart, 1990.

Halliday, Sam. *Sonic Modernity: Representing Sound in Literature, Culture, and the Arts*. Edinburgh: Edinburgh University Press, 2013.

Heredia, Aida. Foreword to *Comrade, Bliss Ain't Playing*, by Josefina Báez. New York: Self-published, 2008.

Heredia, Juanita. *Transnational Latina Narratives in the Twenty-First Century: The Politics of Gender, Race, and Migrations*. New York: Palgrave Macmillan, 2009.

Hernández, Rita Indiana. *Ciencia succión*. Santo Domingo, DR: Amigo del hogar, 2001.

Hernández, Rita Indiana. "El legado." *Vetas* 17 (March 1996).

Hernández, Rita Indiana. "Guest DJ Rita Indiana." Interview by Jasmine Garsd and Félix Contreras. *alt.Latino*, NPR, April 7, 2011. https://www.npr.org/sections/altlatino/2011/04/16/135151650/this-week-on-alt-latino-guest-dj-rita-indiana.

Hernández, Rita Indiana. "La caída." *Vetas* 19 (June 1996).

Hernández, Rita Indiana. "La división." *Vetas* 19 (June 1996).

Hernández, Rita Indiana. *La estrategia de Chochueca*. 3rd ed. San Juan, PR: Editorial Isla Negra, 2006.

Hernández, Tanya Katerí. "The New Census Proposal May Likely Undercount Black People by Ignoring Afro-Latinos. We Can't Let That Happen." *Grio*, March 16, 2023.

https://thegrio.com/2023/03/16/the-new-census-proposal-may-likely-undercount-black-people-by-ignoring-afro-latinos-we-cant-let-that-happen/.

Hernández Medina, Esther. "Josefina Báez y El Nié." *Acento*, January 3, 2023. https://acento.com.do/opinion/josefina-baez-y-el-nie-9169365.html.

Herrera, Isabelia. "In Her New Show, Rita Indiana Confronts All Kinds of Ghosts." *New York Times*, April 12, 2023. https://www.nytimes.com/2023/04/12/arts/music/rita-indiana-tu-nombre-verdadero.html.

hooks, bell. *The Will to Change: Men, Masculinity, and Love*. New York: Washington Square, 2004.

Horn, Maja. *Masculinity after Trujillo: The Politics of Gender in Dominican Literature*. Gainesville: University of Florida Press, 2014.

Hutchinson, Sydney. "Listening Sideways: The Transgenre Work of Rita Indiana." In *Tigers of a Different Stripe*, 173–210.

Hutchinson, Sydney. "Merengue Típico in Santiago and New York: Transnational Regionalism in a Neo-Traditional Dominican Music." *Ethnomusicology* 50, no. 1 (2006): 37–72.

Hutchinson, Sydney. *Tigers of a Different Stripe: Performing Gender in Dominican Identity*. Chicago: University of Chicago Press, 2016.

Indiana, Rita. *Cuentos y poemas (1998–2003)*. Santo Domingo, DR: Ediciones Cielo Naranja, 2017.

Indiana, Rita. "Nueva narrativa." *El País*, January 27, 2014. https://elpais.com/elpais/2014/01/27/eps/1390830451_271183.html.

Indiana, Rita. *Papi*. 2nd ed. Cáceres, Spain: Periférica, 2011.

Indiana, Rita. "Tu afro no cabe en la foto." *El País*, July 28, 2014. https://elpais.com/elpais/2014/07/28/eps/1406564419_461753.html.

Irizarry, Roberto. "Traveling Light: Performance, Autobiography and Immigration in Josefina Báez's Dominicanish." *Gestos* 42 (2006): 81–96.

Itzigsohn, Jose, and Carlos Dore-Cabral. "Competing Identities? Race, Ethnicity and Panethnicity among Dominicans in the United States." *Sociological Forum* 15, no. 2 (2000): 232–247.

Itzigsohn, Jose, Carlos Dore Cabral, Esther Hernández-Medina, and Obed Vazquez. "Mapping Dominican Transnationalism: Narrow and Broad Transnational Practices." *Ethnic and Racial Studies* 22, no. 2 (1999): 316–339.

Jiménez, Blas R. *Afrodominicano por elección, negro por nacimiento: Seudonesayos*. Santo Domingo, DR: Editora Manatí, 2008.

Jiménez Polanco, Jacqueline, ed. *Divagaciones bajo la luna: Voces e imágenes de lesbianas dominicanas / Musing under the Moon: Voices and Images of Dominican Lesbians*. Santo Domingo, DR: Idegraf Editora, 2006.

Johnson, Catalina Maria. "Interview: Rita Indiana at LAMC 2011." Gozamos Chicago. July 25, 2011. YouTube video. https://www.youtube.com/watch?v=VWkb68Ka75c.

Johnson, Gaye Theresa. *Spaces of Conflict, Sounds of Solidarity: Music, Race, and Spatial Entitlement in Los Angeles*. Berkeley: University of California Press, 2013.

Jordan, June. "Where Is the Love?" In *Some of Us Did Not Die*, 275–283. New York: Basic Books, 2003.

Jung, Eun-Young. "Transnational Migrations and YouTube Sensations: Korean Americans, Popular Music, and Social Media." *Ethnomusicology* 58, no. 1 (2014): 54–82.

Kelly, Kim. "A Brief History of American Payola." *Vice*, February 14, 2016. https://www.vice.com/en/article/a-brief-history-of-american-payola/.

Kleeman, Sophie. "Nicki Minaj's New 'Anaconda' Video Is Here—And It's a Huge Letdown." *Mic*, August 20, 2014. https://www.mic.com/articles/96698/nicki-minaj-s-new-anaconda-video-is-here-and-it-s-a-huge-letdown.

Knowles, Beyoncé. "Ring the Alarm." Directed by Sophie Mueller. Sony Music Studios. October 3, 2009. YouTube video. https://www.youtube.com/watch?v=eY_mrU8MPfI.

Krohn-Hansen, Christian. "Masculinity and the Political among Dominicans: The Dominican Tiger." In *Machos, Mistresses, Madonnas: Contesting the Power of Latin American Gender Imagery*, edited by Marit Melhuus and Kristi Anne Stolen, 108–133. London: Verso, 1996.

Krohn-Hansen, Christian. *Political Authoritarianism in the Dominican Republic*. New York: Palgrave Macmillan, 2009.

Kyker, Jennifer. "Listening in the Wilderness: The Audience Reception of Oliver Mtukudzi's Music in the Zimbabwean Diaspora." *Ethnomusicology* 57, no. 2 (2013): 261–285.

La Fountain-Stokes, Lawrence. "Queer Diasporas, Boricua Lives: A Meditation on Sexile." *Review: Literature and Arts of the Americas* 41, no. 2 (2008): 294–301.

La Fountain-Stokes, Lawrence. *Queer Ricans: Cultures and Sexualities in the Diaspora*. Minneapolis: University of Minnesota Press, 2009.

La Fountain-Stokes, Lawrence. "Speaking Black Latino/a/ness: Race, Performance, and Poetry in Tato Laviera, Willie Perdomo and Josefina Báez." In *The AmeRícan Poet: Essays on the Work of Tato Laviera*, edited by Stephanie Alvarez and William Luis, 240–257. New York: Center for Puerto Rican Studies Press, 2014.

La Fountain-Stokes, Lawrence. *Translocas: The Politics of Puerto Rican Drag and Trans Performance*. Ann Arbor: University of Michigan Press, 2021.

Lam, Christina. "Bearing Witness: Alternate Archives of Latinx Identity in Raquel Cepeda's *Bird of Paradise: How I Became Latina*." *Studies in American Culture* 43, no. 1 (2020): 26–42.

Lamar, Kendrick. "Poetic Justice." Track 6 on *Good Kid, M.A.A.D City*. Top Dawg Entertainment, Interscope Records, 2012, compact disc.

Laó-Montes, Agustín. "Afro-Latinidades and the Diasporic Imaginary." *Iberoamericana* 5, no. 17 (2015): 117–130.

Lara, Ana M. "Uncovering Mirrors: Afro-Latina Lesbian Subjects." In *The Afro-Latin@ Reader: History and Culture in the United States*, edited by Miriam Jiménez Román and Juan Flores, 298–313. Durham, NC: Duke University Press, 2010.

Lemieux, Jamilah. "Nicki Minaj's Butt Is Not Your Daughter's Problem." *Ebony*, July 29, 2014. http://www.ebony.com/entertainment-culture/nicki-minajs-butt-is-not-your-daughters-problem-503#axzz38slZjGrm.

Levitt, Peggy. *The Transnational Villagers*. Berkeley: University of California Press, 2001.

Lidskog, Rolf. "The Role of Music in Ethnic Identity Formation in Diaspora: A Research Review." *International Social Science Journal* 55, no. 219–220 (2017): 23–38.

Lipsitz, George. *Footsteps in the Dark: The Hidden History of Popular Music*. Minneapolis: University of Minnesota Press, 2007.

Lipsitz, George. *Time Passages: Collective Memory and American Popular Culture*. Minneapolis: University of Minnesota Press, 2001.

Lira, Cristiane. "Josefina Báez não está de brincadera: Negociando a seu espaço através do Sagrado e da delicadeza." *Karpa* 6 (2013).

López, Héctor. *La música caribeña en la literatura de la postmodernidad*. Mérida, Venezuela: Fondo Editorial "Ramón Palomares," 1998.

Lorde, Audre. *Sister Outsider: Essays and Speeches*. Trumansburg, NY: Crossing Press, 1984.

Los Vecinos. "Volvió Juanita." Track 1 on *Esta Noche!* Algar Records, 1984.

Lugones, María. "Playfulness, 'World'-Travelling, and Loving Perception." *Hypathia* 52, no. 2 (1987): 3–19.

Lunsford, Andrea A. "Toward a Mestiza Rhetoric: Gloria Anzaldúa on Composition and Postcoloniality." *JAC* 18, no. 1 (1998): 1–27.

Lyon, Jacqueline. "Pajón Power: Styling Citizenship and Black Politics in the Dominican Natural Hair Movement." *Ethnic and Racial Studies* 43, no. 12 (2020): 2120–2139.

Madianou, Mirca, and Daniel Miller. *Migration and New Media: Transnational Families and Polymedia*. New York: Routledge, 2013.

Madonna. "Like a Prayer." Track 1 on *Like a Prayer*. Sire, Warner Bros., 1989.

Maguire, Emily. "'Hace[r] encantadora la idea del desencanto': Luis 'Terror' Días en los cuentos de Aurora Arias." In Serrata, *El sonido de la música*, 147–166.

Manuel, Peter. *Caribbean Currents: Caribbean Music from Rumba to Reggae*. Philadelphia: Temple University Press, 1995.

Maríñez, Sophie. "Poética de la relación en Dominicanish de Josefina Báez." *La Torre* 10, no. 35 (2005): 149–160.

Maríñez, Sophie. "The Quisqueya Diaspora: The Emergence of Latina/o Literature from Hispaniola." In *The Cambridge History of Latina/o American Literature*, edited by John Morán González and Laura Lomas, 561–582. New York: Cambridge University Press, 2018.

Martín Martínez, Macarena. "Afro-Caribbean Women Reclaiming Their Bodies and Sexuality: Nicki Minaj and Cardi B's Ambivalent Self Portrayals." *Popular Culture as Transformative Action: Videoclips, Performances, and Speeches in US Popular Culture*. PopMeC Research Blog. November 17, 2020. https://popmec.hypotheses.org/3304.

Martín Martínez, Macarena. "Corporeal Activism in Elizabeth Acevedo's *The Poet X*: Towards a Self-Appropriation of US Afro-Latinas' Bodies." *Revista de Estudios Norteamericanos* 25 (2021): 1–23.

Martínez-Reyes, Consuelo. "Hispanic Caribbean Sexiles." *Oxford Research Encyclopedia of Literature*. November 20, 2018. https://oxfordre.com/literature/view/10.1093/acrefore/9780190201098.001.0001/acrefore-9780190201098-e-393.

Martínez-San Miguel, Yolanda. *Caribe Two Ways: Cultura de la migración en el Caribe insular hispánico*. San Juan, PR: Ediciones Callejón, 2003.

Martínez-San Miguel, Yolanda. "'Con mi música pa' otra parte': Desplazamientos simbólicos dominicanos." In *Caribe Two Ways*, 263–322.

Masiki, Trent. "Post-Soul Latinidad: Black Nationalism in *Mama's Girl* and *Bird of Paradise: How I Became Latina*." *Latino Studies* 20, no. 4 (2022): 475–497.

Mateo, Francis. "Cañemo Revival Blues." Cielo Naranja, 2010. http://www.cielonaranja.com/francismateo.htm.

Mateo, Francis. *Ubre Urbe*. Self-published, 2013.

Mayes, April. "Black Feminist Formations in the Dominican Republic since *La Senten-cia*." In *AfroLatin American Politics*, edited by Kwame Dixon and Ollie Johnson III, 139–160. New Brunswick, NJ: Rutgers University Press, 2019.

McGill, Lisa D. *Constructing Black Selves: Caribbean American Narratives and the Second Generation*. New York: New York University Press, 2005.

McLaughlin, Carolyn, and David Gómez. *South Bronx Battles: Stories of Resistance, Resilience and Renewal*. Oakland: University of California Press, 2019.

Mena, Miguel D. "Ciudades revisadas: La literatura posinsular dominicana." *Revista Iberoamericana* 79, no. 243 (2013): 349–369.

Mena, Miguel D. "Distopías urbanas, el Polígono Central." Cielo Naranja, 2017. http://www.cielonaranja.com/menapoligono.html.

Mena, Miguel D. "Drake's, Raffles, Poco-Loco." In Mena, *Luis Días*, 2nd ed., 65–67.

Mena, Miguel D. "El dominicano, sus imaginarios." In *Poética de Santo Domingo II: Identidad, poder, territorios*, 2nd ed., 17–20. Santo Domingo, DR: Ediciones Cielo Naranja, 2013.

Mena, Miguel D. "El mejor libreto para la dominicanidad manhattanera: Josefina Báez." *Areito*. Suplemento Cultural del periódico *Hoy*. September 17, 2011. https://issuu.com/editorahoy/docs/areito_20110917.

Mena, Miguel D. "¿La ciudad hostil?" Cielo Naranja, 2002. http://www.cielonaranja.com/hostil_mena.htm.

Mena, Miguel D., ed. *Luis Días, ¡Échale gas!* Santo Domingo, DR: El jardín de las delicias, 1999.

Mena, Miguel D., ed. *Luis Días, ¡Échale gas!* 2nd ed. Santo Domingo, DR: Ediciones Cielo Naranja, 2012.

Mena, Miguel D. "Mi delirio." In Mena, *Luis Días*, 2nd ed., 12–17.

Mena, Miguel D. "Y con ustedes Josefina Báez: De La Romana al infinito." Cielo Naranja. Accessed May 10, 2023. http://www.cielonaranja.com/menajosefinabaez.htm.

Méndez, Danny. "The Intricacies of Bliss in Diaspora: Dominican Diasporic Subjectivities in Josefina Báez's *Comrade, Bliss Ain't Playing*." *La Habana Elegante* 52 (2012).

Méndez, Danny. *Narratives of Migration and Displacement in Dominican Literature*. New York: Routledge, 2012.

Moraga, Cherríe. "Entering the Lives of Others: Theory in the Flesh." In *This Bridge Called My Back: Writings by Radical Women of Color*, 40th anniv. ed., edited by Cherríe Moraga and Gloria Anzaldúa, 19. Albany: State University of New York Press, 2021.

Morgan, Joan, and Brittney Cooper. "Keynote with Joan Morgan and Dr. Brittney Cooper at the Hip Hop Literacies Conference 2014." College of Education and Human Ecology, Ohio State University. February 28, 2014. YouTube video. https://www.youtube.com/watch?v=my9pLqUwfK4.

Nash, Jennifer. "Practicing Love: Black Feminism, Love-Politics, and Post-intersectionality." *Meridians: Feminism Race Transnationalism* 19 (2020): 439–462.

The Notorious B.I.G. "Big Poppa." Track 13 on *Ready to Die*. Bad Boy Records and Arista Records, 1994, compact disc.

Oboler, Suzanne. *Ethnic Labels, Latino Lives*. Minneapolis: University of Minnesota Press, 1995.

Ornes, Germán. *Trujillo: Little Caesar of the Caribbean*. New York: Thomas Nelson and Sons, 1958.

Pacheco, Johnny, and El Conde. "Cositas buenas." Track 2 on *Tres de leche y dos de azúcar.* Fania Records, 1973.

Pacini Hernandez, Deborah. *Bachata: A Social History of a Dominican Popular Music.* Philadelphia: Temple University Press, 1995.

Pacini Hernández, Deborah. "*La lucha sonora*: Dominican Popular Music in the Post-Trujillo Era." *Latin American Music Review / Revista de Música Latinoamericana* 12, no. 2 (1991): 105–123.

"Papi: Entrevista a Rita Indiana, escritora y músico." El Centre de Cultura Contemporánia de Barcelona. September 23, 2011. YouTube video. https://www.youtube.com/watch?v=STiwYxwyEQM.

Pépen, Juan Félix. *La cruz señaló el camino: Influencia de la iglesia en la formación y conservación de la nacionalidad dominicana.* Ciudad Trujillo, DR: Duarte, 1954.

Pérez, Odalís. *La ideología rota: El derrumbe del pensamiento pseudonacionalista dominicano.* Santo Domingo, DR: Centro de Información Afroamericano, 2002.

Pérez, Odalís. *Literatura dominicana y memoria cultural: Ritmos y tiempos de la alteridad.* Santo Domingo, DR: Editora Manati, 2005.

Pérez Firmat, Gustavo. *Life on the Hyphen: The Cuban-American Way.* Austin: University of Texas Press, 2012.

Pérez Rosario, Vanessa. "Latinas Write the New York City Diaspora." *Review: Literature and Arts of the Americas* 89 (2014): 164–171.

Pessar, Patricia R. *A Visa for a Dream: Dominicans in the United States.* Boston: Allyn and Bacon, 1995.

Pinn, Anthony B., and Christopher M. Driscoll. "Introduction: K.Dotting the American Cultural Landscape with Black Meaning." In *Kendrick Lamar and the Making of Black Meaning*, edited by Christopher M. Driscoll, Monica R. Miller, and Anthony B. Pinn, 1–16. New York: Routledge, 2023.

Portes, Alejandro. "The New Latin Nation: Immigration and the Hispanic Population of the United States." In *A Companion to Latino Studies*, edited by Renato Rosaldo and Juan Flores, 15–24. Hoboken, NJ: Blackwell, 2007.

Pratt, Ray. *Rhythm and Resistance: Explorations in the Political Uses of Popular Music.* New York: Praeger, 1990.

Public Enemy. "Prophets of Rage." Track 15 on *It Takes a Nation of Millions to Hold Us Back.* Def Jam Records, 1988, compact disc.

Quinn, Rachel Afi. *Being la Dominicana: Race and Identity in the Visual Culture of Santo Domingo.* Urbana: University of Illinois Press, 2021.

Quiñones, Alfonso. "'7 días con el Pueblo,' un evento que cambió la canción." *Diario Libre*, November 26, 2004. https://www.diariolibre.com/revista/7-das-con-el-pueblo-un-evento-que-cambi-la-cancin-XADL52550.

Quiñonez, Naomi H. "Circles of Women." In *Voices from the Ancestors: Xicanx and Latinx Spiritual Expressions and Healing Practices*, edited by Lara Medina and Martha R. Gonzales, 387–390. Tucson: University of Arizona Press, 2019.

Quintero Rivera, Ángel G. *Cuerpo y cultura: Las músicas "mulatas" y la subversión del baile.* Madrid: Iberoamericana, 2009.

Ramírez, Rafael. *What It Means to Be a Man: Reflections on Puerto Rican Masculinity.* New Brunswick, NJ: Rutgers University Press, 1999.

Regalado, Pedro A. "The Washington Heights Uprising of 1992: Dominican Belonging and Urban Policing in New York City." *Journal of Urban History* 45, no. 5 (2019): 961–986.

Retis, Jessica, and Roza Tsagarousianou, eds. *The Handbook of Diaspora, Media and Culture*. Hoboken, NJ: Wiley-Blackwell, 2019.

Reyes, Israel. *Embodied Economies: Diaspora and Transcultural Capital in Latinx Caribbean Fiction and Theater*. New Brunswick, NJ: Rutgers University Press, 2022.

Rich, Adrienne. "North American Time." In *Your Native Land, Your Life*, 33–36. New York: W. W. Norton, 1986.

Rios, Carmen. "Nicki Minaj's Feminism Isn't about Your Comfort Zone: On 'Anaconda' and Respectability Politics." *Autostraddle*, August 25, 2014. https://www.autostraddle.com/nicki-minajs-feminism-isnt-about-your-comfort-zone-on-anaconda-and-respectability-politics-251866/.

Rivera, Raquel Z. "Between Blackness and Latinidad in the Hip Hop Zone." In *A Companion to Latino Studies*, edited by Juan Flores and Renato Rosaldo, 351–362. Hoboken, NJ: Wiley-Blackwell, 2011.

Rivera, Raquel Z. "Hip-Hop, Puerto Ricans, and Ethnoracial Identities in New York." In *Mambo Montage: The Latinization of New York*, edited by Agustín Laó-Montes and Arlene Dávila, 235–261. New York: Columbia University Press, 2001.

Rivera, Raquel Z. *New York Ricans from the Hip Hop Zone*. New York: Palgrave Macmillan, 2003.

Rivera-Servera, Ramón. "A Dominican York in Andhra." In *Caribbean Dance from Abakuá to Zouk: How Movement Shapes Identity*, edited by Susanna Sloat, 152–161. Gainesville: University Press of Florida, 2005.

Rivera-Velázquez, Celiany. "A una década de la importancia de ser Rita Indiana: La incursión en videorte, sonido, y performance de la montra del Caribe hispano." In Bustamante Escalona, *Rita Indiana*, 293–328.

Rivera-Velázquez, Celiany. "The Importance of Being Rita Indiana-Hernández." In *Globalizing Cultural Studies: Ethnographic Interventions in Theory, Method, and Policy*, edited by Cameron McCarthy, 205–227. New York: Peter Lang, 2007.

Rodríguez, José. "Años germinales en Convite," in Mena, *Luis Días*, 2nd ed., 18–21.

Rodríguez, Néstor E. "De La Romana a Washington Heights: El azar trashumante de Josefina Báez." *Revista Surco Sur* 2, no. 4 (2011): 71–74.

Rodríguez, Néstor E. *Divergent Dictions: Contemporary Dominican Literature*. Coconut Creek, FL: Caribbean Studies, 2011.

Rodríguez, Néstor E. "Dos artículos sobre *La estrategia de Chochueca*." In Bustamante Escalona, *Rita Indiana*, 31–38.

Rodríguez, Néstor E. *Escrituras de desencuentro en la República Dominicana*. Mexico City: Siglo XXI Editores, 2005.

Rodríguez, Néstor E. "Rita Indiana Hernández y la novísima narrativa dominicana." Cielo Naranja, 2005. http://www.cielonaranja.com/nestorchochueca.htm.

Rodríguez, Néstor E. "Terror y sus maneras de hacerse el muerto." *80 Grados*, July 8, 2011. http://www.80grados.net/terror-y-sus-maneras-de-hacerse-el-muerto/.

Rodríguez, Néstor E. "Un-Imagining the Dominican Nation." In *Divergent Dictions: Contemporary Dominican Literature*, 63–98. Coconut Creek, FL: Caribbean Studies Press, 2011.

Rose, Tricia. *Black Noise: Rap Music and Black Culture in Contemporary America*. Hanover, CT: Wesleyan University Press, 1994.

Roth, Wendy D. *Race Migrations: Latinos and the Cultural Transformation of Race*. Stanford, CA: Stanford University Press, 2012.

Saldaña-Portillo, María Josefina. "Epilogue: Latino Literature: The Borders Are Burning."

In *The Cambridge History of Latina/o Literature*, edited by John Morán González and Laura Lomas, 737–747. New York: Cambridge University Press, 2018.

Saldívar, José David. *Border Matters: Remapping American Cultural Studies*. Berkeley: University of California Press, 1997.

Sander, Sam, Anjuli Sastry Krbechek, Liam McBain, and Jordana Hochman. "There Was Nothing like 'Soul Train' on TV. There's Never Been Anything like It Since." *It's Been a Minute*. NPR, September 28, 2021. https://www.npr .org/2021/09/14/1037118049/soul-train-hanif-abdurraqib.

Santos Febres, Mayra. "Caribe y travestismo." In *El artista caribeño como guerrero de lo imaginario*, edited by Rita De Maeseneer and An Van Hecke, 37–44. Madrid: Iberoamericana, 2005.

Saunders, Tanya L. "The Cuban Remix: Rethinking Culture and Political Participation in Contemporary Cuba." PhD diss., University of Michigan, 2008.

Saunders, Tanya L. *Cuban Underground Hip Hop: Black Thoughts, Black Revolution, Black Modernity*. Austin: University of Texas Press, 2015.

Serrata, Médar, ed. *El sonido de la música en la narrativa dominicana: Ensayos sobre identidad, nación y performance*. Santo Domingo, DR: Instituto de Estudios Caribeños, 2012.

Serrata, Médar. Introduction to Serrata, *El sonido de la música*, 11–19.

Smith, Michael P., and Luis E. Guarnizo, eds. "The Locations of Transnationalism." In *Transnationalism from Below*, 1–34. New Brunswick, NJ: Transaction Publishers.

Smith, Michael Peter, and Luis Eduardo Guarnizo. *Transnationalism from Below*. New Brunswick, NJ: Transaction, 1998.

Smith, Mychal Denzel. "Nicki Minaj's Butt and the Politics of Black Women's Sexuality." *Feministing* (blog), July 29, 2014. http://feministing.com/2014/07/29 /nicki-minajs-butt-and-the-politics-of-black-womens-sexuality/.

Snyder, Robert W. "Crack Years." In *Crossing Broadway: Washington Heights and the Promise of New York City*, 158–195. New York: Cornell University Press, 2015.

Solano, Patricia. "Luis Días explica algunas de sus canciones." Página de Luis Terror Días. Cielo Naranja, 2009. http://www.cielonaranja.com/ldpatricias.htm.

Sterne, Jonathan. *The Audible Past: Cultural Origins of Sound Reproduction*. Durham, NC: Duke University Press, 2003.

Sterne, Jonathan. *The Sound Studies Reader*. New York: Routledge, 2012.

Stevens, Camilla. *Aquí and Allá: Transnational Dominican Theater and Performance*. Pittsburgh: University of Pittsburgh Press, 2019.

Stevens, Camilla. "'Home Is Where Theater Is': Performing Dominican Transnationalism." *Latin American Theater Review* 44, no. 1 (2010): 29–48.

Stokes, Martin. "Music and the Global Order." *Annual Review of Anthropology* 33 (2004): 47–72.

Tallaj, Angelina. "A Country That Ain't Belong to Me: Dominicanyorks, Identity and Popular Music." Guttman Community College Publications and Research No. 93. New York: CUNY Academic Works, 2006. https://academicworks.cuny.edu /nc_pubs/93.

Taylor, Diana. *The Archive and the Repertoire: Performing Cultural Memory in the Americas*. Durham, NC: Duke University Press, 2003.

Tejeda, Darío. *La pasión danzaria: Música y baile en el Caribe a través del merengue y la bachata*. Santo Domingo, DR: Academia de Ciencias de República Dominicana, 2002.

Thompson, Robert. "Hip Hop 101." In *Droppin' Science: Critical Essays on Rap Music and Hip Hop Culture*, edited by William Eric Perkins, 211–219. Philadelphia: Temple University Press, 1996.

Torrado, Lorna. "Desplazamientos bailables: Revisión histórica en la producción musical de Rita Indiana Hernández." In Bustamante Escalona, *Rita Indiana*, 331–350.

Torrado, Lorna. "Sinfonía del desencanto: La destrucción de Ciudad Trujillo en Rita Indiana Hernández." In Serrata, *El sonido de la música*, 235–258.

Torres, Lourdes. "The Construction of the Self in U.S. Latina Autobiographies." In *Third World Women and the Politics of Feminism*, edited by Chandra Talpade Mohanty, Ann Russo, and Lourdes Torres, 271–287. Bloomington: Indiana University Press, 1991.

Torres-Saillant, Silvio. "Dominican-American Literature: Immigrants, Exiles, and Ethnics." In *The Routledge Companion to Latino/a Literature*, edited by Suzanne Bost and Frances R. Aparicio, 423–435. New York: Routledge, 2013.

Torres-Saillant, Silvio. *El retorno de las yolas: Ensayos sobre diáspora, democracia y dominicanidad*. Santo Domingo, DR: Librería Trinitaria y Editora Manatí, 1999.

Torres-Saillant, Silvio. *El retorno de las yolas: Ensayos sobre diáspora, democracia y dominicanidad*. 2nd ed. Santo Domingo, DR: Editorial Universitaria Bonó, 2019.

Torres-Saillant, Silvio. *An Intellectual History of the Caribbean*. New York: Palgrave Macmillan, 2006.

Torres-Saillant, Silvio. *Introduction to Dominican Blackness*. New York: CUNY Dominican Studies Institute, City College of New York, 2010.

Torres-Saillant, Silvio. "The Latino Autobiography." In *Latino and Latina Writers*, edited by Alan West-Durán, 61–79. New York: Charles Scribner's Sons, 2004.

Torres-Saillant, Silvio. "The Tribulations of Blackness: Stages in Dominican Racial Identity." *Callaloo* 23, no. 3 (2000): 1086–1111.

Torres-Saillant, Silvio, and Nancy Kang. "Currents in Dominican American Literature." In *The Oxford Encyclopedia of Latina and Latino Literature*, vol. 1, edited by Louis G. Mendoza, 489–506. New York: Oxford University Press, 2020.

Torres-Saillant, Silvio, and Ramona Hernández. *The Dominican Americans*. Westport, CT: Greenwood, 1998.

Torres-Saillant, Silvio, and Ramona Hernández. "Dominicans: Community, Culture, and Collective Identity." In *One out of Three: Immigrants in New York in the Twenty-First Century*, edited by Nancy Foner, 223–245. New York: Columbia University Press, 2013.

Valerio-Holguín, Fernando. "El orden de la música popular en la literatura dominicana." *Céfiro: A Journal of the Céfiro Graduate Student Organization* 8, no. 1–2 (2008): 101–118.

Van Buren, Thomas, and Leonardo Iván Domínguez. "Transnational Music and Dance in Dominican New York." In *Dominican Migration: Transnational Perspectives*, edited by Ernesto Sagás and Sintia Molina, 244–273. Gainesville: University Press of Florida, 2004.

Vargas, Wilfrido. "El Jardinero." Track 1 on *El Jardinero*. Karen Records, 1984.

Vera-Rojas, María Teresa. "¡Se armó el juidero! Cartografías imprecisas, cuerpos disidentes, sexualidades transgresoras: Hacia una lectura queer de Rita Indiana Hernández." In Bustamante Escalona, *Rita Indiana*, 207–230.

Vicioso, Sherezada "Chiqui." "Discovering Myself: Un Testimonio." In *The Afro-Latin@*

Reader: History and Culture in the United States, edited by Miriam Jiménez Román and Juan Flores, 262–265. New York: Duke University Press, 2010.

Victoriano-Martínez, Ramón Antonio (Arturo). "Memoria y espacios en Santo Domingo." Cielo Naranja. Accessed August 23, 2020. http://www.cielonaranja .com/victorianomemoria.htm.

Victoriano-Martínez, Ramón Antonio (Arturo). *Rayanos y Dominicanyorks: La Dominicanidad del siglo XXI*. Pittsburgh: Instituto Internacional de Literatura Iberoamericana, 2014.

Victoriano-Martínez, Ramón Antonio (Arturo). "'Tienes que conocer tu historia . . .': Una entrevista con Josefina Báez." *Karpa* 3, no. 2 (2010).

Vila, Pablo. "Narrative Identities and Popular Music." In *Music and Youth Culture in Latin America: Identity Construction Processes from New York to Buenos Aires*, 17–80. New York: Oxford University Press, 2014.

White, Theresa Renee. "Missy 'Misdemeanor' Elliott and Nicki Minaj: Fashionistin' Black Female Sexuality in Hip-Hop Culture—Girl Power or Overpowered?" *Journal of Black Studies* 44, no. 6 (2013): 607–626.

Wiarda, Howard. *Dictatorship and Development: The Methods of Control in Trujillo's Dominican Republic*. Gainesville: University of Florida Press, 1968.

Zamora, Omaris. "Before *Bodak Yellow* and Beyond the Post-Soul: Cardi B Performs AfroLatina Feminisms in the Trance." *Black Scholar* 52, no. 1 (2022): 53–63.

Zamora, Omaris. "Black Latina Girlhood Poetics of the Body: Church, Sexuality and Dispossession." *Post 45: The Body of Contemporary Latina/o/x Poetry* (September 20, 2020): 1–15.

Page numbers in italics refer to figures

Archivo General de la Nación, 8
Arias, Aurora, 1, 52, 75, 77, 187n79;
  Emoticons, 58; *Fin de mundo y otros
  relatos*, 58, 60; "Invi's Paradise," 10–11,
  53–54, 58–68; *Invi's Paradise y otros
  relatos*, 58; *Piano lila*, 58; "Poco Loco,"
  10, 53–54, 58–68; *Vida verdadera en el
  Caribe*, 58; *Vivienda de pájaros*, 58
Armstrong, Louis, 138
Arrizón, Alicia, 159
assimilation, 35–36, 103, 105, 148
Atlanta Braves, 163
Austerlitz, Paul, 6, 9, 150
authoritarianism, 9, 37, 56, 61, 82–83.
  See also Balaguer, Joaquín; Trujillo,
  Rafael Leonidas
Ávila, Lorraine, 1, 127

bachata, 12, 56, 63, 145–146, 153–154,
  180n80
Báez, Frank, 1, 181n107, 187n79
Báez, Josefina, 1, 8, 52, *149, 155, 157*;
  Comrade, Bliss Ain't Playing, 13, 131;
  Dominicanish, 8, 12, 74, 131–143,
  154, 158–159, 198n65; and dominicanyork identity, 196n13; *Levente no.
  Yolayorkdominicanyork*, 10, 12, 54,
  74–77, 131, 133, 143–154, 158–159,
  187n72, 198n79, 198n84; "Lista del
  Terror," 10, 74–77
Bailey, Benjamin, 190n31
Bailey, Pearl, 138
balada, 161
Balaguer, Joaquín, 4, 27, 48–49, 78,
  87–88, 181n101, 183n8; aftermath of,
  52, 56, 63, 68, 82; balaguerista city, 63,
  65–66, 68, 78–79, 82, 85; and canción
  protesta, 11, 82; de-balaguerization,
  56; and emigration from Dominican
  Republic, 31, 52; on immigration,
  179n61; and merengue de ruptura,
  9, 37; return to power, 55, 79; rise to
  power, 183n8; violence under, 32, 40,
  79, 94, 183n10. *See also* los doce años
Balaguerato, 4, 43, 49, 52, 57, 82–84
Bayetti-Flores, Verónica, 177n30
Beat Latino, 18
Belén, Ana, 188n90

Belie Belcan, 86
Benítez, Lucecita, 188n90
Ben-Ur, Lorraine, 3
Beyoncé, 117, 119; "Ring the Alarm,"
  120–121
Biblioteca Nacional de España, 8
Bizet, Georges: *Carmen*, 152–153
Black Atlantic, 141
Black-centric schemas, 103
Black feminism, 13, 92–93, 97
Black Latinx girls. *See* Afro-Latina
  girlhood
Black liberation, 42
Blackness, 36, 129, 148, 162; in
  Bird of Paradise, 99–113, 192n80;
  in *Dominicanish*, 137–142; and
  Dominicanness, 40–42, 89–124,
  188n101, 192n80; and latinidad, 12;
  in *Levente no. Yolayorkdominicanyork*,
  152–153; in "Like a Prayer," 137–138;
  in *Papi*, 36, 39–40; in "Poco Loco," 61;
  in *The Poet X*, 92, 113–124; and Spanish language, 190n31; and US Latinx
  identity, 136. *See also* sonic blackness
Blount Danois, Ericka, 140
blues music, 12, 38
bolero, 12, 145, 154, 161
Bonao, Dominican Republic, 75
Bonilla, Frank, 104, 136
border arte, 142
borderlands, 26, 58, 114; Anzaldúa
  on, 8; in "Cañemo Revival Blues," 21,
  25; in *Dominicanish*, 12; Dominican
  Republic/NYC, 12, 15, 17, 20–21, 25,
  31, 58, 162–163; and Josefina Báez,
  125–159; in "Merengue," 49; and
  merengue de ruptura, 38–39, 45; in
  Papi, 31, 38–39, 45; and queerness, 49;
  in "Terror," 74; in *Ubre Urbe*, 20–21
Bosch, Juan, 183n8
Bost, Suzanne, 96
Boxing Championship, 141
Bracero Program, 128
Bronx, NYC, 15, 49, 89, *91*, 108, 176n12
Brooklyn, NYC, 71
Brooks, Daphne, 121
Brown, James, 41, 141
brujería, 41–42

Makeba, Miriam, 141
Mañaná, Miguel, 184n11
Manhattan, NYC, 4, 6, 42, 45, 51, 53, 58, 68, *91*, 97–98, 154; Harlem, 89, 96, 99, 105, 141. *See also* Washington Heights, NYC
Manhattan College, 146
Manuel, Peter, 30
Manuel, Víctor, 188n90
Mao, Dominican Republic, 9, 19, 21, 23, 25
maracas, 65
Maríñez, Sophie, 101–102
Marley, Bob, 66–67
Marte, Melania Luisa, 127
Martínez-San Miguel, Yolanda, 5, 16, 174n21
Martín Martínez, Macarena, 114, 119
masculinity, 25, 32, 35, 48, 66, 181n100, 182n116; in hip-hop, 122; and merengue típico cibaeño, 9, 23; (neo)trujillian, 33, 150
Masiki, Trent, 97, 107, 112
Masucci, Jerry, 140
Mateo, Francis, 1, 46, 163; "Cañemo Revival Blues," 9, 16–19, 21–25, 50; *El Alto*, 19; *Ubre Urbe*, 19–20
Mayes, April, 92
McGill, Lisa, 149
MC Lyte, 93, 109
Meat Puppets, 80, 84
Medrano, Marianela, 1, 127
Melle Mel, 193n88
Melymel, 162
Mena, Miguel D., 28, 144, 178n57
Méndez, Danny, 133, 135, 142, 158
merengue, 6–8, 12, 15, 51, 53, 56, 126, 161–163, 177n30, 198n84, 200n109; in "Cañemo Revival Blues," 16, 18; in *Comrade, Bliss Ain't Playing*, 154; and dominicanidad, 9–10, 17–18, 24, 42, 44, 49; in *La estrategia de Chochueca*, 85; in *Levente no. Yolayorkdominicanyork*, 145, 149–153; in "Merengue," 45–50; in *Papi*, 9, 16, 17, 18, 29–31, 36–44; in "Poco Loco," 63–64; and Trujillo, 185n34
merengue de orquesta, 24

merengue de ruptura, 9, 16, 31, 36–37, 38, 44–45, 162
merengue típico cibaeño, 9, 16, 17, 21–25, 175n30
merenhouse/merenrap, 24, 149
Miller, Daniel, 22
Milly, Jocelyn y Los Vecinos, 15, 39, 41; "Volvió Juanita," 151, 200n109
Minaj, Nicki, 117, 121; "Anaconda," 119–120; "Feeling Myself," 120
Miñoso, Minnie (Saturnino Orestes Armas Miñoso Arrieta), 135–137
misogyny, 25, 96, 129. *See also* domestic violence; patriarchy; sexual violence
Miti Miti, 177n40
modern folk music, 10
modes of listening, 7
Mohr, Nicholasa, 99
Moraga, Cherríe, 126
Moreno, Rita, 126
Moreno Vega, Marta, 99, 106, 126
Morgan, Joan, 109
Morris, Susana, 93, 115, 121
Mota, Jennifer, 162
Movimiento Renovador de la Universidad Autónoma de Santo Domingo, 52
Movimiento Revolucionario, 183n8
MTV, 44; MTV Live, 162
Mujeres Del Movimiento, 162–164
Museo del desorden, 64–65

Nas, 117
Nash, Jennifer, 157
Natera, Cleyvis, 127
National Baseball Hall of Fame, 136
nationalism, 97; Black, 107; Dominican, 29, 36–37, 180n80; US, 2
New Jersey, 137
new mestiza consciousness, 43
New York Mets, 163
ni aquí ni allá, 54
Nicola, Noel, 188n90
noise, 2, 7, 13, 82, 145, 158, 161, 163–164
nostalgia, 9, 20, 23, 43, 49, 70, 89, 151–152, 161–163
Notorious B.I.G., 109; "Big Poppa," 89

Spanish language, 2, 42, 90, 97, 106, 148, 198n65; in *Bird of Paradise*, 111; and Blackness, 190n31; in *Comrade, Bliss Ain't Playing*, 158; in *Dominicanish*, 133–135, 139–140, 143; Dominican Spanish, 134–135, 139; and hip-hop, 96, 108; in *La estrategia de Chochueca*, 85; in *Levente no. Yolayorkdominicanyork*, 146; and returning Dominican émigrés, 52; Spanish-speaking Caribbean, 3, 5, 85, 99, 108, 111, 136
Spencer, Isabel, 181n107
spoken-word poetry, 96, 113–115
Stade du Hai, 141
Starocean, Karol, 187n79
Sterne, Jonathan, 7
Stevens, Camilla, 135
Studio 54, 125–126
subaltern, 30, 53, 55, 58, 62, 65, 67–68, 79, 84, 86, 97
SummerStage, 162

Taínos, 97
Talking Heads, 80
Tallaj, Angelina, 16, 29, 178n53
Taylor, Diana, 129
Tejeda, Dagoberto, 184n11
Tejeda, Darío, 56
terminology of book, 9, 189n9
theory in the flesh, 127
third space, 8, 14, 132, 147
Thomas, Piri, 99, 106
tíguere aesthetics, 35, 179n74
TLC, 93, 109
Torrado, Lorna, 16, 79–80, 82
Torres, Lourdes, 97
Torres-Saillant, Silvio, 16, 25, 45, 69, 86, 92, 126, 176n12, 186n49; on Caribbean spaces, 186n46; on Dominican Blackness, 103; on Dominican cultural production, 7, 25; on *Dominicanish*, 137; on Dominican literature, 6; on dominicanyorks, 36; on emigration, 186n49; on Josefina Báez, 128–130; on Latino autobiography, 192n63; on race and survival, 102
transculturation, 6, 109, 138, 142
translingualism, 138, 142

translocation, 2, 5, 12, 74–75, 99, 142
transnational texts from below, 18
transracial consciousness, 138
Treaty of Basel, 182n118
Trinidad, José Enrique, 184n11
Troyano, Alina, 126
Trujillato, 4, 43–44, 47, 56–57, 181n101
Trujillo, Rafael Leonidas, 4, 27, 52, 57, 181n101; aftermath of, 36, 183n8; and the Catholic Church, 47, 182n118; de-trujillization, 56; on immigration, 179n61; and merengue, 24, 47, 64, 185n34; sonic archive of, 37; and tíguere, 35, 179n74; trujillista city, 63–66, 68, 78–80, 82, 85, 87–88, 183n8; trujillista ideology, 43, 48, 56
Tupac, 109, 123
21 Divisions, 86
Twitter (X), 21, 162

Universidad Autónoma de Santo Domingo, 52, 94
Urban Stages, 19
US Black Americans, 8, 11, 35, 40–42, 107, 137. *See also* African Americans
US Census, 103–104
US occupations, 4; 1916–1924, 64; 1965–1966, 44, 79, 181n103, 183n8, 184n11

vaivén, 15, 26, 30, 54, 58, 99, 141
Valdez, Antonio, 187n79
Valdez, Pedro Antonio, 181n107
Valerio-Holguín, Fernando, 27
Valoy, Cuco, 37–42, 188n90
van Buren, Thomas, 76
Vargas, Wilfrido, 37, 41–42; "El Jardinero," 150–151
Ventura, Johnny, 15, 37, 41–42
Ventura, Miriam, 127
Vicioso, Chiqui, 1
Victoriano-Martínez, Ramón Antonio (Arturo), 134, 135, 147, 199n108
Vila, Pablo, 62, 77
Villalona, Fernando "el Mayimbe," 15, 37–39, 41–42, 161; "Cuando pise

tierra dominicana," 43; "Dominicano soy," 43, 163; "Quisqueya," 43
Virgil, Osvaldo "Ozzie," 163
vital acts of transfer, 129
voodoo, 62
Voorhees, Jason, 31

Washington Heights, NYC, 19–20, 54, 76, 94, 176n12, 187n72, 200n109
West, Kanye (Ye), 122–123
White-centric schemas, 103
whiteness, 11, 36–37, 100, 103–108, 138, 147, 192n80
white supremacy, 138

Wiarda, Howard, 182n118
Withers, Bill, 141
Wu-Tang Clan, 193n88

X. *See* Twitter (X)

Yailin La Más Viral, 162
Yarull, Miguel, 187n79
Yendry, 162
YouTube, 26

Zamora, Omaris, 12, 93, 114
Zona Colonial, 19, 54, 60, 73, 79, 86
Zoot Suit Riots, 128